—— Praise for ——
The Comprehensive Clinician's Guide to Cognitive Behavioral Therapy

"*The Comprehensive Clinician's Guide to Cognitive Behavioral Therapy* is truly a one-stop shop for any student or professional who intends to practice CBT in its most authentic and evidence-based form. Sokol and Fox have struck a perfect balance between an elegant academic volume and a clear and concise resource complete with excellent worksheets woven throughout the text. The forthcoming praise and success of this book is well deserved."

-Aaron T. Beck, MD,
University Professor Emeritus of Psychiatry,
University of Pennsylvania

"This is a marvelous addition to the literature supporting therapists in learning and applying Cognitive Behavioral Therapy written by two master clinicians and educators. The client worksheets alone would be worth the purchase of the book, even for experienced clinicians. The text is practical, straightforward, and filled with specific examples of the principles in practice."

-Donna M. Sudak, MD,
Immediate Past President, American Association
of Directors of Psychiatric Residency Training

"Clear, practical, broad, and entirely evidence-based, *The Comprehensive Clinician's Guide to Cognitive Behavioral Therapy* is rightly named and is a volume which belongs on the shelf of any clinician wishing to understand the practice of contemporary CBT. Students and trainees will find the book to be a useful primer on CBT, whereas seasoned clinicians will find wisdom in the author's spare, focused approach. They direct our attention to what is most important in practice, ensuring high-fidelity CBT. This guide is optimistic in tone, emphasizing the role of "confidence" as a foundation of clinical change. Combining elements of efficacy and hope, "confidence" is something clinicians and their patients may gain from this simple volume."

-Mark Reinecke, PhD,
Professor Emeritus of Psychiatry and Behavioral Sciences,
Northwestern University

"Ranging from anxiety disorders to psychosis and everything in between, this book is your go-to resource guide for applying the principles of CBT to a variety of clinical issues and diagnoses. Written in a manner that is easily accessible, this book provides you with the step-by-step tools needed to put theory into practice. This indispensable guide is a must have for every clinician's library. I highly recommend it!"

-Lynn McFarr, PhD,
Founder of CBT California (CBTC),
Professor of Health Sciences at UCLA David Geffen School of Medicine

The Comprehensive Clinician's Guide to

COGNITIVE BEHAVIORAL THERAPY

Depression • Bipolar • Anxiety • Anger
Substance Abuse • Personality Disorders
PTSD • Self-Harm • Suicidality • Psychosis

Leslie Sokol, PhD and **Marci G. Fox**, PhD

Copyright © 2020, 2019 Leslie Sokol and Marci G. Fox

Published by
PESI Publishing & Media
PESI, Inc.
3839 White Ave
Eau Claire, WI 54703

Cover Design: Amy Rubenzer
Editing: Jenessa Jackson, PhD
Layout: Bookmasters and Amy Rubenzer

Proudly printed in the United States of America

ISBN: 9781683733201

All rights reserved

ABOUT THE AUTHORS

 **Leslie Sokol, PhD,** a licensed psychologist, is an internationally recognized leader in the field of cognitive behavioral therapy with more than 35 years of experience in practice, teaching, and research. She was a past Director of Education and one of the principal instructors at the internationally acclaimed Beck Institute for Cognitive Behavior Therapy in Philadelphia. She has taught cognitive therapy to professional and paraprofessional groups, both nationally and internationally, on a multitude of CBT topics.

Dr. Sokol served as Chairman of Behavioral Science for the Mercy Suburban Hospital Family Practice Training Program for over 20 years. She is a distinguished founding fellow of the Academy of Cognitive Therapy and a past president. Currently, she serves as Chairman of its Credentialing Committee. She is a fellow of the Association for Behavioral and Cognitive Therapies (ABCT) and a board member at large of the International Association of Cognitive Psychotherapy (IACP). Dr. Sokol is on the Meet the Experts panel for *Psychology Today*, as well as an invited member of the *Psychology Today* and Penguin Speakers Bureaus. She currently maintains a private practice in the Philadelphia suburbs.

Dr. Sokol has coauthored numerous books and book chapters. Her most current co-authored books are: *Teaching and Supervising Cognitive Behavioral Therapy*; *Think Confident, Be Confident for Teens: A Cognitive Therapy Guide to Overcoming Self-Doubt and Creating Unshakable Self-Esteem*; *Think Confident, Be Confident: A Four-Step Program to Eliminate Doubt and Achieve Lifelong Self-Esteem*; and *The Think Confident, Be Confident Workbook for Teens: Activities to Help You Create Unshakable Self-Confidence and Reach Your Goals*. For more information, visit her website at www.thinkconfidentbeconfident.com.

 **Marci G. Fox, PhD,** a licensed psychologist, has been in private practice almost 25 years and specializes in cognitive behavioral therapy with teens and adults. She has worked with the Beck Institute for Cognitive Behavior Therapy in Philadelphia for almost the same amount of time. As an Academy of Cognitive Therapy Certified Trainer/Consultant and Adjunct Faculty Member at the Beck Institute, she trains individuals in cognitive behavioral therapy both nationally and internationally. She is actively involved in training thousands of mental health professionals nationally to increase their competency in cognitive behavior therapy.

Dr. Fox has a founding fellow distinction, as well as invited placement on the board of examiners and credentials committee, with the Academy of Cognitive Therapy. She has lectured nationally and internationally for years on cognitive therapy, as well as on confidence and self-esteem. Dr. Fox is an invited member of the *Psychology Today* and Penguin Speakers Bureaus. She has coauthored the following books: *Think Confident, Be Confident: A Four-Step Program to Eliminate Doubt and Achieve Lifelong Self-Esteem*; *Think Confident, Be Confident for Teens: A Cognitive Therapy Guide to Overcoming Self-Doubt and Creating Unshakable Self-Esteem*; and *Teaching and Supervising Cognitive Behavioral Therapy*. Dr. Fox has published in peer-reviewed journals and has diverse publications in the area of cognitive behavioral therapy. She has been interviewed for articles in multiple national magazines and is often interviewed by many national and international radio stations. Her practice is in Boca Raton, Florida. For more information, visit her website at www.thinkconfidentbeconfident.com.

DEDICATION

To Aaron T. Beck, MD
The pioneer and champion of cognitive behavioral therapy and our beloved mentor

TABLE OF CONTENTS

Acknowledgements xiii
Introduction xv

Chapter 1: The Cognitive Model 1
    The Cognitive Model 1
    Underlying Self-Doubt Beliefs 10

Chapter 2: Cognitive Conceptualization: Understanding the Client 11
    Personality: What We Value 11
    Values and Doubt Labels 18
    Doubt Labels 20
    The Role of History and Life Experiences 20
    Ineffective Compensatory Actions 23
    Doubt Labels and Behavior: Guidelines or Assumptions 24
    Doubt Conceptualization Model 26

Chapter 3: Goal-Directed Therapy 33
    Problem List 33
    Treatment Goals 34
    Session Structure 37
        The Beginning 37
        The Agenda 40
        The Middle of the Session 42
        Summaries 43
        Homework 43
        End of the Session 45
    Self-Assessment 48

Chapter 4: Case Write-Up 53
    Case Write-Up Instructions 53
    Case Write-Up Example 58

Chapter 5: Depression 69
    The Cognitive Model and Key Component Treatments 69
    Assessment 69
        Mood Scales 69

- Behavioral Activation 70
  - The First Step: Behavioral Assessment 70
  - The Tool: The Activity Schedule 71
  - Activity Schedule: The Learning 74
  - Key Concepts in Behavioral Activation 75
  - Considering Bipolar Disorder 88
- Cognitive Restructuring 88
  - Eliciting Automatic Thoughts 89
  - Evaluating Automatic Thoughts 91
  - Reframing the Doubt Label 107
  - Identifying and Evaluating Conditional Assumptions 111
  - Considering Bipolar Disorder 111
- Sustaining and Growing Confidence Through Action 111

Chapter 6: Anxiety 113
- The Cognitive Model of Anxiety 113
- Cognitive Restructuring 115
  - The Probability Error 115
  - The Catastrophic Error 116
  - The Resource Error 117
- Exposure-Based Strategies 118
  - Key Components of Exposure Interventions 119
  - Potential Pitfalls 120
- Interventions for Specific Anxiety Disorders 121
  - Generalized Anxiety Disorder 121
  - Social Anxiety Disorder 124
  - Panic Disorder 129
  - Specific Phobia 139
  - Illness Anxiety Disorder 141
  - Obsessive Compulsive Disorder 142
  - Post-Traumatic Stress Disorder 147
  - Summary: Anxiety Disorders 150

Chapter 7: Anger 151
- The Cognitive Model of Anger 151
- Anger Arousal 160
- Assertive Communication 162
- Effective Restraint 164
- Putting It All Together: Diverting Anger 166
- Self-Confidence 167

Chapter 8: Substance Use Disorders **169**
- Motivation and Buy-In 169
- The Cognitive Model of Relapse 172
  - Triggering Stimuli 172
  - Underlying Drug-Related Beliefs 172
  - Substance-Biased Automatic Thoughts 173
  - Increased Urges and Cravings 173
  - Permission-Giving Beliefs 177
  - Instrumental Strategies 177
  - Lapses or Relapses 177
  - The Cognitive Model of Abuse 177
- Vulnerability to Relapse 182

Chapter 9: Personality Disorders, Self-Harm, and Suicidality **185**
- The Cognitive Model of Personality Disorders 185
  - Personality Disorders and Core Beliefs 186
- Key Treatment Components 187
  - Establish Goals 188
  - Increase Motivation and Develop Buy-In 189
  - Build a Confident Self-View 193
  - Modify Ineffective Action 208
- Self-Harm 211
  - Cognitive Model of Self-Harm 211
  - Intervention 212
- Suicidality 218
  - Intervention 218
- Summary 228

Chapter 10: Psychosis **229**
- Psychotic Disorders 229
- The Cognitive Model of Psychosis 229
- Interventions for Psychosis 230
  - Negative Symptoms 231
  - Hallucinations 232
  - Delusions 238
- CBT and Medicine 239

References **241**

ACKNOWLEDGEMENTS

A big thank you to our readers. We are passionate about cognitive behavioral therapy (CBT) and have witnessed the significant impact it has made in the lives of our clients and the clients of the mental health professionals we train and supervise all over the world. CBT works!

We are forever grateful to Aaron T. Beck, MD, the pioneer of cognitive therapy. Thank you for being our mentor and for allowing us to work so closely with you for so many decades. We are especially grateful for Dr. Beck's contributions to the field of psychosis in improving the quality of life for so many. His latest thinking and validated interventions for psychosis are discussed in Chapter 10. We are also fortunate and thankful to have had Aaron P. Brinen, PhD, a partner in Dr. Beck's work and vision, significantly contribute to our chapter on psychosis to discuss their new CT-R approach. A big thank you as well to Greg K. Brown, PhD for sharing his most current work on suicide, including his Safety Planning Intervention.

We'd also like to thank our families for supporting us through the writing process. Thank you to our children—Chad, Alex, Max, Jesse, Ethan, and Carly—for your enthusiastic support, fun breaks, and laughs. We adore you! Thank you to our amazing husbands, Bob and Stu. You make everything better and the world a brighter place.

Thank you to Emily Krumenauer for promoting CBT, reuniting us with PESI, and introducing us to Karsyn Morse who believed in this book and helped make it better with her editorial suggestions. To Jenessa Jackson, PhD, you are the most talented, diligent, and helpful editor we have ever had the pleasure to work with. A huge thank-you for your painstaking work! We are grateful to PESI for giving us this platform and the enthusiasm of Valerie Whitehead, who is our new advocate for CBT at PESI.

INTRODUCTION

WHY WE WROTE THIS BOOK

The Comprehensive Clinician's Guide to Cognitive Behavioral Therapy provides clinicians with a cognitive conceptualization for a multitude of psychological disorders based within the principles of cognitive behavioral therapy (CBT), as well as a variety of CBT-based interventions for addressing these specific difficulties. Our experiences as clinicians, trainers, and supervisors in large-scale CBT dissemination projects have allowed us to create a book that meets the needs of clinicians in community mental health, private practice, and hospital and organizational settings, as well as the needs of supervisors, trainers, and teachers in training programs, practicum settings, and in the classroom. The principles in this book are based solely on the principles of CBT as intended by Dr. Aaron T. Beck. Having had the privilege of being mentored directly by Dr. Beck and working collaboratively with him for over 30 years, we are able to bring his ideas to mental health professionals in an easy-to-understand, practical format.

WHAT IS IN THIS BOOK

This book combines the most current principles of CBT for depression and provides a framework for applying these principles to a variety of clinical issues and diagnoses. Chapter 1 provides a thorough introduction to the principles of CBT, followed by a more specific discussion of the doubt conceptualization model in Chapter 2. Chapter 3 discusses the typical structure of goal-oriented therapy, including how to identify problems, set treatment goals, and structure typical CBT sessions. Chapter 4 presents the guidelines and format for developing a case formulation and accompanying case write-up as delineated by the Academy of Cognitive Therapy, with a sample case write-up included in the chapter.

Chapters 5 and beyond provide a framework for understanding the principles of CBT as they are applied to depression, bipolar disorder, anxiety, anger, substance abuse, personality disorders, self-harm and suicidality, and psychosis. In particular, each chapter discusses how each of these clinical issues can be understood through the lens of the cognitive model, in which distorted thinking patterns lead to the development of dysfunctional behavior. We then discuss specifically tailored treatment strategies for each of these issues within a CBT framework, including a variety of step-by-step plans, interactive in-session and out-of-session exercises, and pre-populated coping cards to clearly demonstrate how to put theory into practice. At the core of each of these interventions is a focus on helping clients increase their self-confidence. Building confidence and eliminating self-doubt is the foundation of treatment and a focal point of the interventions we present for each diagnosis and difficulty. This book is not intended as a script to be followed but, rather, as a case-conceptualization-driven guide that can be creatively and flexibly tailored to the specific needs of each individual.

WHO IS THIS BOOK FOR?

This book is designed to help clinicians of all levels of CBT proficiency better serve their clients by gaining expertise in delivering the evidence-based principles of CBT. It is intended for mental health professionals, students, trainers, supervisors, teachers, and clinicians looking for a guide to solidify and grow their clinical knowledge of CBT. This inclusive CBT guidebook equips mental health professionals with the tools needed to teach their clients how to be their own CBT therapist. Indeed, CBT's most powerful contribution to mental health recovery is the power that it gives to the client in preventing relapse and sustaining recovery. By helping clients learn effective coping skills and building their confidence, CBT gives them tools to be their own therapist and guide as they navigate life. Therefore, this book is a versatile resource for any reader seeking to gain an explicit understanding of psychological problems, as it empowers individuals to be in charge of how they think, feel, and behave.

1
THE COGNITIVE MODEL

THE COGNITIVE MODEL

Cognitive behavior therapy is based on the cognitive model of psychopathology, which hypothesizes that people's emotions, body responses, and behaviors are influenced by their perception of events (Beck, 1964). According to the model, situations do not inherently determine what people feel or how they behave. Rather, it is how people *perceive* these situations that determine how they react and respond (Beck, 1964; Ellis, 1962). Therefore, a situation in and of itself cannot cause distress per se. In contrast, it is the interpretation of that situation that drives the distress. A simple schematic of the cognitive model is as follows:

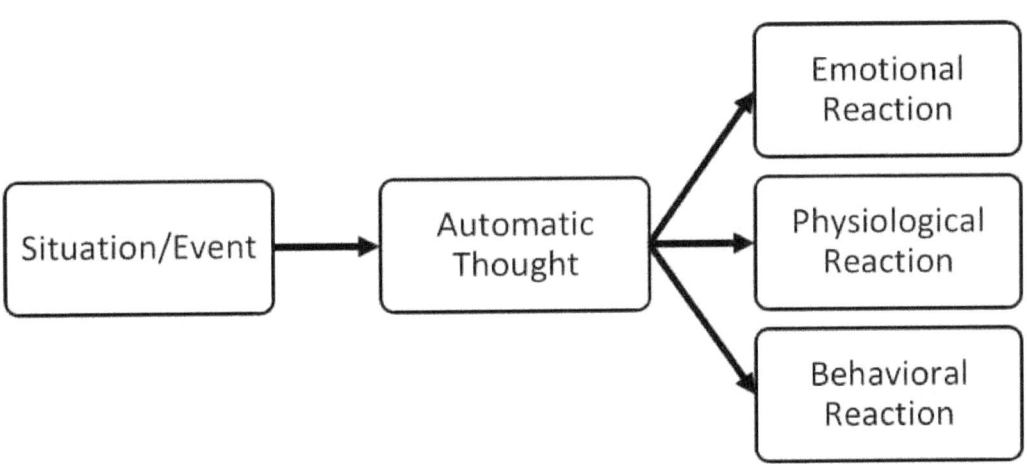

To better understand the cognitive model, let's put it into practice with a hypothetical example. Imagine that a wedding invitation is sent to a family of three. The dad opens the invitation and thinks, "This is great. I might get to see people I haven't seen in a while. This will be so much fun!" He feels happy and energized, and he puts the date on his calendar. The mom, on the other hand, thinks, "I don't want to go. I've gained so much weight. People will judge me. I have no energy. I will never be up for this. I cannot go." She feels down and depressed, her body feels sluggish, and she hides the invitation in the drawer. Their son finds the invitation in the drawer and thinks, "My parents are going to make me go, and this is the worst possible date. I will have to miss the big fraternity rush. If I don't show up and make a good impression, then I probably won't get an invite to pledge. I'll be the only one of my friends not in Greek life. This is a disaster." He feels anxious, notices his heart pounding as sweat starts to roll down his face, and he starts pacing back and forth trying to come up with the best excuse not to attend.

In this example, the invitation serves as an *external* trigger, which causes the mom, dad, and son to each have different automatic thoughts about the situation. In turn, they each experience different emotions and body responses, which influence their behavior. However, *internal* triggers influence our emotions and behaviors as well.

For example, the son may start to focus on his heart rate, shortness of breath, and tingling sensations in his hands. In turn, he may think, "I'm having a heart attack," and call 911 in a panic. Both internal and external triggers can elicit negative automatic thoughts, which drive distress and problematic behavioral choices.

There are several ways to teach clients the cognitive model and increase their understanding of how thoughts influence their ensuing emotions, body responses, and behaviors. For example, you can take an innocuous situation, such as walking into a coffee shop or handing in an assignment, and help clients consider several possible automatic thoughts that someone might have in each situation. Then, direct them to imagine the potential emotional, physiological, and behavioral reactions that someone might have to that automatic thought. Alternatively, you can use an example from the client's life, such as a car stopping short in front of them or a situation in which they were running late, and ask them to describe their automatic thoughts about the situation. Then, you can help clients connect how these thoughts are related to their emotional, physiological, and behavioral reactions. You may even wish to add any automatic thoughts and reactions you have personally experienced. The goal is simply to help clients understand the connection between perception and reaction.

Early in therapy, worksheets can be used to help clients identify their thoughts, feelings, and behaviors in gaining an understanding of the cognitive model. The following pages contain several exercises you can use with your clients to guide them through this process. Whenever possible, it is better to have clients complete these worksheets in session before asking them to try it on their own.

Client Worksheet

UNDERSTANDING THE COGNITIVE MODEL

· · · · · ·

According to the cognitive model, for every situation that we experience in life, we have automatic thoughts, which influence how we feel, how our body responds, and how we behave. Here is what the cognitive model looks like:

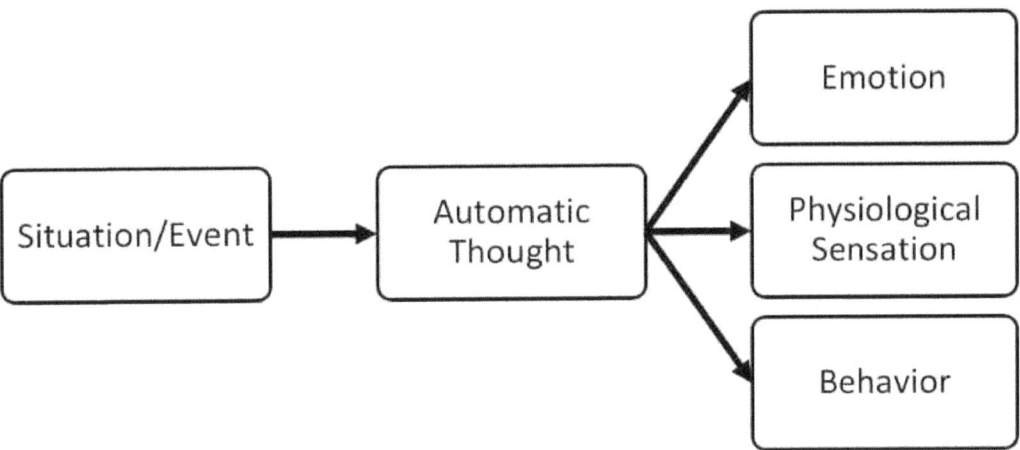

Automatic thoughts are powerful because the manner in which we interpret a situation drives how we react to that situation. For example, let's say that a dog is running toward you on the street (*situation/event*). If you think to yourself, "That dog is going to bite me!" then you'd probably feel scared (*emotion*), your heart would start racing (*physiological response*), and you would probably run away (*behavior*). However, in the same exact situation, if you were to think, "What a cute dog!" then you might feel happy (*emotion*), you might smile (*physiological sensation*), and you might approach the dog to pet it (*behavior*).

As another example, let's say you are meeting a friend for dinner, who is now 30 minutes late (*situation/event*). If you think to yourself, "She isn't coming," then you'd probably feel disappointed (*emotion*), a tear might well up in your eye (*physiological sensation*), and you might decide to head home (*behavior*). Alternatively, in the same situation, if you were to think, "She's probably running late as usual or traffic must be horrendous for her to be this late," then you might feel accepting (*emotion*), relaxed (*physiological sensation*), and decide to sit at the bar and have a drink until she gets there (*behavior*).

Therefore, the same exact situation can result in different emotional, physiological, and behavioral reactions—depending on the automatic thoughts that you have about the situation. Let's practice. For the three situations that follow, try interpreting each situation from two different perspectives. For each situation, come up with two different automatic thoughts that someone might have about the situation, as well as the ensuing emotions, body sensations, and behaviors that are associated with that automatic thought.

Situation 1: You text your friend, and two days pass without a response.

Interpretation 1:

    Automatic thought: _____

    Emotion: _____

    Physiological sensation(s): _____

    Behavior(s): _____

Interpretation 2:

    Automatic thought: _____

    Emotion: _____

    Physiological sensation(s): _____

    Behavior(s): _____

Situation 2: Your boss requests a meeting.

Interpretation 1:

    Automatic thought: _____

    Emotion: _____

    Physiological sensation(s): _____

    Behavior(s): _____

Interpretation 2:

    Automatic thought: _____

    Emotion: _____

    Physiological sensation(s): _____

    Behavior(s): _____

Situation 3: You arrive home, and multiple unknown cars are in your driveway.

Interpretation 1:

    Automatic thought: _____

    Emotion: _____

    Physiological sensation(s): _____

    Behavior(s): _____

Interpretation 2:

    Automatic thought: _____

    Emotion: _____

    Physiological sensation(s): _____

    Behavior(s): _____

Client Worksheet

AWARENESS OF THOUGHTS

· · · · ·

We constantly experience thoughts throughout the day. Our brains are active all the time, so thoughts constantly pop up or pass through our minds. Most people never think to question their thoughts and just accept them as true. However, our perceptions are not always accurate. We make errors, and those thinking errors impact our mood, body, and actions. The first step in addressing those thinking errors is simply to become more aware of our thoughts. By paying attention to what we are thinking, we can start to evaluate—and ultimately change—any incorrect or unhelpful thoughts. The following activity is intended to help you become more conscious and mindful of your thoughts so that you can begin this process.

Sit quietly for the next two minutes. Look around or close your eyes. Try to make yourself aware of the thoughts popping into or passing through your mind. Record what you notice.

_____

_____

_____

Sit quietly for another two minutes. Think back to an upsetting moment. What thoughts are going through your mind?

_____

_____

_____

Sit quietly for another two minutes. Think back to a time that made you happy. Recall the thoughts you had about this situation. The next time that you feel down, try to reflect on this happy memory.

The Cognitive Model

> **REMIND YOUR CLIENTS:**
>
> Thoughts are not always true.
>
> Thoughts are not facts.
>
> Thoughts can be subjective.
>
> Thoughts can be biased by past experiences or by what we hear, read, or see.

Once clients have completed the prior two worksheets in session, have them apply the cognitive model to a personal situation they have experienced in their life. First, ask clients to identify a time when they experienced a strong negative reaction to a situation or event, such as sadness, anger, fear, or any other unpleasant emotion. Then, have clients use the following worksheet to describe the triggering situation, as well as their accompanying thoughts and reactions (e.g., emotions, body responses, behaviors) to that situation. By completing this exercise, clients will learn how their thoughts influence how they feel and behave.

A word of caution: Asking clients to pay attention to distressing thoughts can exacerbate distress! To protect your clients from experiencing unnecessary distress with this exercise, make sure they have a good understanding of the notion that thoughts are not facts. Just because they have a thought does not make it true. Clients must fully embrace this notion before attempting this exercise. In addition, practice this worksheet with your clients together in session before sending them out to explore negative automatic thoughts for homework.

Client Worksheet

APPLY THE COGNITIVE MODEL:
Connect Thoughts and Reactions

• • • • • •

As you've learned, your perception of a situation influences your reaction to that situation. In order to help get you into the habit of connecting your automatic thoughts to your reactions, think of a recent situation (either today or in the last several days) when you noticed a shift in your mood or in the way your body felt.

Step 1: Identify the Trigger

Identify the specific trigger that caused you distress. If you're not sure, then think back to what exactly "set you off." That is, think of the prompting event that caused a change in your mood or how your body felt. For example, if someone canceled plans with you, you don't need to recount the whole story. Rather, just write the specific trigger (e.g., "I received a text from my friend saying that plans were canceled, but I later saw on social media that they were out with other friends.").

_____
_____
_____

Step 2: Identify the Automatic Thought

When this happened, what went through your mind? That's the automatic thought.

_____
_____
_____

Step 3: Map Your Reaction

Write the emotional, physiological, and behavioral reactions you had in response to this automatic thought.

1. Emotion: How did it make you feel?

   _____

   _____

2. Physiological Response: What body sensations did you experience?

   _____

   _____

3. Behavior: What actions did you take?

   _____

   _____

UNDERLYING SELF-DOUBT BELIEFS

Although the cognitive model maintains that automatic thoughts influence how we react and respond to situations, another important layer adds to the model: underlying self-doubt beliefs. The manner in which we perceive specific situations (and, in turn, the automatic thoughts we have about those situations) are shaped by our underlying beliefs about ourselves, the world, and others (Beck, 2011; Dobson, 2012). When these underlying beliefs are plagued by self-doubt, it can result in the creation of doubt labels, which act like a filter, biasing the way we view and interpret situations.

Doubt labels (also known as core beliefs) reflect the negative names we call ourselves when our self-doubt is activated (Sokol & Fox, 2009). For example, consider a student who is confused by the material being taught in class. Although he wants to ask the teacher for clarification, he refrains from raising his hand because he believes that he is the only person who is confused, and he is convinced that asking a question will further demonstrate his stupidity to everyone in the class. In this case, the student's doubt label is that he is "stupid," and this is what is driving him to think that he is the only one confused. Instead of considering the possibility that other students don't understand the material, that the teacher is doing a poor job explaining the material, or that the material is genuinely difficult, the student assumes that it's his fault. His belief that he is stupid is what has led him to this conclusion. If the student accepts this conclusion, he will refrain from asking for clarification, which will cause him to perform poorly in the class and serve as a self-fulfilling confirmation of his stupidity.

Therefore, to reduce dysfunctional thinking and behavior, it is important not only to identify and evaluate negative automatic thoughts but also to identify and reframe the doubt labels that are driving these thoughts. For example, if the student in the previous example did not harbor the underlying belief that he is stupid, then he would not automatically assume that he is the only student confused by the material. In turn, he would have the courage to ask the teacher for clarification, which would increase his chances of performing well in the class and confirm a more positive self-concept. Chapter 2 goes into further detail on doubt labels and what drives them so that you can begin to gain a better understanding of how your clients' personal beliefs shape their thoughts, feelings, and behaviors.

2

COGNITIVE CONCEPTUALIZATION: UNDERSTANDING THE CLIENT

From the first conversation forward, you need to gain information from your clients that allows you to understand how they view their experiences and themselves. While it is easier to obtain information regarding the automatic thoughts, feelings, and behaviors associated with a specific situation, uncovering the client's doubt labels, and the assumptions related to these underlying doubt labels, is more challenging. However, doing so is vital to understanding their vulnerability to distress. Therefore, this chapter focuses on helping you develop a comprehensive cognitive conceptualization of your clients so you can more easily uncover and address these underlying core beliefs.

PERSONALITY: WHAT WE VALUE

Sociotropy and autonomy are two personality styles that confer vulnerability to depression (Beck, 1983). **Sociotropy** reflects a desire for social connectedness and is characterized by excessive investment in interpersonal relationships. People who are sociotropic seek out positive social feedback, want confirmation that they are loved and accepted, and place significant value on close relationships. In contrast, **autonomy** reflects a desire for independence, freedom from others, and personal rights. People with an autonomous personality value goal achievement, participation in meaningful activities, and a strong desire for accomplishment and control.

Although sociotropy and autonomy reflect opposite personality styles, these two personality dimensions are not dichotomous. Rather, they fall on a continuum, move over time, and are influenced by external circumstances (e.g., marriage, childbirth, school, first job, career). Although most people fall closer to the middle of the continuum over time, some people become even more extreme in their values.

In addition, even if a person highly values both domains, one personality style is likely to dominate, and this preference is expressed as early as infancy. For example, the baby who wants to be held all the time and needs to be in close proximity with a loved one in order to sleep is sociotropic, while the baby who can self-soothe and sit for hours entertained by a screen or a fish tank is more autonomous. Similarly, consider the sociotropic four-year-old—whose parents sign them up for an activity but the child refuses to participate unless their friends are signed up too—in contrast with the autonomous child, who is more than willing to participate in that activity even if they have no friends doing it. Or the sociotropic adolescent, who waits to see what their friends sign up for before committing to an activity, versus the autonomous adolescent, who signs up for the activity of their choosing regardless of what others are doing.

These personality styles continue to develop into adulthood, where our values play a significant role in the choices we make when compromise is necessary. For example, when we are presented with a choice that involves an interpersonal-related goal (e.g., wedding, birthday celebration, child's musical performance, or sporting event) versus an achievement-related goal (e.g., work, lecture, exercise class, hobby, learning a new skill), our values shape our choices. When people fall toward the extreme ends of the continuum, then they don't experience much internal conflict because their preferred choice is clear. However, when they fall more toward the middle—where value is placed on *both* social and achievement goals—then the choice becomes more difficult, and this triggers feelings of distress.

Therefore, identifying what clients value can help us understand which situations are more likely to contribute to distress and how the processing of those situations plays a role in the shaping of their beliefs, assumptions, and behaviors. Envision the person who has had major surgery with significant temporary restrictions on mobility. At first, everyone is visiting, bringing gifts, and making a fuss. The sociotropic personality feels loved and important, and is happy, while the more autonomous person feels miserable because their mobility is compromised, and they must rely on others for help. Weeks later, when the visiting stops and the mobility returns, the sociotropic person feels sad, whereas the autonomous person feels rejuvenated as they regain their independence.

Similarly, imagine a group of second graders who have just received their scores on a reading test. Student A gets a 97 percent and places in the top reading group, Student B gets an 87 percent and places in the second group, and Student C gets a 70 percent and places in the lowest group, thus requiring that he participate in extra tutoring. Depending on these students' personality styles, they could all potentially be affected by their scores—or they may not be affected at all. For example, if these students are more socially inclined, then they may not care about their scores (and the students with the lowest scores may even be pleased if many of their friends scored similarly!). On the other hand, if these students are more autonomous, then Student A may be pleased with a score of 97 percent (or be upset that it was not a perfect score), Student B may be disappointed or even devastated to not make it to the top group, and Student C may be crushed over his performance.

Simply put, the conclusions that we start to develop about ourselves are shaped by how we process these early experiences. Our processing of our disappointments, challenges, and conflicts shapes the development of our self-view. When people receive constant disappointments or always seem to experience conflict in the areas they value, it negatively impacts their core beliefs, which creates self-doubt and makes them more vulnerable to distress. Thus, understanding your client's underlying doubt labels is a critical component of successful CBT.

To determine where your clients fall along the continuum of sociotropy and autonomy, use the following three worksheets to gauge their personality style and determine how it has affected their self-view.

Client Worksheet

VULNERABILITY QUIZ

• • • • • •

The following quiz is intended to help you identify what it is that you value in life. By determining what bothers you (and also what doesn't bother you), you can help identify what it is that you value. Read each of the following statements, and circle "yes" or "no" to indicate whether you are bothered by each scenario.

You are bothered by . . .

1. Criticism, real or imagined, regarding your performance — YES NO
2. Rejection, real or imagined — YES NO
3. Feeling as if you have no control of the plans — YES NO
4. Disagreement with another person — YES NO
5. A loss of mobility — YES NO
6. Being left out or excluded — YES NO
7. Having your goals thwarted — YES NO
8. Someone being upset with you — YES NO
9. Being told, rather than asked, to do something — YES NO
10. Feeling awkward in a social situation — YES NO
11. Not living up to your own expectations — YES NO
12. Criticism, real or imagined, regarding a social interaction — YES NO
13. Difficulty completing what you want to do — YES NO
14. Not having calls or texts returned — YES NO
15. Having no say in a matter — YES NO
16. Being rejected — YES NO
17. An inability to get what you want done — YES NO
18. Feeling distant from someone — YES NO
19. Not delivering your best work — YES NO
20. Not looking your best — YES NO

Look at all the odd numbers, and add up the odd "yes" responses that you circled: _____

Look at all the even numbers, and add up the even "yes" responses that you circled: _____

Copyright © 2019 Leslie Sokol & Marci G. Fox, *The Comprehensive Clinician's Guide to Cognitive Behavioral Therapy*. All Rights Reserved

A higher score on *even* numbers means that social situations matter to you, so when you experience social conflicts or challenges, then you feel upset. A higher score on *odd* numbers means that achievement-oriented situations matter more to you, so when you experience disappointments or challenges related to your accomplishments, then you feel upset. An equally high score on *both* odd and even numbers means that both social and achievement-oriented situations matter to you, and when you experience challenges in either of these areas, then you feel upset.

When you feel upset, is the cause more social or achievement related in nature (or both)? What can you conclude about what bothers you and what you value?

_____

_____

_____

_____

Client Worksheet

SHAPING EXPERIENCES

• • • • • •

Our life experiences, especially early on, play a role in developing our self-concept. These life events can sow early seeds of self-doubt, fortify existing doubt, or completely modify our self-concept. Often we are unaware of the impact of life events. Think back through your life and try to recall how specific experiences may have negatively affected the way you see yourself now. The more negatively recalled experiences you have increases the likelihood that self-doubt will grow.

1. Did it take you longer to learn to crawl or walk?   YES   NO
2. Did it take you longer to talk?   YES   NO
3. Did you have a difficult time separating from your parents?   YES   NO
4. Did you struggle socially in school?   YES   NO
5. Did you have academic difficulty in classes?   YES   NO
6. Were you placed in different levels of classes or groups than your friends?   YES   NO
7. Were you held back?   YES   NO
8. Did you get cut from a team or club?   YES   NO
9. Were you not invited to parties or social events?   YES   NO
10. Did you have specific struggles with your siblings?   YES   NO
11. Did you have difficulties with your parents?   YES   NO
12. Did you have financial stress in your family?   YES   NO
13. Have you been exposed to an accident or natural disaster?   YES   NO
14. Were you hospitalized or needed surgery?   YES   NO
15. Did you lose a friend through an argument?   YES   NO
16. Have you had your heart broken?   YES   NO
17. Have you been passed over or fired from a job?   YES   NO
18. Did you get into trouble at school or with the law?   YES   NO
19. Have you been significantly affected by an event on the news or in your community?   YES   NO
20. Have you been impacted by bullying?   YES   NO
21. Have you ever been subject to physical, sexual, emotional, or verbal abuse?   YES   NO

22. Have you been affected by a diagnosis you received? YES NO

23. Have you had to care for sick or impaired relatives or friends? YES NO

Notice how many items you endorsed as a "yes." Keep in mind that the more negative experiences a person has had, the more likely it is that their self-concept will be negatively impacted. What's the conclusion? What effects did any of these or any other situations have on your self-concept?

___

___

___

___

Client Worksheet

MESSAGES PERCEIVED

• • • • • •

The messages that we receive from the people around us—those close to us or passerbys in our lives—can have a direct or indirect effect on the way we view ourselves. When we receive positive messages, we feel good about ourselves. However, when we receive negative or mixed messages (including messages that we perceive as negative), then this can negatively interfere with our sense of self.

For example, if your parents always referred to you as "the social one" or "the athlete" (instead of the "smart one"), then you may have concluded this means "I'm dumb." Similarly, if your teacher referred to you as "the hard worker," then you may have concluded "I'm average" or "I don't measure up." Or, your ex-partner may have said that you are "nice," causing you to believe "I'm not good enough or undesirable." These messages don't have to come from the people around us; they also come from the media. For example, magazines display pictures of thin women in bathing suits and athletic men with muscular physiques, which may send the message that you are unattractive. These messages are made even more explicit if your parents called you worthless, stupid, ugly, or any other negative label.

What kind of negative messages did you hear growing up and throughout your life?

_____

_____

_____

_____

What conclusions did these messages cause you to make about yourself?

_____

_____

_____

_____

VALUES AND DOUBT LABELS

We all have insecurity lurking inside us. For people who have a positive view of themselves and a strong sense of self-esteem, this insecurity only arises when they are faced with a particularly challenging or stressful situation. However, for others, self-doubt is always lurking, and these doubt labels take charge of how people perceive themselves and the world around them. Left unchecked, this self-doubt can take over and negatively influence how people interpret and respond to specific situations, resulting in significant psychological impairment (e.g., depression, anxiety, psychosis, substance abuse). Identifying and labeling a client's most negative and pervasive doubt labels is critical in gaining a full understanding of the client. Moreover, uncovering these doubt labels is a necessary component of successful treatment, as it is the first step in getting clients to ultimately evaluate and modify these labels.

Identifying doubt labels is easier when you know what the client values. The more socially-oriented client will tend to have doubt labels that revolve around themes of social acceptance—such as lovability, attractiveness, and decency—while the more achievement-oriented client will experience doubt around themes of capability—such as competency, independence, and strength. Clients who place a high value on sociotropy and autonomy may have doubt across both domains.

You can use the following worksheet to determine the doubt labels that your clients use to describe themselves. The adjectives on the top half represent doubt labels with a sociotropic theme of being undesirable, whereas the adjectives on the bottom half reflect doubt labels with an autonomous theme of being incapable or incompetent. Keep in mind that it is possible for clients to have only one nasty name they call themselves, or they may have multiple nasty names that may or may not cut across themes.

Client Worksheet

FIND YOUR DOUBT LABELS

• • • • •

Circle all the names that you tend to call yourself when you are upset or under stress.

Unlikeable	Unlovable	Not good enough
Undesirable	Outcast	Hideous
Odd	Plain	Uninteresting
Unattractive	Boring	Quiet
Shy	Disgusting	Unworthy
Insignificant	Ugly	Weird
Uncool	Loner	Bad
Awkward	Don't measure up	Fat
Unwanted	Mediocre	Strange
Helpless	Weak	Incompetent
Incapable	Powerless	Failure
Average	Loser	Not good enough to succeed
Dumbass	Dumb	Lazy
Inferior	Stupid	Idiot
Fraud	Ineffective	Useless
Dud	Feeble	Vulnerable
Inept	Senseless	Special needs
Retarded	Unskilled	Worthless

DOUBT LABELS

When talking with clients about specific situations that have triggered distress, identifying whether their automatic thoughts are related to social themes of love and acceptance (sociotropy), achievement and control (autonomy), or both will help guide you in probing for the underlying doubt label. The downward arrow technique is a valuable tool to help you uncover this underlying meaning. It asks the client to look at the personal meaning of the situation. The following list of potential downward arrow questions focuses on eliciting personal meaning, followed by two examples.

- "What does that mean?"
- "What does that say about you?"
- "What does that mean about you?"
- "What does that mean to you?"

Example 1:
Situation:	A client does not receive an invitation to a party.
Automatic thought:	"I'm the only one I know who wasn't invited."
Downward arrow question:	"What does that mean about you?"
Automatic thought:	"She doesn't like me."
Downward arrow question:	"What does it mean about you if she doesn't like you?"
Doubt label:	"I'm unlikeable."

Example 2:
Situation:	A client's workload has just been increased.
Automatic thought:	"I will never be able to get all this work done."
Downward arrow question:	"What does it say about you that you won't be able to get the work done?"
Automatic thought:	"I can't handle it."
Downward arrow question:	"What does it mean about you that you can't handle it?"
Doubt label:	"I'm incompetent."

Be prepared that eliciting the doubt label may not be easy. It may be that this negative label is still burgeoning and not easy to access, or it is buried deep inside. In addition, acknowledging this doubt label might be upsetting, so clients may wish to avoid this topic altogether. Alternatively, it may be that clients lack insight and are not aware of this underlying doubt label, or they may have not thought about it. If you find that clients are having difficulty coming up with answers when using the downward arrow technique, help them access their doubt label by using the **Find Your Doubt Labels** worksheet as a prompt. Invite them to refer back to their answers on the worksheet and see if any of the labels they previously identified may be responsible for these negative automatic thoughts.

THE ROLE OF HISTORY AND LIFE EXPERIENCES

Our history and life experiences shape and reinforce the views we have about ourselves and the world. Sometimes, individuals face horrific life circumstances, such as abuse, neglect, abandonment, poverty, and homelessness, which plant the seeds for self-doubt to flourish. For example, a woman who views herself as strong and capable, but becomes a victim of rape or assault, may now think of herself as weak and helpless. Similarly, the child of an alcoholic, who is physically abused and told that he is worthless, may conclude that he is a bad person. At the same time, not everyone who is exposed to trauma will develop underlying self-doubt beliefs. For example, another child growing up in a household characterized by abuse and alcoholism may recognize that she is an innocent victim and that the abuse is in no way a reflection of her character. Only those who ascribe personal meaning to the trauma will experience disruptions in their core beliefs.

In addition, even life experiences not associated with serious trauma can negatively impact our self-view. For example, think back to the student who didn't get a perfect grade or wasn't picked for the highest reading group, who now thinks that he is "dumb." Think of a child who lives with a family of musicians or athletes, but who lacks skills in these areas and concludes that she is "defective." Or the child on the playground who is picked last for a game of tag and now believes that he is "not good enough." The events that happen to us throughout our lives, whether they are traumatic or not, impact how we develop our sense of self.

Therefore, to understand and address your clients' self-doubt, it is important to identify the significant life events that played a role in shaping these doubt labels to begin with. To do so, use the following worksheet to help your clients understand the origins of their self-doubt. When completing the worksheet, begin by asking clients when they first started thinking about themselves this way. This historical approach offers a significant clue into the development of their self-concept. You may also ask them if any particular memories are significant and, if so, whether any of these memories played a role in how they view themselves now.

Early on, make sure to help clients understand how they came to see themselves in this light and to offer the possibility that the conclusions they made may not be accurate. Remember that it is not the historical event or trauma per se that caused them to develop self-doubt but, rather, their *interpretation* of that event and the personal meaning they ascribed to it. By helping your clients complete this worksheet, you can begin to see the distortions and biased conclusions that your clients have made.

Client Worksheet

CONNECT YOUR DOUBTS WITH THE PAST

• • • • • •

Think back to an early vivid memory and ask yourself, "What negative idea about myself might have existed at that time?" For example, perhaps you had a serious illness that required an extended time in the hospital and caused you to miss school, leading you to believe that you are weak, vulnerable, or helpless. As another example, perhaps you tried out for a sports team at an early age and didn't make it, causing you to believe that you are a failure, not good enough, or average. Alternatively, maybe you already know what your doubt belief is but aren't sure the specific event that triggered this belief. If so, try and recall an early memory where this negative idea about yourself existed.

Identify the doubt belief(s):

_____

What is your earliest memory of harboring this belief? Describe that memory here.

_____

_____

_____

What additional life events may have contributed to the development of this doubt belief?

_____

_____

_____

Cognitive Conceptualization: Understanding the Client

INEFFECTIVE COMPENSATORY ACTIONS

Compensatory behaviors are strategies we use to face life's challenges. Some of these behavioral strategies help us to cope, whereas others work against us. For example, avoidance, quitting, and distraction are all ineffective strategies that prevent us from addressing what is important or even necessary. Similarly, being passive, manipulative, or defensive are all ineffective communication strategies that lead to misunderstandings and compromises our needs. In addition, seeking perfection, attempting to control the situation, and worrying are all strategies that work against us. Given that mistakes are inevitable, perfectionistic demands are unattainable and plant the seeds for self-doubt.

In contrast, strategies that are typically effective in helping us achieve our goals include problem solving, prioritizing, staying focused, being assertive, self-soothing, exercising, asking for help, developing realistic standards, and turning off worry. However, even these strategies do not work all the time or in every situation. The ability to change our behaviors when whatever we are doing is not working is the key to wellness. For example, when a team approach on a committee project is not producing desired results, then taking complete control of the project might make sense. Similarly, if someone has just completed several hours of sustained work and needs a break, then watching TV is not avoidance.

However, when clients experience a trigger that activates their self-doubt, they tend to use strategies out of habit regardless of their effectiveness. They may also act in ways that they otherwise would not. These actions may lead to negative consequences or may compromise their values. For example, they may engage in self-harm, attempt suicide, or abuse substances. Alternatively, they may exploit or attack others, or engage in passive communication, which are all strategies that may work in the short run but have long-term costs. The following is a list of some common compensatory actions that individuals often engage in when self-doubt is activated.

Ineffective Compensatory Actions	
Avoidance	**Self-Harm**
Avoiding	Cutting
Quitting	Suicide attempts
Distracting	Substance abuse
Ineffective Communication	**Perfectionism**
Being passive	Seeking perfection
Manipulating	Controlling
Defending	Pleasing
Acting aggressively	Worrying

To get a better understanding of the behaviors your clients use to cope with their insecurities, look back at their answers on the **Apply the Cognitive Model: Connect Thoughts and Reactions** worksheet (page 8), and note which behaviors they exhibited in response to this trigger. You want to understand if this behavior represents a pattern, so ask your clients if this response is typical. You can also ask them about other distressing situations and see if they use other strategies when faced with a challenge.

DOUBT LABELS AND BEHAVIOR: GUIDELINES OR ASSUMPTIONS

The behavioral strategies clients use to cope are guided by the conditional rules, attitudes, and assumptions they have about themselves, which are known as intermediate beliefs (Beck, 2011). These intermediate beliefs are usually in the form of conditional "if, then" statements, which link the doubt label with the behavioral action. For example, clients who harbor the doubt label that they are undesirable may assume, "If I behave perfectly, then people will like me." In this case, the core belief that they are socially undesirable (doubt label) is driving them to seek perfection (behavioral strategy) as a means of compensating for their perceived undesirability. Clients who believe they are incompetent may also use perfectionism as a compensatory strategy, but their assumption is different: "If I am perfect, then I can prove I am competent."

The preceding examples are positive assumptions because they specify a behavioral strategy that can (in the client's mind) lead toward a *desirable* outcome. However, assumptions can also be negative, such that the conditional statement expresses how failing to behave a certain way will result in *negative* consequences. For example, "If I am not perfect, then people will reject me" or "If I am not perfect, then people will see how incompetent I am." Whether assumptions are positive or negative, they serve to drive ineffective compensatory strategies because clients believe that these strategies are protective in helping them avoid their feared outcome. The following worksheet may help your clients identify the positive and negative assumptions that drive their behavior.

Client Worksheet

IDENTIFY THE ASSUMPTION
· · · · · ·

Our doubt labels impact the attitudes, rules, and assumptions we have about the ways we believe we should behave. For example, if we have the doubt label that we are "unlovable," then we might believe that we have to put on our "game face" at all times to make and keep friends. In addition, we may believe that if we assert ourselves, then we might make someone unhappy, which activates the doubt that we are "unlovable."

This worksheet can help you identify the positive and negative assumptions that are driving your behaviors. Use your answers on previous worksheets as a guide, and identify the positive and negative assumptions associated with your doubt label.

Positive Assumptions

If I (state the behavior), then (state the positive impact on the doubt).

Example: If I *keep my opinions to myself*, then *people will want to hang out with me*.

   If I *drink wine*, then *I will feel better and be in control*.

   If I *am perfect*, then *people won't find me incompetent*.

   If I _____, then _____.

Negative Assumptions

If I (state the behavior), then (state the negative impact on the doubt).

Example: If I *don't keep my opinions to myself*, then *people won't like me*.

   If I *don't do everything for myself by letting people help*, then *I'll lose all control*.

   If I *am not perfect*, then *people will see how incompetent I am*.

   If I _____, then _____.

DOUBT CONCEPTUALIZATION MODEL

Once you have identified a client's doubt labels, life experiences, compensatory behaviors, and underlying assumptions, put these pieces together to develop a doubt conceptualization model, which provides a comprehensive picture of who the client is, how they define themselves, and what makes them tick. A thoughtful conceptualization will include a consideration of the client's cultural, social, and economic background, as well as other relevant factors that impact treatment. By developing this conceptualization, you can better understand the framework from which your clients view the world, themselves, and others, which will assist you in formulating a diagnosis, identifying goals, developing a treatment plan, and selecting the most appropriate cognitive-behavioral intervention.

The following page contains a sample doubt conceptualization model for a client who experiences the doubt label that she is unlovable, followed by a blank template you can use with your clients. As you can see from the sample doubt model, the client's doubt label was largely shaped within the context of her family life, which was characterized by a dysfunctional relationship with her parents and constant social comparisons to her siblings. As the client's doubt label developed over time, she began to believe that she could never assert her needs and that she always had to be perfect for others to like her. In turn, these assumptions drove her to become perfectionistic, passive, and people pleasing in the context of interpersonal relationships.

Sample Worksheet

DOUBT CONCEPTUALIZATION MODEL

• • • • • •

Shaping Experiences

Hardworking, highly critical father with demanding expectations

Emotionally distant mother

Challenging brother is the favored child in the family and is always in the spotlight

Three older sisters always receiving compliments on their appearance

Doubt Labels

"I am unlovable."

Guidelines or Assumptions

"If I am complimented, then I am lovable."

"If I am ignored, then I won't be loved."

"If I always say 'yes,' then people will love me."

"If I assert myself, then people won't love me."

"If I am perfect, then people will love me."

"If I am not perfect, then people will reject me, which means I am unlovable."

Compensatory Ineffective Actions

Try to be perfect

Never assert myself and say "yes" to everyone

Stay quiet and well behaved

Client Worksheet

DOUBT CONCEPTUALIZATION MODEL

· · · · · ·

Shaping Experiences

Doubt Labels

Guidelines or Assumptions

Compensatory Ineffective Actions

Cognitive Conceptualization: Understanding the Client

As discussed in Chapter 1, how we perceive specific situations—along with the automatic thoughts we subsequently have about those situations—is influenced by our underlying doubt labels. In other words, how we view any given situation can be negatively altered by self-doubt. Therefore, after developing a doubt conceptualization of your client, return to the cognitive model to see how the client's doubt labels influence a variety of situation-specific automatic thoughts.

Returning to the previous example of the client who believes she is unlovable, we can use the cognitive model and our doubt conceptualization of the client to help explain how her self-doubt influences the manner in which she interprets and responds to her experiences. The diagrams on the following page illustrate how this doubt conceptualization can influence the outcome of three different scenarios. At the root of each of these scenarios is the client's core belief that she is incapable of being loved and that she is not good enough. This doubt label causes her to perceive her world through a lens of doubt, in turn affecting her feelings, thoughts, and behaviors. Following this sample diagram is a blank template you can use with your own clients to see how their doubt labels affect how they react and respond to certain situations.

Sample Worksheet

SITUATION-SPECIFIC AUTOMATIC THOUGHTS

・・・・・

Scenario 1

Doubt Label
"I'm unlovable."

↓

Assumptions
"If I am ignored, then I won't be loved."

↓

Event
On a date and her date is looking at something behind her head

→

Automatic Thought
"He wants to be with the person he is looking at behind me. He is going to break up with me."

→

Emotion
Sadness, anxiety

Physiological Sensation
Shaky, pit in stomach

Behavior
Smiles and pretends like everything is fine. After the date, she never talks to him again, fearing that he will reject her

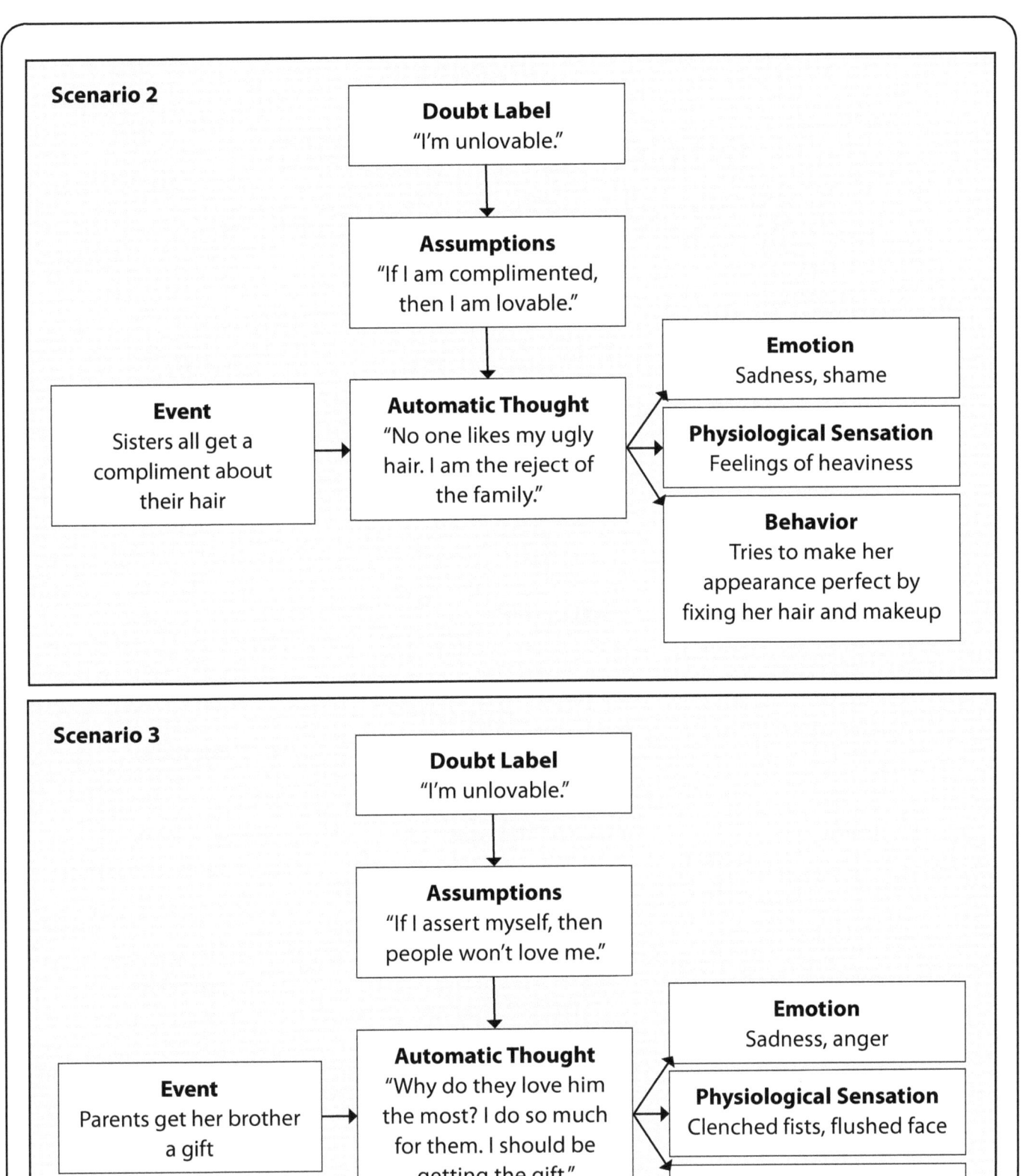

Client Worksheet

SITUATION-SPECIFIC AUTOMATIC THOUGHTS

· · · · · ·

```
        ┌──────────────────┐
        │   Doubt Label    │
        │                  │
        └────────┬─────────┘
                 ↓
        ┌──────────────────┐
        │   Assumptions    │
        │                  │
        └────────┬─────────┘
                 ↓                          ┌──────────────────────┐
┌───────────┐   ┌──────────────────┐  ──→   │      Emotion         │
│           │   │                  │        └──────────────────────┘
│   Event   │──→│ Automatic Thought│  ──→   ┌──────────────────────┐
│           │   │                  │        │ Physiological Sensation │
└───────────┘   └──────────────────┘  ──→   └──────────────────────┘
                                            ┌──────────────────────┐
                                            │      Behavior        │
                                            └──────────────────────┘
```

Copyright © 2019 Leslie Sokol & Marci G. Fox, *The Comprehensive Clinician's Guide to Cognitive Behavioral Therapy*. All Rights Reserved

3
GOAL-DIRECTED THERAPY

PROBLEM LIST

Therapy is intended to help reduce the distress clients are experiencing and improve their ability to function in their day-to-day lives. However, vague goals lead to vague therapy. In order for therapy to be effective, the treatment plan needs to be driven by specific, concrete goals—and to establish these goals, you first need to clearly define the client's problems.

The first question to ask clients who are seeking treatment is, "What brings you in today?" or "What is your chief complaint?" You want to identify the issues in the client's life that are a source of distress or conflict so that you can create a problem list. Problem lists typically have two to six items but can be much longer. A complete problem list should include all of the things in the client's life that are contributing to this distress, including difficulties that are psychological, interpersonal, occupational, educational, medical, legal, housing, or leisure related in nature.

A problem list does not merely contain a list of topics that are bothering the client. Rather, it provides an understanding of *how* these specific areas are a problem for the client (or why someone else thinks these areas are a problem for the client). For example, the following is an inadequate problem list because it only describes the broader problem area of concern and gives us no information as to what the specific problem is:

- Anxiety
- My husband
- My kids
- Self-esteem

To elicit the specific problems at hand, you need to clarify and more clearly define these initial difficulties. A dialogue that accomplishes this goal might look as follows:

Therapist: "What is your chief complaint?"
Client: "Anxiety is my biggest problem."
Therapist: "How is anxiety a problem for you?"
Client: "It keeps me from doing things."
Therapist: "What does it keep you from doing?"
Client: "I cannot go anywhere because I'm afraid I might have horrible anxiety."
Therapist: "So anxiety is a problem because it prevents you from doing the things that you would like to do. Is the feeling of anxiety itself a problem as well?"
Client: "Yes, I do everything I can to try and avoid those feelings."
Therapist: "What is your worst fear about those feelings?"
Client: "I am going to have a heart attack and die."

Now the client's first problem (anxiety) is more fully understood as a fear of having a heart attack and phobic avoidance. As the therapist, you can more clearly define the remaining three problems by asking *how* each of those are a problem for the client. For example, perhaps the husband is a problem because he thinks the client is using anxiety as an excuse and is fed up with her refusals. Perhaps the client has reported her kids as a problem because she has started to limit their activities out of concern that she is inadvertently going to make them fearful as well. Lastly, perhaps self-esteem is a problem because she believes she is failing in every aspect of her life and questions her self-worth, leading her to question every decision she makes. By asking probing questions, you can better define the problem.

Keep in mind that clients may be brought into treatment against their will. Often, clients show up to treatment because they have been pushed to go by partners, parents, employers, teachers, or court mandates. Regardless of whether clients come to treatment of their own volition or are there as a result of some other party, developing a clearly-defined problem list is the first step in treatment.

For clients who are pushed into therapy, you can begin by asking them why someone else thinks they need to be there and guiding them in understanding why treatment makes sense. For example, consider a woman who comes into therapy because her employer has told her that she has an anger management problem. The woman believes that she does not need therapy and thinks it is ridiculous that she is being forced to go. The therapist might first ask if she values her job and wants to remain an employee. Then, the therapist might ask if she tends to feel annoyed and frustrated (especially at work) and, if so, how she acts when that happens. Through this process, the therapist can hopefully help the client see that her anger may be getting the best of her and that working on it may be a necessary pain to keep the job she is invested in keeping. Getting the client to buy in to and engage in treatment is the first step in developing a problem list.

TREATMENT GOALS

Treatment goals follow directly from the problem list, as they represent a solution to the difficulties the client has identified. In general, goals that are specific and measurable are the most ideal. Clearly-defined goals allow for clear paths of intervention. A client's goals should also be realistic and personal, meaning that these goals should not involve an attempt to change others. Therapy goals are not about changing other people. Therefore, when developing treatment goals, it is crucial for clients to understand that they have no control over how other people act, think, or speak. Therapy goals are personal, not imposing.

Therapy goals such as "find a spouse," "get rich," or "get a job" are not something that therapy can produce. On the other hand, taking the necessary steps to increase the likelihood of obtaining those outcomes is an appropriate therapy goal. We cannot find clients a spouse, but we can help them overcome their fear of talking to people or their fear of rejection, and we can help them see themselves in a way that gives them the courage to go after what they want.

To make goals concrete, realistic, and specific, start by having clients define each goal and ask them to describe what it would look like to achieve this goal. You can use guided discovery to move clients from an abstract understanding of their desired outcome to one that is more clearly defined, as well as to move them from unrealistic expectations to those that are more realistic. For example, if a client says, "I just want to be happy," then you can help list the specific behaviors that the client can engage in to increase the likelihood of being happier, such as "reconnect with friends" and "increase pleasant activities."

Continuing with the previous example of the anxious client, the development of treatment goals might look as follows: You might address her first identified problem (anxiety) by asking if she would like to be able to face all the things she is afraid of and then having her make a list of all those things. You can then work with her to gradually confront and challenge these fears. The client's second problem involves her husband's lack of understanding and the demands he is placing on her. Given that the goal of therapy cannot involve changing

Goal-Directed Therapy

his behavior, a more appropriate goal may be to reduce the negative impact of these demands on the client, as well as to help her consider alternative viewpoints, such as the possibility that her husband may think he is helping by behaving this way. Similarly, another valid goal may be to help the client learn ways to assert herself and set limits, or to seek out couples counseling if marital discord continues to be a problem for her.

In order to address the client's third problem (e.g., her children and the impact that her anxiety is having on them), an appropriate therapy goal might involve finding ways for her children to participate in activities, regardless of whether she accompanies them, with the ultimate goal being for her to join in on these activities as well. It may also be helpful to give her coping tools to prevent her from inadvertently transferring any unnecessary anxiety onto her children. Finally, to increase the client's self-esteem, you can work with the client to help her see herself in a more realistically positive light, which would entail learning to take credit for all she does. Instead of questioning every decision she makes, you can help the client learn to feel confident in her decision-making abilities by teaching her assertiveness and social skills.

To help your clients create a problem list and develop accompanying treatment goals to address these problems, you can use the worksheet on the following page.

Client Worksheet

DEVELOP A PROBLEM AND GOAL LIST

· · · · · ·

With the help of your therapist, use this worksheet to develop a list of problems and accompanying goals that you'd like to work on in treatment. Keep in mind that a problem is defined as an issue that is causing you distress, interfering with your functioning, or preventing you from achieving your objectives. The aim is to make these issues less of a problem for you. Having concrete, realistic goals will help to guide treatment and inform the specific interventions that will be most useful for you.

Problems

Make sure to clearly define *why* the problem is a problem.

1. _____
   _____

2. _____
   _____

3. _____
   _____

4. _____
   _____

5. _____
   _____

Goals

Make sure your goals are personal, realistic, and measurable.

1. _____
   _____

2. _____
   _____

3. _____
   _____

4. _____
   _____

5. _____
   _____

SESSION STRUCTURE

As CBT clinicians, we are here to intervene. We are not here simply to provide support, listen, or allow the client to have a cathartic experience. In CBT, therapy has a defined beginning, numerous middle sections, and an end. This structure maximizes the amount of time we have in session so that work can get accomplished. It ensures that critical topics get the time they deserve while making sure that appropriate interventions still take place. Providing clients with the rationale for this structure can help gain their cooperation. While you can certainly encourage clients to take greater responsibility for the session over time, the overall burden of responsibility still lies with you as the therapist. In addition, although adhering to the session structure is important, at the same time, do not be rigid. Respect your therapeutic judgment and prioritize accordingly when life-threatening issues arise.

If clients have had previous therapy experience, educate them as to how this course of treatment will be different. Doing so is especially relevant if they have been in supportive therapy. Let clients know that CBT is goal-oriented, directive, and problem solving in nature. Explain that they will participate in establishing goals and setting problem-focused agendas. Encourage them to take notes (in writing, electronically, or via audio recording) from the onset of treatment to increase their engagement and provide them with opportunities for learning rehearsal. Most importantly, make sure clients know that they will be expected to participate as a critical member of their treatment team. You want clients to see that making connections between their thoughts, feelings, and behaviors requires active participation both in session *and* between sessions.

The Beginning

Every CBT session should start with a check-in that establishes the workload ahead. It also serves as the bridge between sessions so that the therapeutic work is cumulative, and it serves as an opportunity for the therapist to build and maintain a solid therapeutic alliance. Typically, a mood check opens the session, which allows for therapists to gauge how the client is doing compared to previous sessions. Although many therapists perform this mood check by asking, "How are you doing?", open-ended questions like this don't necessarily yield reliable information. Rather, using a standardized, Likert-response-style scale—like the Beck inventories for anxiety, hopelessness, and depression (Beck & Steer, 1993a, 1993b; Beck, Steer, & Brown, 1996)—is preferable, but even a one-item Likert scale can provide more reliable information about your client's state of mind than asking a general question.

You can evaluate mood on a scale of 0 to 10 by asking how the client's overall mood is this week, or by asking about specific moods (e.g., how depressed, anxious, hopeless, suicidal, angry, etc. the client has been this past week). In severe depression, it is also helpful to ask how clients are feeling that very day and then to reassess how they are feeling at the end of the session, as it's important to make sure they do not leave the session in worse shape than when they arrived.

You can use the following worksheet at the beginning of each session to gauge your client's overall mood. Prior to giving clients the worksheet, write in the three main moods they tend to experience under "Mood 1," "Mood 2," and "Mood 3." Then, ask clients to rate how intensely they are experiencing each of these three different emotions on a 0 to 10 scale, as well as to describe what response anchors of 0, 5, and 10 look like in their life.

Client Worksheet

MOOD CHECK

• • • • • •

Describe how you are feeling today. Rate how intensely you are experiencing the following three emotions on a 0 to 10 scale, with 0 being not at all and 10 being the most you have ever felt that emotion. Then, describe what it looks like when you are experiencing that emotion at an intensity of 0, 5, and 10. An example for sadness is illustrated in the box below.

> **Example: Sadness**
>
> 0   1   2   3   ④   5   6   7   8   9   10
>
> Not at all   Moderately   The most
>
> 0 = I get up and go to work on time, do my job, and recognize my hard work. I make plans with friends and smile. I go to the gym and take care of stuff.
>
> 5 = I struggle to get to work. I have a hard time seeing the good stuff that happens at work, and I have to push myself to return texts and calls to friends.
>
> 10 = I can't get out of bed and go to work. I can't stop thinking about how bad things are and how I'm all alone. I stop taking care of myself and sometimes can't even get myself to shower or eat anything but cookies and ice cream.

Mood 1: _____

0   1   2   3   4   5   6   7   8   9   10

Not at all   Moderately   The most

0 = _____

_____

_____

5 = _____

_____

_____

10 = _____

_____

Mood 2: _____

| 0 | 1 | 2 | 3 | 4 | 5 | 6 | 7 | 8 | 9 | 10 |

Not at all   Moderately   The most

0 = _____

_____

_____

5 = _____

_____

_____

10 = _____

_____

_____

Mood 3: _____

| 0 | 1 | 2 | 3 | 4 | 5 | 6 | 7 | 8 | 9 | 10 |

Not at all   Moderately   The most

0 = _____

_____

_____

5 = _____

_____

_____

10 = _____

_____

_____

The Agenda

In addition to allowing for a mood check, the beginning of the session is also a time to check in on the impact of previous sessions and see if anything from the last session has impacted the client's week. To obtain this information, explicitly ask the client if anything significant has happened in the past week that warrants further discussion. Do not assume that this is something the client will automatically talk about; you must ask. In addition, the beginning of the session is a time to check in on medication and homework. However, this is only a check-in. If a discussion is warranted, then it becomes an item on the agenda, which is the most important part of the beginning of the session.

The agenda reflects a list of the most important items that clients are working on as a means of achieving their treatment goals. Typically, the agenda has a few items, but it may have only one item, or it may comprise quite a few issues. The agenda is meant to be problem-focused rather than a global list of topics. For example, instead of "talking about the client's boyfriend," the agenda item might be "figuring out if this relationship is in the client's best interest." Similarly, instead of "talking about work," the agenda item might be "finding ways to address the client's feelings of inadequacy and feeling overwhelmed." Although an agenda is intended to be problem-focused, sometimes the client's difficulty cannot be defined until you have a discussion to get at the root of the matter.

The agenda is meant to be a collaborative process, but that does not mean that therapists cannot make suggestions. For example, less engaged clients can be offered choices or guided to see what might make sense to work on together. The fact that the agenda is collaborative simply means the client has agreed that working on the identified problems makes sense. Once a collaborative agenda is established, the items are prioritized to ensure time is allocated for the most important items on the list. However, if the client wishes to address all the items, then it is the therapist's responsibility to manage the time to do so.

There are several important things to remember about the agenda. First, make sure the agenda is realistic for the time allotted. A standard therapy session is 45 to 50 minutes. If the mood check, review of previous homework, and medication and weekly check-in take about five to seven minutes (and the end of session review takes approximately five to seven minutes), then you have about 30 minutes to work on the agenda items. Choosing one to three items to work on tends to be realistic, depending on how much time is required to cover each item comprehensively. Prioritize the agenda items with the client and decide together the amount of time to work on each one.

Second, if the homework will take more than five or so minutes to review, then include it as an agenda item. Make sure the agenda item relevant to homework is defined as a problem and does not simply involve the topic of reviewing the homework assignment. For example, you might instead decide to focus on the obstacles that prevented the client from doing the assignment, the challenges they experienced while doing it, or the learning that they gained as a result. To guide this discussion, you might say, "In discussing the homework today, it sounds like it would make sense for us to talk about strategies to help you follow through on getting your paperwork done." Following these guidelines will help make your sessions more focused and increase the effectiveness of treatment.

To develop the agenda at the start of each session, you can use the following worksheet in collaboration with your clients.

Client Worksheet

SET THE AGENDA

• • • • • •

To help your session be goal directed, list the agenda items you'd like to talk about today. In order to be clear about what you'd like to focus on in session, make sure these agenda items are specific and concrete.

For example, instead of "Talk about my significant other," a more specific agenda item might be, "Figure out if my romantic relationship is in my best interest." Then, work with your therapist to prioritize each agenda item to determine which items you'd like to tackle first in session.

Finally, decide with your therapist how much time you'd like to spend on each item. Remember, there is only a limited amount of time in each session, so think about what is most important for you today.

Agenda Items   **Priority**   **Time Allotted**

1. _____ _____ _____

2. _____ _____ _____

3. _____ _____ _____

Copyright © 2019 Leslie Sokol & Marci G. Fox, *The Comprehensive Clinician's Guide to Cognitive Behavioral Therapy*. All Rights Reserved

The Middle of the Session

Once the agenda items are set, the middle of the therapy session begins, which is where the work is done. The middle of the session is a time when you work to understand and address the "what" regarding each agenda item. In other words, for each agenda item that the client has listed, identify *what* is driving the issue at hand. Get specifics regarding the difficulties and struggles clients are experiencing with regard to each agenda item. Help clients define what is getting in the way. In particular, clarify whether it is the client's thinking patterns, behaviors, or both that are contributing to their difficulties. The following table provides an example of two difficulties a client may have identified as agenda items, as well as the accompanying "what" components (e.g., thoughts and behaviors) that are driving these difficulties.

Define the "What" for Each Agenda Item

Agenda item	What is getting in the way? Thoughts, behaviors, or both?
1. Can't get things done	Thinking: "I always think I'll just do it later." Behavior: Procrastination (watches TV, checks social media)
2. Perceives criticism from Mom	Thinking: "My mom should just shut up." Behavior: Fights with Mom, yells, insults, and ignores Mom's wishes

Once you have identified the "what" for each agenda item, move on to discussing the "how" regarding each item. That is, brainstorm *how* clients can address this specific issue. Part of this process involves helping clients determine the accuracy or helpfulness of their thoughts and behaviors, and how they can modify any thoughts or behaviors that are maladaptive in nature.

Remember, all psychological problems involve problems in thinking, so cognitive restructuring can help clients evaluate their thought processes. Use the process of guided questioning to help clients modify distorted or unhelpful thoughts so they can see situations in a less biased and more helpful way. Thought registers, pie charts, cost-benefit analyses, looking at things through another person's eyes, seeing alternative viewpoints, looking at continuums, labeling thought distortions, and looking at the evidence are some of the ways to restructure thoughts.

To address your clients' ineffective behaviors, consider CBT strategies that target the problematic behavior, such as exposure-based techniques, running experiments to test hypotheses, collecting behavioral data, role-playing, or behavioral activation—to name a few. The overall goal is to identify the specific skills that clients can use to overcome whatever maladaptive thinking or behavior patterns are contributing to their difficulties.

Define the "How" for Each Agenda Item

Agenda item	What specific skills can the client use to address this issue?
1. Can't get things done	Thinking: Replace "give-up" thinking with "go-to" thinking Behavior: Set a goal, plan, resist distractions, and follow the plan
2. Perceives criticism from Mom	Thinking: Replace the "should" statement with a preference statement (e.g., "I'd like it if . . . ," "It would be nice if . . . ," etc.) Behavior: Practice assertiveness by expressing feelings and letting Mom know what she is doing that is upsetting. Instead of ignoring Mom's wishes, consider compromise.

Summaries

Throughout the session, summarize what the client has learned. Providing brief, periodic summaries after each agenda item—as well as an overall summary once the agenda is complete—is critical to effective treatment because it reinforces what has been learned in the session. In addition, you want clients to be able to summarize what they have learned in their own words to make sure they have gained something from the experience.

Elicit a summary statement by asking the client, "What have you gained from this conversation?" or "What do you think is the takeaway from our conversation?" Eliciting this summary based on content, not process, is crucial. It is not, "We talked about your husband today," but, "In talking about your husband, what did you learn?" Ideally, you want clients to be able to provide this summary in their own words and without your guidance. However, if they are unable to, a second option is to guide clients toward a conclusion. For example, you might say, "We talked about how your husband doesn't show you that he cares in a way that you would prefer, but how does he *think* he shows that he cares about you?" As a last resort, you can also explicitly tell clients what you were hoping they gained from the conversation (e.g., "Remember we concluded that your husband *does* care about you, just not in the way you wish").

To help clients retain and rehearse what they have learned, ask them to record these summaries in writing, electronically, or verbally. For example, clients can write these summaries down in a notebook, small index card, or piece of paper; send themselves a text message; put a message in the notes section of their phone; or leave themselves a recorded message.

Summarize the Takeaways from Each Agenda Item

Agenda item	What is the takeaway?
1. Can't get things done	Therapist: "What do you think the takeaway from our conversation is?" Client: "My thoughts get in the way of acting. It's important to replace goal-interfering thoughts with goal-orienting thoughts and to use them to push myself to act. I feel better when I take care of what I need to by following my plan."
2. Perceives criticism from Mom	Therapist: "What do you think the takeaway from our conversation is?" Client: "When I calmly and assertively express myself to my mom, things go a lot better, and I feel less angry. Compromise has helped me get what I want and keeps Mom happy too."

Homework

For clients to fully absorb what they have learned in session, they must put this learning into practice between sessions. It is for this reason that homework is such an important part of CBT. Homework is a measure of how invested clients are in the change process, which is why homework adherence is associated with better treatment prognosis. When clients complete homework, it validates that they have embraced the treatment model and are working toward self-efficacy. It extends and increases therapy contact by having them apply the principles they were taught in session to the real world. It serves as an opportunity to gather data, run experiments, and rehearse new viewpoints learned in session. In other words, homework offers an opportunity for clients to put abstract concepts into practice, and it often provides the necessary behavioral data for cognitive change to take place. Most importantly, homework also aids in relapse prevention because *everything* is homework when therapy is finished.

Homework should never be assigned in a generic manner but should grow organically based on each client's needs. Therefore, make sure to involve the client in the process of setting the homework. Doing so ensures that the homework assignment is individually tailored to the client, which increases the likelihood of compliance. Make sure to clearly explain the rationale behind the homework so that clients fully understand why they should take it on. This is especially important in the case of dependent clients, who seek therapist approval and often blindly comply with homework assignments without understanding its rationale, which causes them to gain less from the homework experience. Similarly, more autonomous clients will want to play a more active role in choosing their homework assignment, and providing them with the rationale behind the assignment will enhance the quality of their choice.

In addition, you can increase homework compliance by providing clients with detailed instructions about the nature of the homework assignment (e.g., place, time, frequency, duration). It is also helpful to have clients consider starting the assignment as soon as they leave the office. To help clients entertain this possibility, you can ask questions such as, "What were you planning on doing when you leave here?" or "What might be the advantages of doing the assignment we just agreed on right now?" Equally important is asking, "How likely are you to do the homework?" You want clients to leave the office believing they will do it. If clients respond with, "I'll try" or "It's 50-50," then consider modifying the homework or finding out what the obstacles might be. In these cases, you can also begin the assignment in session. For example, if a client's homework assignment is to complete a particular application (e.g., school, job, housing), but the client has been putting off doing so, then the application process could be started in the office.

Directly Link the Homework to the Problem

Agenda item	Homework
1. Can't get things done	• Review all the reasons to follow through on my plan (e.g., I'll gain a sense of accomplishment; it might boost my self-esteem, especially if I take credit for any amount I get done; it will reduce pressure and stress; I'll have more fun because I won't be focused on what I haven't done). • Follow my plan to spend every day from 5-7 p.m. taking care of the specific things I've been putting off. • Replace any "give-up" thoughts (e.g., "I'll do it later") with "go-to" thoughts (e.g., "Putting it off makes me feel worse, and I miss out on fun" or "If I wait, then it may never happen").
2. Perceives criticism from Mom	• Practice assertively communicating with Mom by explicitly telling her how I feel and what I want, wish for, or prefer. Be open to compromise.

Sometimes, real obstacles interfere with homework compliance, and when this occurs, it is appropriate for therapists to help problem solve and address these barriers. More often, though, obstacles are a result of psychological difficulties, lack of buy-in, lack of understanding regarding the assignment, or hopelessness. Regardless, when homework is not done the first time around, a discussion of obstacles is warranted. Unless the specific assignment is an important component of clients' recovery, the most practical intervention is to modify the homework. If the specific assignment is crucial, such as exposure work, then you might try finding a way to do the assignment with the client first. In addition, you can ask the client to seek out the assistance of a friend or family member who can aid in the exposure, and you can also remind the client of the treatment goals that were identified at the start of treatment and discuss how doing the assignment is crucial in achieving these goals.

Goal-Directed Therapy

End of the Session

The end of the session is the wrap-up. Clinicians often think of this as the time to discuss homework, but that discussion should have followed each problem on the agenda after it was addressed. Rather, the end of the session is an opportunity to get overall feedback, reiterate the key points of learning, provide a summary, and review the planned homework. Asking clients for overall feedback ensures that you are not rubbing them the wrong way, overwhelming them, or in any way making them unhappy. Be mindful when clients spontaneously provide you with feedback, as asking for feedback when they have already provided it gives clients the message that you are not paying attention or listening to them.

In addition, if clients provide you with positive feedback by stating that the session was helpful, ask "What made it helpful?" If they tell you the session helped them talk through their problems and that you are the only person they have ever told this to, then this reflects a strong therapeutic relationship. However, positive feedback doesn't necessarily mean that clients have gained the ability to cope or experienced a reduction in distress associated with their identified problems. When an intervention takes place, clients should ideally be able to articulate what they have specifically learned that will help them function better in the upcoming week. Often, it is necessary for the therapist to guide clients to this understanding—and, when needed, even spell it out for them. Summarizing the content of learning demonstrates that an intervention has taken place.

To help you incorporate the basic CBT session structure into your practice, the following two pages provide an example of a therapy note that you can use to summarize your sessions with clients.

Clinician Worksheet

THERAPY NOTE
· · · · · ·

Client: _____   Date: _____

Session #: _____   Session length: _____

Mood check: _____
_____

Medication check: _____
_____

Homework compliance: _____
_____

Agenda item 1: _____

    Key thoughts and behaviors ("what"): _____
_____

    Skill to change or build ("how"): _____
_____

    Brief summary/takeaway: _____
_____

    Relevant homework: _____
_____

Agenda item 2: _____

    Key thoughts and behaviors ("what"): _____
_____

    Skill to change or build ("how"): _____
_____

    Brief summary/takeaway: _____
_____

    Relevant homework: _____
_____

Overall summary of main points: _____
_____

Overall feedback about session: _____
_____

Homework: _____
_____

Work for future sessions: _____
_____

Next appointment date: _____

SELF-ASSESSMENT

The Cognitive Therapy Scale—also known as the Cognitive Therapy Rating Scale (CTRS)—is a good way for therapists to assess their clinical competency in administering CBT (Young & Beck, 1988). It measures the extent to which therapists are adhering to the CBT model, as well as their proficiency in delivery CBT. Therefore, it's considered a measure that assesses both fidelity and competency.

The CTRS contains 11 items that measure fidelity and competency across a variety of areas. In particular, it measures therapists' ability to (1) collaboratively establish and follow an agenda, (2) elicit feedback and summaries throughout the session and at the end of the session, (3) understand the client through the lens of the cognitive model, (4) establish interpersonal effectiveness and rapport, (5) demonstrate collaboration throughout, (6) pace the work effectively, (7) use the basic principles of guided discovery, (8) identify and address the key cognitions and behaviors, (9) formulate and deliver a coherent and promising CBT change strategy, (10) apply the techniques in a reasonable way, and (11) define and discuss relevant homework.

You can use the CTRS provided on the following pages to assess your own CBT proficiency. A score of 40 or greater indicates clinical competency in CBT (Young & Beck, 1988). Although work samples are typically scored by an independent, objective, and trained rater, you can score your own work sample by using the anchors on the scale as a guide. When used in supervision, supervisors can rate the therapist's application of CBT in session and go through each of the subscales with the therapist to improve his or her CBT skills. Over time, the supervisor can train the therapist on the use of the CTRS, and both the supervisor and therapist can rate the same session and review it together to improve fidelity to the cognitive model and enhance proficiency in CBT. Therapists can also read through the scale and accompanying manual and continue to self-score sessions, or a group can rate a volunteer's session to increase inter-rater reliability within a specific organization. The scale and accompanying CTRS Manual (Young & Beck, 1980) are also available on the Academy of Cognitive Therapy's website: www.academyofct.org.

Supervisor/Clinician Self-Assessment Worksheet

COGNITIVE THERAPY SCALE

• • • • • •

Therapist: _____ Client: _____ Date of Session: _____

Directions: For each time, assess the therapist on a scale from 0 to 6, and record the rating on the line next to the item number. Descriptions are provided for even-numbered scale points. If you believe the therapist falls between two of the descriptors, select the intervening odd number (1, 3, 5). For example, if the therapist set a very good agenda but did not establish priorities, assign a rating of a 5 rather than a 4 or 6.

If the descriptions for a given item occasionally do not seem to apply to the session you are rating, feel free to disregard them and use the more general scale below:

0	1	2	3	4	5	6
Poor	Barely Adequate	Mediocre	Satisfactory	Good	Very Good	Excellent

Please do not leave any item blank. For all items, focus on the skill of the therapist, considering how difficult the client seems to be.

PART I. GENERAL THERAPEUTIC SKILLS

___1. **Agenda**

   0   Therapist did not set agenda.
   2   Therapist set agenda that was vague or incomplete.
   4   Therapist worked with client to set a mutually satisfactory agenda that included specific target problems (e.g., anxiety at work, dissatisfaction with marriage).
   6   Therapist worked with client to set an appropriate agenda with target problems, suitable for the available time. Established priorities and then followed agenda.

___2. **Feedback**

   0   Therapist did not ask for feedback to determine client's understanding of, or response to, the session.
   2   Therapist elicited some feedback from client but did not ask enough questions to be sure client understood therapist's line of reasoning during the session *or* to ascertain whether client was satisfied with the session.

- 4 Therapist asked enough questions to be sure that client understood therapist's line of reasoning throughout the session and to determine client's reactions to the session. Therapist adjusted his or her behavior in response to the feedback, when appropriate.
- 6 Therapist was especially adept at eliciting and responding to verbal and nonverbal feedback throughout the session (e.g., elicited reactions to session, regularly checked for understanding, helped summarize main points at end of session).

____ **3. Understanding**

- 0 Therapist repeatedly failed to understand what client explicitly said and thus consistently missed the point. Poor empathic skills.
- 2 Therapist was usually able to reflect or rephrase what client explicitly said, but repeatedly failed to respond to more subtle communication. Limited ability to listen and empathize.
- 4 Therapist generally seemed to grasp client's internal reality as reflected by both what client explicitly said and what client communicated in more subtle ways. Good ability to listen and empathize.
- 6 Therapist seemed to understand client's internal reality thoroughly and was adept at communicating this understanding through appropriate verbal and nonverbal responses to client (e.g., the tone of therapist's response conveyed a sympathetic understanding of client's message). Excellent listening and empathic skills.

____ **4. Interpersonal Effectiveness**

- 0 Therapist had poor interpersonal skills. Seemed hostile, demeaning, or in some other way destructive to the client.
- 2 Therapist did not seem destructive but had significant interpersonal problems. At times, therapist appeared unnecessarily impatient, aloof, insincere, *or* had difficulty conveying confidence and competence.
- 4 Therapist displayed a *satisfactory* degree of warmth, concern, confidence, genuineness, and professionalism. No significant interpersonal problems.
- 6 Therapist displayed *optimal* levels of warmth, concern, confidence, genuineness, and professionalism, appropriate for this particular client in this session.

____ **5. Collaboration**

- 0 Therapist did not attempt to set up a collaboration with client.
- 2 Therapist attempted to collaborate with client but had difficulty *either* defining a problem that client considered important *or* establishing rapport.
- 4 Therapist was able to collaborate with client, focus on a problem that both client and therapist considered important, and establish rapport.

6   Collaboration seemed excellent; therapist encouraged client as much as possible to take an active role during the session (e.g., by offering choices) so they could function as a team.

___ 6. **Pacing and Efficient Use of Time**

0   Therapist made no attempt to structure therapy time. Session seemed aimless.

2   Session had some direction, but therapist had significant problems with structuring or pacing (e.g., too little structure, inflexible about structure, too slowly paced, too rapidly paced).

4   Therapist was reasonably successful at using time efficiently. Therapist maintained appropriate control over flow of discussion and pacing.

6   Therapist used time efficiently by tactfully limiting peripheral and unproductive discussion and by pacing the session as rapidly as was appropriate for client.

PART II: CONCEPTUALIZATION, STRATEGY, AND TECHNIQUE

___ 7. **Guided Discovery**

0   Therapist relied primarily on debate, persuasion, or "lecturing." Therapist seemed to be cross-examining client, putting client on the defensive, or forcing his or her point of view on client.

2   Therapist relied too heavily on persuasion and debate, rather than guided discovery. However, therapist's style was supportive enough that client did not seem to feel attacked or defensive.

4   Therapist, for the most part, helped client see new perspectives through guided discovery (e.g., examining evidence, considering alternatives, weighing advantages and disadvantages) rather than through debate. Used questioning appropriately.

6   Therapist was especially adept at using guided discovery during the session to explore problems and help client draw own conclusions. Achieved an excellent balance between skillful questioning and other modes of intervention.

___ 8. **Focusing on Key Cognitions or Behaviors**

0   Therapist did not attempt to elicit specific thoughts, assumptions, images, meanings, or behaviors.

2   Therapist used appropriate techniques to elicit cognitions or behaviors; however, therapist had difficulty finding a focus *or* focused on cognitions or behaviors that were irrelevant to client's key problems.

4   Therapist focused on specific cognitions or behaviors relevant to the target problem. However, therapist could have focused on more central cognitions or behaviors that offered greater promise for progress.

6 Therapist skillfully focused on key thoughts, assumptions, behaviors, etc. that were most relevant to the problem area and offered considerable promise for progress.

___9. **Strategy for Change** (Note: For this item, focus on the quality of therapist's strategy for change, not on how effectively the strategy was implemented or whether change actually occurred.)

0 Therapist did not select cognitive-behavioral techniques.

2 Therapist selected cognitive-behavioral techniques; however, either the overall strategy for bringing about change seemed vague *or* did not seem promising in helping client.

4 Therapist seemed to have a generally coherent strategy for change that showed reasonable promise and incorporated cognitive-behavioral techniques.

6 Therapist followed a consistent strategy for change that seemed promising and incorporated the most appropriate cognitive-behavioral techniques.

___10. **Application of Cognitive-Behavioral Techniques** (Note: For this item, focus on how skillfully the techniques were applied, not on how appropriate they were for the target problem or whether change actually occurred.)

0 Therapist did not apply any cognitive-behavioral techniques.

2 Therapist used cognitive-behavioral techniques, but there were *significant flaws* in the way they were applied.

4 Therapist applied cognitive-behavioral techniques *with moderate skill.*

6 Therapist *skillfully* and resourcefully employed cognitive-behavioral techniques.

___11. **Homework**

0 Therapist did not attempt to incorporate homework relevant to cognitive therapy.

2 Therapist had significant difficulties incorporating homework (e.g., did not review previous homework, did not explain homework in sufficient detail, assigned inappropriate homework).

4 Therapist reviewed previous homework and assigned "standard" cognitive therapy homework generally relevant to issues dealt with in session. Homework was explained in sufficient detail.

6 Therapist reviewed previous homework and carefully assigned homework drawn from cognitive therapy for the coming week. Assignment seemed "custom tailored" to help client incorporate new perspectives, test hypotheses, experiment with new behaviors discussed during session, etc.

Total _____

CASE WRITE-UP

CASE WRITE-UP INSTRUCTIONS

A case write-up is a comprehensive way to understand your clients, their diagnosis, and their difficulties. According to the format used by the Academy of Cognitive Therapy, a case write-up consists of four sections: a case history, case formulation, treatment plan, and course of treatment. The **case history** section provides a general overview of the client's background, including information regarding the chief complaint; history of present illness; past psychiatric, personal, social, and medical history; current mental status; and applicable diagnoses. Support for the client's diagnosis should be demonstrated throughout each section of the case history so that the diagnosis is a foregone conclusion.

The **case formulation** follows the case history, which provides a cognitive conceptualization of the client. This section includes information regarding any significant events that may have precipitated the current disorder, a cross-sectional view of current cognitions and behaviors (e.g., automatic thoughts, emotions, behaviors), a longitudinal view of cognitions and behaviors (e.g., core beliefs, underlying assumptions), the client's strengths and assets, and a working hypothesis that connects the treatment conceptualization to the intervention. Before completing the cross-sectional and longitudinal sections of the case formulation, a doubt conceptualization (see Chapter 2) must first be completed to provide the information necessary to understand the client's cognitive and behavioral functioning.

The treatment plan and course of treatment represent the last two sections of the case write-up. The treatment plan section contains the client's problem list, treatment goals, and plan for treatment. Having a clearly-defined treatment plan section is important, as it makes therapy an easier task for the clinician and maximizes the likelihood that therapy will be effective. Finally, the course of treatment section addresses issues encountered throughout the course of CBT. In particular, this section contains information regarding the nature and quality of the therapeutic relationship, the primary CBT interventions used (along with the rationale for using these strategies based on the client's conceptualization), any difficulties encountered, how these difficulties were understood and handled based on the conceptualization of the client, and the treatment outcome or progress to date.

Like the CTRS, the case write-up is as an effective tool for enhancing CBT skill acquisition, as a strong write-up requires a good understanding of clients and their problems, as well as a comprehensive plan of intervention. Developing an effective case formulation and treatment plan requires therapists to understand the basic principles of the cognitive model and apply them to individual cases with specific diagnoses in mind. For this reason, the Academy of Cognitive Therapy has developed a case write-up scoring sheet to assess clinical competency in CBT. This rating scale assesses adherence to specific elements of the case conceptualization, in which each item is scored as "absent," "present but inadequate," or "present and adequate." A score of 20 out of a possible 24 points demonstrates adherence. A copy of this case conceptualization scoring sheet is available for download from the Academy of Cognitive Therapy website. You can also find a detailed outline of the case write-up instructions on the following pages.

Clinician Tips

CASE WRITE-UP

• • • • • •

I. Case History (Suggested number of words: 750)

General instructions: The case history should briefly summarize the most important background information that you collected in evaluating this client for treatment. Be succinct in describing the case history.

A. Identifying information

Provide a fictitious name to protect the confidentiality of the client. Use this fictitious name throughout the case history and formulation. Describe the client's age, gender, ethnicity, marital status, living situation, and occupation.

B. Chief complaint

Note the chief complaint in the client's own words.

C. History of present illness

Describe present illness, including emotional, cognitive, behavioral, and physiological symptoms. Note environmental stressors. Briefly review treatments (if any) that have been tried for the present illness.

D. Past psychiatric history

Briefly summarize past psychiatric history, including substance abuse.

E. Personal and social history

Briefly summarize the most salient features of personal and social history. Include observations on formative experiences, traumas (if any), support structure, interests, and use of substances.

F. Medical history

Note any medical problems (e.g., endocrine disturbances, heart disease, cancer, chronic medical illnesses, chronic pain) that may influence psychological functioning or the treatment process.

G. Mental status observations

List three to five of the most salient features of the mental status exam at the time treatment began. Include observations on general appearance and mood. *Do not* describe the entire mental status examination.

H. *DSM-5*® diagnoses

Provide ICD-10 or *DSM-5* diagnoses.

II. Case Formulation (Suggested number of words: 500)

General instructions: Describe the primary features of your case formulation using the following outline.

A. Precipitants

Precipitants are large-scale events that may play a significant role in precipitating an episode of illness. A typical example is a depressive episode precipitated by multiple events, including failure to be promoted at work, death of a close friend, and marital strain. In some cases (e.g., bipolar disorder, recurrent depression with strong biological features), there may be no clear psychosocial precipitant. If no psychosocial precipitants can be identified, note any other features of the client's history that may help explain the onset of illness.

The term *activating situations*, used in the next part of the case formulation, refers to smaller-scale events and situations that stimulate negative moods or maladaptive bursts of cognitions and behaviors. For example, a client who is depressed following the precipitating events described earlier may experience worsening of her depressed mood when she's at work, when she's with her husband, or when she attends a class that she used to attend with her friend who died.

Which *precipitants* do you hypothesize played a significant role in the development of the client's symptoms and problems?

B. Cross-sectional view of current cognitions and behaviors

The cross-sectional view of the case formulation includes observations of the predominant cognitions, emotions, and behaviors (and physiological reactions if relevant) that the client demonstrates in the present (or demonstrated prior to making substantive gains in therapy). Typically, the cross-sectional view focuses more on the surface cognitions (e.g., automatic thoughts) that are identified earlier in therapy than underlying schemas, core beliefs, or assumptions that are the centerpiece of the longitudinal view described next.

The cross-sectional view should give your conceptualization of how the cognitive model applied to this client early in treatment. List up to three current activating situations or memories of activating situations. Describe the client's typical automatic thoughts, emotions, and behaviors (and physiological reactions if relevant) in these situations.

C. Longitudinal view of cognitions and behaviors

This portion of the case conceptualization focuses on a longitudinal perspective of the client's cognitive and behavioral functioning. The longitudinal view is developed fully as therapy proceeds and the therapist uncovers underlying schemas (core beliefs, rules, assumptions) and enduring patterns of behavior (compensatory strategies).

What are the client's key schemas (core beliefs, rules, or assumptions) and compensatory behavioral strategies? For clients whose premorbid history was not significant (e.g., a bipolar client with no history of developmental issues that played a role in the generation of maladaptive assumptions or schemas), indicate the major belief(s) and dysfunctional behavioral patterns present only during the current episode. Report developmental antecedents relevant to the origin or maintenance of the client's schemas and behavioral strategies, or offer support for your hypothesis that the client's developmental history is not relevant to the current disorder.

D. Strengths and assets

Describe in a few words the client's strengths and assets (e.g., physical health, intelligence, social skills, support network, work history, etc.).

E. Working hypothesis (summary of conceptualization)

Briefly summarize the principal features of the working hypothesis that directed your treatment interventions. Link your working hypothesis with the cognitive model for the client's disorder(s).

III. Treatment Plan (Suggested number of words: 250)

General instructions: Describe the primary features of your treatment plan using the following outline.

A. Problem list

List any significant problems that you and the client have identified. Usually, problems are identified in several domains (e.g., psychological/psychiatric, interpersonal, occupational, medical, financial, housing, legal, and leisure). Problem lists generally have two to six items, sometimes as many as eight or nine items. Briefly describe the problems in a few words or, if previously described in detail in the history of present illness, just name the problem here.

B. Treatment goals

Indicate the goals for treatment that have been developed collaboratively with the client.

C. Plan for treatment

Weaving together these goals, the case history, and your working hypothesis, briefly state your treatment plan for this client.

IV. Course of Treatment (Suggested number of words: 500)

General instructions: Describe the primary features of the course of treatment using the following outline.

A. Therapeutic relationship

Detail the nature and quality of the therapeutic relationship, any problems you encountered, how you conceptualized these problems, and how you resolved them.

B. Interventions or procedures

Describe three major cognitive therapy interventions you used, providing a rationale that links these interventions with the client's treatment goals and your working hypothesis.

C. Obstacles

Present one example of how you resolved an obstacle to therapy. Describe your conceptualization of why the obstacle arose and note what you did about it. If you did not encounter any significant obstacles in this therapy, describe one example of how you were able to capitalize on the client's strengths in the treatment process.

D. Outcome

Briefly report on the outcome of therapy. If the treatment has not been completed, describe progress to date.

CASE WRITE-UP EXAMPLE

The pages that follow illustrate how to put case write-up into practice by providing a sample case write-up for a 28-year-old man named George. As previously discussed, the first component of the case write-up involves filling out the doubt conceptualization model to understand how the client's history shaped the development of the doubt label, guidelines or assumptions, and ineffective compensatory actions. It is only once the therapist has put together these pieces cohesively that a case write-up can be completed. Therefore, the example provided first includes a description of George's doubt conceptualization, followed by his accompanying case write-up. After the case example is a blank case write-up template that you can use to conceptualize and formulate a treatment plan with your own clients.

Sample Worksheet

DOUBT CONCEPTUALIZATION MODEL:
GEORGE
• • • • • •

Shaping Experiences

Cautious and guarded parents

A highly anxious father who worried all the time

Doted on by family

Doubt Labels

"I am vulnerable."

Guidelines or Assumptions

Positive: "If I don't have physical sensations, then I'm okay."

"If I am with people who will take care of me, then I will be okay."

"If I avoid things that make me anxious, then I will be okay."

Negative: "If I experience physical sensations, then I'm vulnerable."

"If I am alone, then I won't be okay."

"If I put myself in stressful situations, then I'll be vulnerable."

Compensatory Ineffective Actions

Avoidance (e.g., avoids work, social situations, and self-disclosure)

Constantly checks his pulse for reassurance

Stays close to family for protection

SITUATION-SPECIFIC AUTOMATIC THOUGHTS:
GEORGE

Scenario 1

Doubt Label
"I am vulnerable."

↓

Assumptions
"If I put myself in stressful situations, then I'm vulnerable."

↓

Event
At a movie with his girlfriend
→
Automatic Thought
"There is something wrong with me. I can't handle this. I'm going to die."

Emotion
Anxiety

Physiological Sensation
Shortness of breath, feeling out of control

Behavior
Leaves the movie

Scenario 2

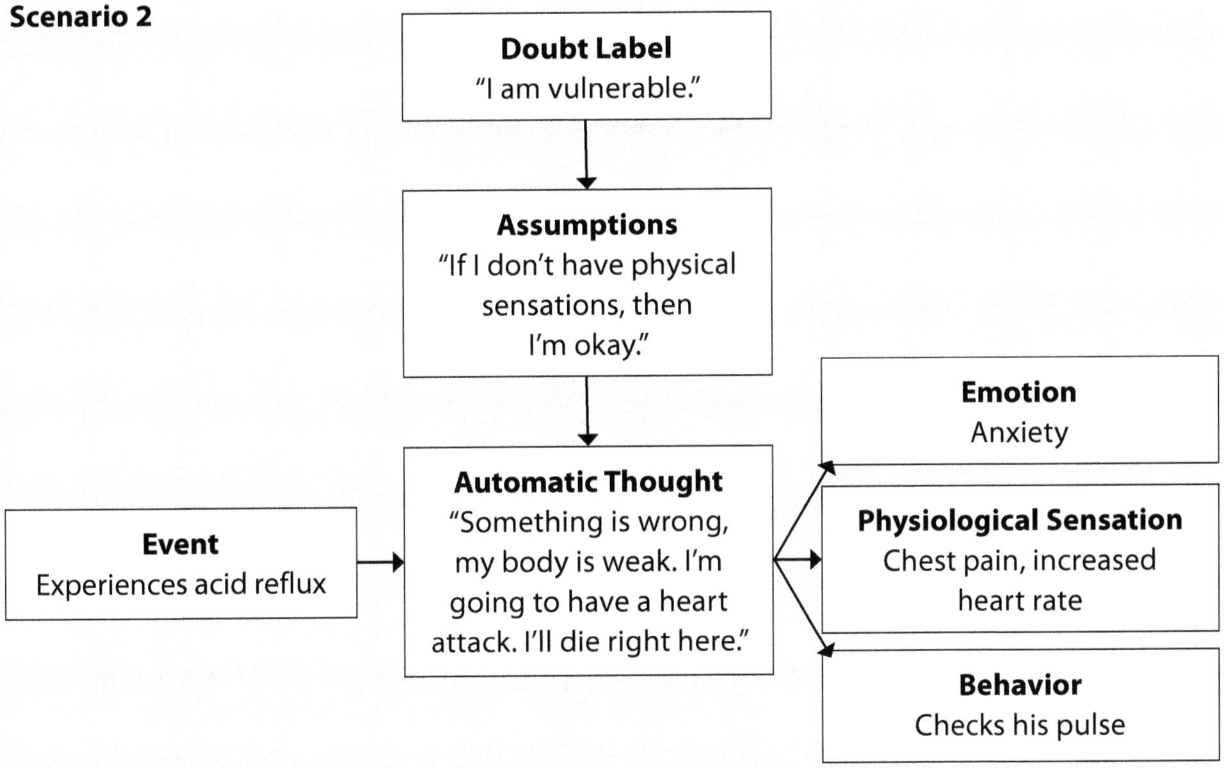

Doubt Label
"I am vulnerable."

↓

Assumptions
"If I don't have physical sensations, then I'm okay."

↓

Event
Experiences acid reflux → **Automatic Thought**
"Something is wrong, my body is weak. I'm going to have a heart attack. I'll die right here."

→ **Emotion**
Anxiety

→ **Physiological Sensation**
Chest pain, increased heart rate

→ **Behavior**
Checks his pulse

Scenario 3

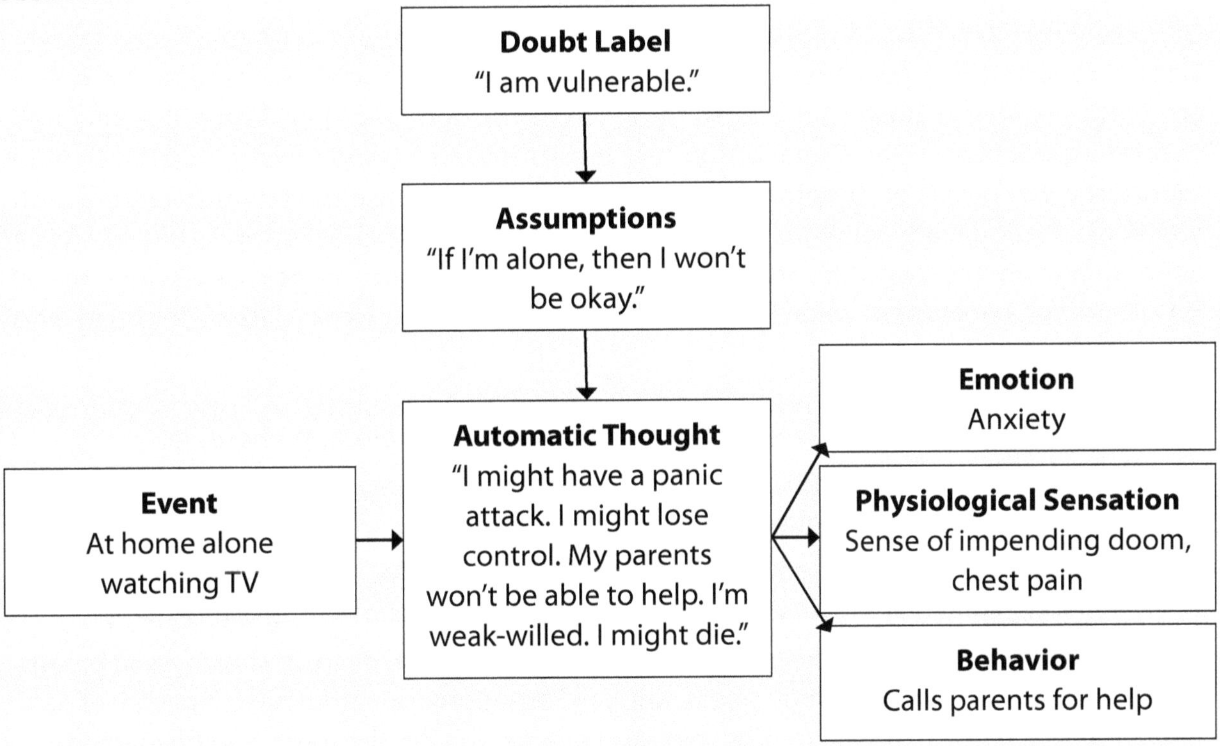

Doubt Label
"I am vulnerable."

↓

Assumptions
"If I'm alone, then I won't be okay."

↓

Event
At home alone watching TV → **Automatic Thought**
"I might have a panic attack. I might lose control. My parents won't be able to help. I'm weak-willed. I might die."

→ **Emotion**
Anxiety

→ **Physiological Sensation**
Sense of impending doom, chest pain

→ **Behavior**
Calls parents for help

Sample Worksheet

CASE WRITE-UP:
GEORGE

• • • • •

Case History

Identifying information

George is a 28-year-old, single Black male who has recently graduated from the police academy and is a rookie policeman. He lives at home with his parents and sister.

Chief complaint

George sought treatment after an incident on the force where he noticed a vicious burning sensation rising in his throat and thought, "Something is wrong, really wrong. I'm scared. I'm not okay. It's getting harder to breathe. My heart is pounding harder and harder. I can't hear what my partner is saying. I can't speak. I'm here but not here. I need help, but I can't call out. I'm dizzy and nauseous. I'm having a heart attack. I won't make it to the hospital because my partner doesn't know what's happening." Now living in dread, he fears the feelings returning.

History of present illness

George reported that his panic attacks began six months ago while training at the police academy. He was evaluated in a hospital emergency room and sent home. He was told that he experienced a panic attack after test results revealed good physical health. George reported a worsening of symptoms two months ago in response to feeling paralyzed with fear while getting ready for work. He reported full-blown panic attacks approximately twice a month and limited-symptom attacks roughly two to three times a week. He decided to call for a therapy appointment when he realized that he barely functioned outside his home and needed to act.

- Emotional symptoms: frightened, anxious, worried, sad, irritable, apprehensive
- Cognitive symptoms: believed something was wrong with him ("I'll have a heart attack, and I'll die") and worried about having more panic attacks
- Behavioral symptoms: checked pulse, spent most of his time at home with family, isolated from friends, limited activities with his girlfriend, sought reassurance, and took naps
- Physiological symptoms: increased heart rate, gastrointestinal distress, shortness of breath, sweating palms, shakiness, drowsiness, tingling sensations, dry mouth, weakness, feelings of unreality, nausea, muscle tension, pins and needles in legs, dizziness, and headaches

The major stressors in George's life were work and his social life. Due to his embarrassment about the panic attacks, he kept them a secret, aside from his immediate family knowing. This caused him to feel isolated from his colleagues, friends, and girlfriend. He reported increased anxiety about his role as a policeman, as that had been a lifelong dream he had recently achieved.

Past psychiatric history

George went to see his family physician, who suggested a few months of medical leave and prescribed him Ativan to take as needed and an antidepressant. However, he was uncomfortable taking psychotropic medications. George indicated that he was briefly in insight-oriented therapy several months ago for treatment of his panic but did not find it helpful. He was also in psychotherapy for treatment of night terrors at the age of 13, which are currently in full remission. George had no history of psychiatric hospitalizations, suicide attempts, or emotional, verbal, physical, or sexual abuse. He did not report smoking, drinking, or using illicit drugs.

Personal and social history

In terms of relevant childhood data, George was the youngest of four children. He reported close relations with his parents and described them as loving, supportive, and protective. He indicated that his father was a worrier who also fretted about his health. George's paternal and maternal grandmothers were treated for depression.

George reported that he had always wanted to be a policeman. However, he did indicate feeling anxious about finally achieving the lifelong dream of being on the police force. Although he reported having friends, there was no one that he was particularly close to or confided in. He was in a new relationship with a woman at the time of therapy.

Medical history

George sought treatment recently for chronic acid reflux. His comprehensive medical examination for admission to the police academy revealed that he was in good physical health.

Mental status observations

George was fully oriented with anxious mood.

ICD-10 diagnosis

F40.01   Panic Disorder

Case Formulation

Precipitants

The precipitating event for the client's panic disorder may have been his admission to the police academy. He had dreamed of becoming a policeman since he was a little boy.

George put a lot of pressure on himself to succeed. He also believed that his anxiety was stronger than he was and that his body was being physically harmed by it. As a result, beliefs centering on vulnerability and weakness were activated. This caused increased anxiety and fear, leading to panic episodes. Trying to hide his difficulties from others also heightened his anxiety. Further, increased self-criticism and isolation may have contributed to his dysphoria.

Cross-sectional view of current cognitions and behaviors

During the initial evaluation, George described a situation in which he took his girlfriend to the movies. As he was paying for the tickets, he felt his heart pounding and experienced nausea, dizziness, shakiness, and weakness in his legs. His automatic thoughts were: "There's something wrong with me," "I can't handle this," and "I'm going to die." In turn, he felt anxious and made his girlfriend leave the movie.

In another situation, George started experiencing increased discomfort due to an acid reflux episode at work. His automatic thoughts were: "Something is wrong," "My body is weak," "I'm going to have a heart attack," and "I'll die right here." As his anxiety increased, he found himself checking his pulse at several-minute intervals.

In a third situation, he was at home alone watching television when he became anxious that no one was around. His automatic thoughts were: "I might have a panic attack," "I might lose control," "My parents won't be able to help," "I'm weak-willed," and "I might die." He felt anxious and called his parents for reassurance.

Longitudinal view of cognitions and behaviors

George grew up with parents who were cautious and guarded in their approach to life. His father especially displayed a tendency to focus on the possible dangerous consequences of actions and activities and the uncertainty of one's health. As a result, George developed internal rules based on these family messages and seemed to develop the core belief (e.g., doubt label) that he was vulnerable. To cope with this self-doubt, his positive conditional assumptions were: "If I don't have physical sensations, then I'm okay," "If I am with people who will take care of me, then I will be okay," and "If I avoid things that make me anxious, then I will be okay." His negative conditional assumptions took this form: "If I experience physical sensations, then I'm vulnerable," "If I am alone, then I won't be okay," and "If I put myself in stressful situations, then I will be vulnerable."

To try to keep his core belief of "I am vulnerable" from being activated, George developed compensatory strategies of avoidance and staying close to his security source. He started limiting his activities, including taking a leave of absence from work and staying close to home. He reported that he isolated himself from his friends and limited social plans with his girlfriend. George spent most of his time at home with his family and avoided doing anything without them. He constantly checked his pulse to make sure he was okay. He also napped to avoid his fears.

Strengths

George was extremely motivated for treatment. He actively collaborated in setting the agenda, participating in the session, and designing homework assignments. He also displayed above average intelligence and had a good support system of family members.

Working hypothesis

Learning from his cautious parents, George displayed a tendency to overestimate the danger in situations and downplayed his ability to cope. Internal sensations triggered fear, consequent and more severe physiological sensations of tachycardia, shortness of breath, nausea, shakiness, and sweating. Focusing internally on physical sensations made them more intense. His negative conditional assumptions made being in stressful situations (e.g., work) challenging, and his self-doubt of being vulnerable was constantly activated. Fearing the worst, any symptom was dreaded and avoided, resulting in compromised functioning in work and his social life.

Treatment Plan

Problem list

1. Panic attacks
2. Anticipatory anxiety
3. Avoidance of colleagues and friends
4. Use of psychotropic medication—George stated that he did not want to become dependent on medication for his anxiety.
5. Work—returning after a leave of absence

Treatment goals

1. Recognize the difference between anxiety and panic
2. Handle anxiety better by strengthening strategies to deal with it
3. Extinguish panic attacks
4. Stop taking psychotropic medications
5. Feel comfortable about going back to work
6. Be social again

Plan for treatment

George was taught the cognitive model and the role of his thoughts in how he responded and reacted to situations. Using his personal experiences, he was able to see the effect of cognitions on his emotions, physical reactions, and behavior. He was then able to see the effect of changing his thinking on his mood, body, and behavior by replacing his automatic thoughts with more rational alternative responses. We linked this old style of thinking to the cognitive model of anxiety and panic to help him recognize his tendency to interpret benign stimuli as threatening, dangerous, or disastrous. The treatment plan also aimed to help George reconnect socially with friends and colleagues and return to work.

Course of Treatment

Therapeutic relationship

We had a good working relationship. George was extremely motivated in treatment, which helped expedite treatment.

Interventions/procedures

1. Educated George on the cognitive model of anxiety and the panic cycle. By developing a working model of his experience and his disorder, it became clear to George that the treatment strategy would allow him to gain the necessary tools for recovery.
2. Taught George how to use the risk/resource ratio to realistically evaluate threats and resources, which reduced his anxiety and sense of vulnerability.
3. Interoceptive exposure exercises were used in session to activate autonomic arousal in the body. The rationale was to simulate a panic attack to help George recognize that the symptoms are uncomfortable but not dangerous.

Obstacles

One obstacle in treatment was George's reluctance to do a homework assignment that involved putting himself in a situation that would increase the likelihood of having a panic attack. We went over the advantages and disadvantages of doing this exercise versus not doing it. We then came up with a rationale for doing it based on the results of the advantages discussed, and he completed the exposure.

Outcome

George responded well to his six-session treatment. He left treatment no longer fearful of his bodily sensations and no longer avoiding social situations or his job.

Template

CASE CONCEPTUALIZATION WRITE-UP

· · · · · ·

I. CASE HISTORY (Suggested number of words: 750)

   A. Identifying information:

   B. Chief complaint:

   C. History of present illness:

      Emotional symptoms:

      Cognitive symptoms:

      Behavioral symptoms:

      Physiological symptoms:

      Stressors:

   D. Psychiatric history:

   E. Personal and social history:

   F. Medical history:

   G. Mental status check:

   H. ICD-10 or *DSM-5* diagnoses:

II. CASE FORMULATION: (Suggested number of words: 500)

   A. Precipitants:

   B. Cross-sectional view of current cognitions and behaviors:

   C. Longitudinal view of cognitions and behaviors:

   D. Strengths:

   E. Working hypothesis (Summary of conceptualization):

III. TREATMENT PLAN: (Suggested number of words: 250)

   A. Problem list:

   B. Treatment goals:

   C. Plan for treatment:

IV. COURSE OF TREATMENT (Suggested number of words: 500)

   A. Therapeutic relationship:

   B. Interventions/procedures:

   C. Obstacles:

   D. Outcome:

5
DEPRESSION

THE COGNITIVE MODEL AND KEY COMPONENT TREATMENTS

Thinking tends to be negatively biased among clients with depression, and this bias is demonstrated in three major spheres of thinking. Namely, clients with depression experience a negative view of the self, the future, and the world (Beck, Rush, Shaw, & Emery, 1987). For example, they may view themselves as worthless (self), believe that nothing will ever get better (future), and assume that no one cares about them (world). This triad of negative biases is associated with paralysis of will, depressed mood, suicidal wishes, increased dependency, avoidance, and social withdrawal (Beck et al., 1987).

This cognitive triad occurs regardless of the etiology of the depression and, significantly, is amenable to treatment regardless of the etiology as well. A key component of treatment for depression involves **cognitive restructuring**, which involves identifying, evaluating, and modifying these distorted and exaggerated negative automatic thoughts into more realistic, positive, and rational beliefs. Another important component of treatment involves **behavioral activation**. Behavioral withdrawal and inactivity in depression play a role in fueling negative biases and preventing recovery. Therefore, getting clients activated and socially reconnected is often a necessary first step in treating depression and can provide the necessary data for cognitive change to take place, along with improving mood. This chapter examines the principles of cognitive restructuring and behavioral activation in greater detail, and also discusses how to best assess the extent of your clients' depressive symptoms so you can structure and prioritize treatment accordingly.

ASSESSMENT

Mood Scales

Mood scales are a helpful way to assess the severity of depressive symptoms. Many readily available objective self-report measures provide a reliable and valid assessment of mood, including the Beck Depression Inventory-II (Beck, Steer, & Brown, 1996) and the Burns Brief Mood Survey (Burns, 1995). However, an alternative to these more formal mood measures is simply to ask clients to provide a subjective rating of their mood using a Likert scale. Depending on the difficulties clients are experiencing, you can ask them to rate their level of irritability, agitation, frustration, anger, anxiety, or hopelessness on scale from 0 (not at all severe) to 10 (severe).

Mood measures serve multiple purposes. First, clients with depression often fail to recognize the progress they have made as they move from severe depression to moderate depression to recovery. By completing weekly mood scales, clients have an objective marker that allows them to see their progress as it unfolds. Second, obtaining a weekly measure of mood at the start of a session provides opportunities to discuss variables that either improved or worsened the client's mood. Third, using mood measures throughout and at the end of a session can provide data regarding the effectiveness of the treatment strategy. For example, let's say you are working with a client who reports a low mood of 2, but then reports a mood of 4 after talking about what is sprouting in her garden. Logically, you can infer that it might make sense for that client to schedule more time gardening, as simply thinking about it seems to have a positive impact on mood. Similarly, for high-risk clients, a reported decrease in mood at the end of a session serves as an indicator that immediate intervention is necessary.

Fourth, the assessment of mood can help guide the focus of the session. For example, when a low mood is reported, issues associated with that low mood may need to be prioritized and addressed. Has the client acknowledged suicidal or homicidal ideation? Is the mood significantly affecting the client's sleep? Is the client reporting dramatic weight loss or gain, or problematic eating (e.g., diabetic clients ignoring their sugar intake)? Is the mood affecting the client's daily functioning, such as hygiene or mobility? Addressing suicidal or homicidal risk is always a top priority, as clients cannot get better if they are not alive to work on their problems, hospitalized with medical issues, or incarcerated. Additionally, dysfunctional eating, poor hygiene, and lack of sleep also put clients at risk (e.g., anorexia can result in cardiac issues and sleep deprivation can result in fatigue, irritability, and psychosis). By assessing the client's mood, you can identify and prioritize issues such as these, many of which are amenable to CBT intervention. For issues that pose more serious problems, ancillary services may be necessary (e.g., pharmacotherapy), and a consultation for these services may be warranted.

To obtain an assessment of mood, you can ask clients for a weekly or daily measure of their mood. For example, you can ask clients to rate their average mood over the past week on whatever specific mood(s) you are tracking and evaluating (e.g., depression, hopelessness, anger, anxiety). A sample Likert scale for this type of mood rating could look as follows:

Not at all			**Mild**			**Moderate**				**Severe**
0	1	2	3	4	5	6	7	8	9	10

Alternatively, or in addition to this weekly mood rating, you can ask clients to keep a daily log of their overall mood, using a Likert scale such as this:

Poor			**Below Average**			**Average**			**Good**			**Excellent**
0	1	2	3	4	5	6	7	8	9	10		

BEHAVIORAL ACTIVATION

The First Step: Behavioral Assessment

The first step in starting the process of behavioral activation is to determine the extent to which your client is behaviorally active. You need to ascertain a clear picture of your clients' daily activities to assess their level of functioning. An important component of this is to assess the level of pleasure, mastery, and social interaction associated with these activities. That is, you need to determine whether these activities are enjoyable, provide a sense of accomplishment, and involve other people. These three qualities are essential for well-being and protect against depression. In contrast, when clients' schedules are unbalanced, they spend too much time alone or are overly focused on attending to other responsibilities (e.g., their job, other people) instead of themselves. When this happens, it is difficult for clients to find joy in their life, and depression prevails.

Keep in mind that clients with depression have negatively-biased memories and often misreport data. For example, they may report doing nothing (when, in fact, they may have accomplished multiple tasks), or they may report no changes in their mood (when, in fact, different situations elicit different emotions). Therefore, to obtain a more objective assessment of your client's activity level, you can walk through what their day looked like prior to coming into session, or you can help them examine their activity level for the previous day. Writing down the activities of their actual day helps clients draw more objective conclusions about how active they were. Going forward, you can ask clients to provide mood ratings on a daily activity schedule, with these mood check-ins eventually corresponding to various pleasant, masterful, and social activities. Through this process, clients learn to recognize fluctuations in their mood and identify activities or times associated with worsened versus improved mood.

The Tool: The Activity Schedule

The activity schedule is the tool of choice for getting a behavioral assessment of your client's activity. The activity schedule asks clients to track their activities over the course of their week and to record their corresponding mood at the time. It gives you a baseline measure of what clients are doing throughout the day and how these activities are impacting their mood so you can determine whether they require increased activity, mastery, pleasure, or social connections to improve their mood.

The best way to introduce this tool is to provide a clear rationale for why you are asking them to complete this information. Emphasize to clients that the activity schedule will allow you to see how active they are and whether their mood responds to specific activities or people, which will help guide therapy. It is best to initiate the completion of this tool in session and to ask clients to complete it every day from the time they awake until they go to sleep, and to repeat this each day until their next visit.

Day 1 starts when clients awaken the morning of the session. That way, you and the client can begin retrospectively filling out the schedule together in session to describe how the client's day has been so far. The advantage of starting the activity schedule in session is that it helps explain to clients exactly what information is being asked of them and demonstrates how doable the exercise is. It also lets you gauge how likely clients are to complete the activity schedule on their own.

Explain to clients that they will be recording what they are doing at each hour of the day and rating their mood at the time on a scale of 0 to 10, with 0 being "the worst mood" and 10 "the best mood." The following page contains an activity schedule that you can use with your clients. This worksheet can be completed once as an assessment tool to evaluate your client's baseline activity level, or it can be used repeatedly to self-monitor and enhance behavioral activation.

Client Worksheet

ACTIVITY SCHEDULE

Over the next week, record what you are doing at each hour of the day and what your mood is at that time. Use the following rating scale to describe your mood:

Poor	Below Average	Average	Good	Excellent
0 1	2 3 4	5 6	7 8	9 10

	MON	TUES	WED	THUR	FRI	SAT	SUN
6–7 a.m.							
7–8 a.m.							
8–9 a.m.							
9–10 a.m.							
10–11 a.m.							
11–12 p.m.							
12–1 p.m.							
1–2 p.m.							

	MON	TUES	WED	THUR	FRI	SAT	SUN
2–3 p.m.							
3–4 p.m.							
4–5 p.m.							
5–6 p.m.							
6–7 p.m.							
7–8 p.m.							
8–9 p.m.							
9–10 p.m.							
10–11 p.m.							
11–12 a.m.							
12–6 a.m.							

Activity Schedule: The Learning

Once clients have completed the activity schedule, the goal is to use it productively. Remember, just completing the exercise is an accomplishment and deserves recognition and credit. The first question is to ask clients what they gained from doing the exercise and what they learned. As the therapist, it's likely that you may have to guide them to additional learning and help them reach conclusions. For example, looking at a partial glimpse of the following completed activity schedule, what conclusions could you help the client gain?

	Sunday	**Monday**	**Tuesday**	**Wednesday**
11–12 p.m.	Woke/had coffee M = 2	Woke/ate healthy breakfast M = 3	Woke/ate junk M = 1	Woke/ate healthy breakfast M = 3
12–1 p.m.	Sat in kitchen M = 1	Sat and did nothing M = 2	Filled bird feeder M = 3	Took shower/got dressed M = 3
1–2 p.m.	Read M = 2	Read M = 2	Sat outside and read M = 3	Went to grocery store M = 3
2–3 p.m.	Read M = 2	Tried to nap M = 1	Ate healthy lunch M = 3	Tried to nap M = 2
3–4 p.m.	Ate unhealthy lunch M = 1	Laid in bed M = 1	Tried to nap M = 1	Laid in bed M = 2
4–5 p.m.	Daughter called and talked M = 4	Ate junk food M = 1	Laid in bed M = 1	Ate healthy dinner M = 3
5–6 p.m.	Tried to nap M = 2	Knitted M = 3	Watched TV M = 1	Went to walking group M = 4
6–7 p.m.	Laid in bed M = 1	Scooped the cat litter M = 3	Went back to bed M = 1	Went to exercise class M = 5

Looking at this sample activity schedule, here are some interesting discussion points you could use with your client:

- "There seem to be activities that are associated with your mood being low and even sinking. For example, when you try to nap or lay in bed, you are isolated and alone, which makes you feel worse, just as eating unhealthy food or watching TV does."
- "On the other hand, having a conversation with your daughter, walking, and especially taking an exercise class out of the house with other people raised your mood substantially."
- "What does this tell us about what goals we may want to work toward? What things clearly are not helping? Helping you engage in activities that promote a better mood are exactly what you will be working toward."

Once the difficulty becomes evident—whether it be behavioral inactivity, an unbalanced schedule, lack of social interaction, or too much time in bed—the activity schedule becomes a tool in mobilizing the client to address the underlying problem. In particular, it serves as a starting point for intentionally planning activities that clients can gradually begin incorporating into their schedule. Developing a schedule is a crucial component of treatment because many clients with depression have withdrawn from life, resulting in job loss, interpersonal detachment, and shrinking responsibilities (e.g., failing to assist with child care, meal preparation, or shopping). This isolation facilitates inactivity and serves to perpetuate their negative view of themselves, the world, and the future. When clients have no obligation to leave their bed or home, depression continues to prevail.

Helping clients see the merit of a schedule can help facilitate action. The first step is to identify reasons why following a schedule makes sense. The following are some potential reasons to follow a schedule, but brainstorm with your clients to see if they can identify any additional reasons that it might be of benefit to them:

1. A schedule is an appointment for wellness, and following it is an accomplishment in itself.
2. A schedule is a way to defeat hopelessness and depression.
3. "Doing" results in a better day.
4. "Doing" might get clients interested in more doing.
5. A schedule keeps clients from getting worse, and that is a plus in their favor.

Once you've helped clients understand the value in creating a schedule, the second step is enabling them to understand the key concepts that underlie the principles of behavioral activation. By helping clients understand these key concepts, you maximize the likelihood that they will be successful.

Key Concepts in Behavioral Activation

Key Concept 1: Action Precedes Motivation

The most important concept in behavioral activation is *action precedes motivation*. Clients with depression falsely assume that they cannot initiate activity until they feel better, have more energy, or develop the motivation or desire to do so. However, the truth is none of those factors are real obstacles to action. Lack of motivation and energy are common features of depression, but they are not obstacles to action.

If a client is sitting in front of you, then you have data to support this point. It is unlikely that this client felt like coming to the appointment, had energy that morning, or suddenly felt the depression lift. Yet, here they are, providing evidence against their belief that energy, motivation, and a positive mood are necessary for action to take place. Rather, action in the face of depression is what leads to energy, motivation, and a positive mood. Having clients remind themselves of this idea helps battle the inertia of depression. The following is a coping card that clients can reference whenever they need this reminder.

> Coping Card
>
> **ACTION-ORIENTED THOUGHTS**
>
> - Action comes before motivation. I don't have to feel like it to do it. Just do it.
> - Accept that depression is stealing my motivation, so it will be harder to do things.
> - Just reminding myself to act will help.
> - I can do things even when I don't feel like it.
> - I can do things even when I don't want to.
> - If I tell myself, "Just do it," then I will likely feel better.
> - I can force myself to act so I can battle this depression.
> - I can remind myself that I am not going to want to or feel like it, but that doesn't have to stop me from just doing it.
> - Action precedes motivation.

Key Concept 2: Success Is in the Effort, Not the Outcome

Often, people judge success based on the outcome of their actions. However, the outcome is often out of our control, influenced by extraneous variables, and not always a reflection of effort. For example, consider a client who has been isolating herself from others and decides to take initiative by calling multiple friends to have lunch, only to find out that all of them are unavailable. Is this a success or a failure? This is a success, as the goal was to connect, and that is not diminished by the unavailability of others. Or consider a client who gets on the treadmill for the first time in months and believes he failed since he only lasted a few minutes. This is also an example of success, regardless of how long the client lasted. Getting on that treadmill was the goal, and given how much effort it took and how difficult it was for the client to do that, the accomplishment was real. Success is in the *doing*, not in the result. Therefore, regardless of what happens, it is the trying—the effort—that wins. Recognizing this concept is an essential part of building confidence in clients with depression.

Depression steals energy, clouds thinking, and makes everything more challenging. Thus, the effort required to do things is greater. Small tasks require substantial effort for clients with depression. For example, getting out of bed, putting on clean clothes, doing the dishes, and calling back a friend are all small tasks that require much more effort in the face of depression. However, clients with depression often negate these successes, especially when they continue to feel depressed despite the efforts that they have put forth. Instead of judging success on the outcome, success is in the doing. Success means that clients put in the effort and did what they set out to do. Any amount of doing is better than doing nothing, and any amount of doing deserves recognition of success. In addition, taking action often results in small changes in mood, which provides clients with evidence that they are getting better. You can help clients recognize that their successes are a reflection of their efforts by providing them with the following coping card.

Coping Card

RECOGNIZING SUCCESS

- Success is in the doing.
- Every step is an accomplishment.
- Effort deserves a reward.
- The outcome is out of my control, but the effort is on me.
- Taking action is the success and not the outcome.

Key Concept 3: Establish a Goal and a Rationale

When working with depressed clients to mobilize them toward action, their goal may be vague (e.g., do things that help combat depression) or very specific (e.g., accept an invitation to be with friends this week). It is less critical how specific the goal is and more important that clients believe the goal is in their best interest. When clients believe that a goal is in their best interest, they believe that it makes sense for them to work on that goal, which increases their buy-in.

Accepting that a goal "makes sense" is different from telling yourself that you "have to" or "should" do it. If clients view their goal as a requirement or demand, then they will likely experience frustration and anger, which will block them from taking action to begin with. In contrast, establishing a good rationale for the goal will increase the likelihood of their buying in. You can use the following coping card to increase buy-in and help clients remind themselves that tackling their goal is in their best interest.

Coping Card

BUY-IN

- I don't have to do this, but it makes sense for me to tackle this goal.
- It is not that I should do this but that it makes sense for me to do this.
- I can choose to do this even if I don't want to.

Another way to help clients realize that working on a particular goal makes sense is to ask them to come up with list of reasons for, or advantages to, working on that goal. Doing so helps them think through the ways that their life will be different, or could be different, if this goal were to come to fruition. The **Establish a Goal with a Rationale** worksheet on the following page can be used for this purpose.

Client Worksheet

ESTABLISH A GOAL WITH A RATIONALE

• • • • • •

Identify a specific goal that can chip away at your depression. Think about positive ways your life would be different if you worked on this specific goal, as that will fuel your investment to work on that goal.

What is your goal? _____

_____

List at least five reasons why working toward this goal makes sense. What are the real and potential advantages of achieving this goal?

1. _____
2. _____
3. _____
4. _____
5. _____

Key Concept 4: Have a Plan and Put It on the Schedule

The activity schedule provides you with an idea of your client's baseline level of activity, as well as which activities improve (or worsen) your client's mood. Once you have this information, you can develop a plan to intentionally plan activities that clients can gradually begin incorporating into their schedule.

The most important part of the plan is scheduling it, because without a specific plan or schedule, the odds of change occurring are unlikely. For example, imagine that a friend asks you to have dinner sometime. Dinner "sometime" typically means that it is not going to happen. If that friend instead asks, "Would you like to have dinner on Friday night?" or "Here are a few dates that I am free to have dinner. Do any of these work for you?", then the odds of dinner happening are more likely. Similarly, scheduling activities toward the designated goal on the activity schedule increase the odds of it occurring.

A plan includes the specifics of the goal. It includes details regarding the where, what, when, how much, and how long. For example, clients with a lack of social connectedness can plan times to see friends, or clients who spend too much time in bed can plan energizing activities to do throughout the day. If you want to maximize the likelihood that something will happen, then schedule it.

At the same time, simply because a client plans an activity doesn't guarantee that it won't get canceled, disrupted, or squashed for a number of valid (and invalid) reasons. The key is to continue rescheduling the activity for as long as it takes until the goal happens. The task of scheduling is an accomplishment in itself. It says, "I am working on this, and I am working on getting better."

As clients begin incorporating planned activities in their activity schedule, make sure they record whether they follow through with the plan, along with their mood. They can continue to record everything else they do on the same activity schedule. Keep in mind that small tasks are accomplishments and thus require recognition. In addition, it is often helpful for clients to start recording ratings other than mood on the schedule, such as how pleasurable the activity was and how much accomplishment they experienced, using a similar 10-point rating scale. Remember, a daily dose of both accomplishment and pleasure is necessary for battling depression and maintaining mental health, as is social interaction.

However, experiencing pleasure is especially challenging for clients with depression, particularly those who are anhedonic. These clients have stopped participating in pleasurable activities, which means that the ingredients for pleasure are missing. In addition, it is not uncommon for clients to experience a variety of obstacles (e.g., limited finances, lack of transportation, no child care, injury, health problems) that make participating in pleasurable activities difficult. Finding alternative, simple, accessible, and inexpensive pleasurable activities is a helpful way to start. Here are some possibilities:

- Soaking in a bathtub or taking a shower
- Listening to music
- Lying in the sun
- Walking in the woods, beach, or neighborhood
- Going for a bike ride
- Striking up a conversation
- Petting one's pet
- Stretching
- Connecting with someone through phone, text, email, or social media
- Watching a movie
- Reading

Key Concept 5: Self-Talk—Change "Give-Up" Thoughts to "Go-to" Thoughts

"Give-up" thoughts are those thoughts that pop into our head, which we blindly believe and lead us to quit or avoid taking action. They serve as roadblocks to working on our plan and achieving our goals. The following are some examples of give-up thoughts:

- "I'll do it later."
- "It's not going to help."
- "I can't do this."
- "I am too tired."
- "I'd rather take a nap."
- "I'll do it tomorrow."
- "I don't feel like it."
- "It's too hard."
- "I'll never get better."

In contrast to give-up thoughts, "go-to" thoughts are rational, objective, and goal directed. They drive clients toward action and their goals. The following are some examples of how go-to thoughts can be used to replace give-up thoughts.

"I'll do it later." ⟶ "If I put it off, then the odds are that I'm never going to do it. Doing it later means never."

"I don't feel like it." ⟶ "The truth is I don't feel like it, but that doesn't have to get in my way. I can do things I don't want to do or feel like doing simply by doing it."

"It's not going to help." ⟶ "I don't know if it will help or not until I do it. Doing nothing isn't working so I might as well try another strategy."

"I can't do this." ⟶ "Telling myself that I can't do this keeps me from trying. I have done lots of things that I thought I couldn't do. I'll start taking action and follow the plan to see if I can."

Clients with depression struggle with give-up thoughts because they hold a negative view of the future, which generates feelings of hopelessness and creates a major obstacle to mobilization. Therefore, defeating that hopelessness is the goal. Ironically, the best way to defeat hopelessness is to use behavioral data from mobilization, as it is difficult for clients to see the biases in their thinking without the behavioral facts. Clients with depression work against themselves, avoiding action and holding onto their unrealistic thoughts. Helping clients mobilize themselves provides the data needed to address the negative biases of depression that get in the way of action. Clients can learn to remove this obstacle by replacing their give-up thoughts will more realistically helpful go-to thoughts.

You can use the following worksheet with your clients to help them identify their give-up thoughts and turn these into go-to thoughts that mobilize them for action. Make sure to pay special attention to any give-up thoughts they have identified that are connected to hopelessness and fear. Hopelessness leads clients to believe that all action is futile (e.g., "Why bother? Nothing will help"), and fear perpetuates avoidance and sabotages action (e.g., "Something bad will happen if I try").

Once clients have identified their give-up thoughts, help them formulate replacement go-to thoughts. Keep two considerations in mind when helping clients formulate these go-to thoughts. First, the principles, "Success is in the doing, not the outcome" and "Action precedes motivation" should drive the development of these thoughts. It is important for these reframes to be guided by an understanding that doing anything is better than doing nothing, that any amount done is a gain, and that every small step is an accomplishment. In addition, these reframes should be driven by the understanding that clients don't have to feel a certain way in order to take action. Action only requires doing, and people can do things even if they are tired and depressed.

Second, it is helpful to engage in a guided discussion of the merit of these go-to thoughts. Work with the client to develop a list of all the reasons that taking action makes sense in order to fortify the go-to thought. Instead of thinking the give-up thoughts (e.g., "It can wait, I'll do it later") help clients think of go-to thoughts to get them moving (e.g., "Remember all the reasons it makes sense to do this. It cannot wait. If I do it later, then everything I want to gain cannot happen").

Once clients understand the exercise, every time they experience a new give-up thought, ask them to write down that thought and try replacing it with a go-to thought.

Client Worksheet

REPLACE "GIVE-UP" THOUGHTS WITH "GO-TO" THOUGHTS

• • • • • •

Give-up thoughts are beliefs that go through your mind that make you want to give up or avoid taking action. These are thoughts that pop into your head when you think about doing a task. Give-up thoughts are ineffective because they keep you stuck. What are some give-up thoughts you have?

1. _____
2. _____
3. _____
4. _____
5. _____

In contrast to give-up thoughts are go-to thoughts. These thoughts are more rational and realistic. They drive you toward action and help you reach your goals. To help you get unstuck and move toward your goals, try replacing the give-up thoughts you previously identified with go-to thoughts.

Give-up Thought	**Go-to Thought**
1. _____ ⟶	1. _____
2. _____ ⟶	2. _____
3. _____ ⟶	3. _____
4. _____ ⟶	4. _____
5. _____ ⟶	5. _____

Key Concept 6: Take Credit

Taking credit for our accomplishments is one way to help overcome depression. However, clients with depression tend to disqualify or minimize their efforts because of the negative lens through which they view themselves and the world. In particular, they downplay their accomplishments by drawing comparisons to where they are now versus where they were previously at a higher level of functioning, as well as by comparing themselves with the "nondepressed" world.

To help clients with depression appreciate their accomplishments, have clients compare themselves now to when they were at their worst. Remind them to take credit for every step they make toward a goal, rather than waiting until they complete the goal. Finally, taking credit involves asking clients to pat themselves on the back and recognize the positive meaning that their actions reflect. For example, consider a woman who hasn't left her house in weeks and makes it to the grocery store to pick up a few essential items. She might think, "This is no big deal, lots of people are shopping and buying a lot more stuff than I am. So what that I was able to buy a few things?"

Alternatively, if she reminds herself that getting to the store was a big deal for her, as it took lots of courage and effort, then she can take credit for doing something she thought she couldn't do. She can prove to herself that she *can* do difficult things even if it feels awful to do so. By reframing her thinking and looking at her actions from this different lens, she can recognize that going to the store was a huge accomplishment for her that deserves a lot of credit.

Therefore, when clients accomplish something they have previously been unable or unwilling to do, they need to take credit for this accomplishment and acknowledge the efforts that went into it. Knowing how hard it was to act and accomplish a goal deserves more credit than less. On the following page is a worksheet that you can use both in session and for homework to have clients pay attention to their accomplishments and acknowledge their efforts. By completing this worksheet on a daily basis, clients can solidify their learning and experience increases in positive mood as they take credit for their actions.

Client Worksheet

CREDIT LIST

• • • • • •

Remember to take credit for your accomplishments, no matter how big or small they are. Accomplishments do not always involve big, grand gestures. They can be as small as successfully getting out of bed and getting your day started, or calling back a friend who you haven't spoken to in awhile. Recognizing the effort that went into accomplishing this activity deserves credit. Every day, try to identify at least one activity you have accomplished and also note the amount of effort required, or challenges that you had to overcome, to accomplish this activity. Finally, write down what this accomplishment says about you as a person.

Activity accomplished	Amount of effort or challenges overcome	What does this accomplishment say about you or your ideas?
1.		
2.		
3.		
4.		
5.		
6.		
7.		

Key Concept 7: Reward

When we accomplish a goal, rewarding ourselves can be a motivating factor that drives behavior and facilitates action. However, rewards are complicated in that they can either promote ongoing helpful behavior or result in behavior that only happens once. *External rewards*, which are incentives that are tangible or physical in nature, tend to do the latter and are usually less effective in promoting meaningful behavior change. For example, promising ourselves screen time, self-pampering, dessert, or a new outfit are all forms of external reinforcement that, although appreciated, may not perpetuate further action. In addition, external reinforcers fail to boost self-esteem because our focus is on obtaining the external reward, as opposed to intrinsically valuing our accomplishment. External rewards are temporary.

In contrast, *intrinsic rewards* are a more effective tool in driving behavior change because they promote self-confidence and a sense of personal achievement. Intrinsic rewards involve the sense of satisfaction or accomplishment that we feel upon completing a difficult task. It is the feeling we experience on the inside when we recognize our efforts and appreciate why it made sense to work toward a goal. Intrinsic rewards promote self-confidence and combat depression because they validate our efforts and give a sense of meaning and accomplishment to doing hard, challenging work.

However, it can sometimes be difficult for clients to recognize the intrinsic reward of getting active and putting forth effort in the face of depression. The following is a coping card that you can give to clients to remind themselves of the intrinsic rewards of continuing to attend therapy and putting in the hard work to move toward recovery.

Coping Card

REWARD YOURSELF

- The reward is the good feeling on the inside.
- The reward is the sense of accomplishment I feel.
- The reward is my mood improving.
- The reward is the little bit of pleasure I feel.
- The reward is my self-confidence growing.

Key Concepts: Putting It All Together

Use the **Getting Mobilized: The Master Plan** worksheet on the following page to help your clients synthesize all of the key concepts associated with behavioral activation and mobilize them toward action. The worksheet asks clients to think through all the steps needed to take action and battle against their depression, including identifying a goal, listing the advantages of achieving this goal, specifying a plan, putting the plan on a schedule, replacing give-up thoughts with go-to thoughts, taking credit for their accomplishments, and reminding themselves of the reward.

Client Worksheet

GETTING MOBILIZED:
THE MASTER PLAN

• • • • • •

1. Identify your goal: _____

   _____

2. List at least five possible advantages of this goal:

   1. _____
   2. _____
   3. _____
   4. _____
   5. _____

3. What is your plan to achieve this goal? List all the details: _____

   _____

   _____

   _____

4. Put the plan on your schedule.

5. Identify give-up thoughts and replace them with go-to thoughts.

Give-up Thought	**Go-to Thought**
1. _____	1. _____
2. _____	2. _____
3. _____	3. _____

6. Take credit by describing the effort involved in implementing this plan: _____
   _____
   _____

7. Remind yourself of the reward: Feeling better, experiencing pleasure, growing more confident.

Considering Bipolar Disorder

For clients with bipolar disorder, maintaining regular patterns of sleep, nutrition, and activity is critical to sustaining wellness. Their fragile biological system is vulnerable to dysregulation, which makes inconsistent or extreme schedules more dangerous. Taking the red eye or staying up late makes the next day tough for everyone, but for clients diagnosed with bipolar disorder, it can stimulate significant mood dysregulation. Additionally, events that unravel most anyone—such as missing a train or flight, getting stuck somewhere because someone forgets to pick us up, or receiving a bill we were not expecting—only temporarily impact the average person. The arousal elicited by these situations diminishes once the problem resolves. In contrast, clients with bipolar disorder may experience extended emotional arousal over the course of many days.

When clients with bipolar disorder are in the depressed phase of the disorder, mobilizing them through behavioral activation is addressed in the same fashion as it is with unipolar depression. However, in the manic or hypomanic phase, the goals of the activity schedule are different. When clients experience mania, they have an inflated view of themselves, the future, and their experiences, which leads to overaction, overmobilization, increased independence, recklessness, and risk taking (Newman, Leahy, Beck, Reilly-Harrington, & Gyulai, 2001). Therefore, rather than adding activities to the schedule, it is important to decrease them.

For example, instead of sleeping less, they are pushed to stay in bed longer. Instead of working more, they are encouraged to set limits and adhere to a scheduled quit time. Mealtimes are planned, and clients are urged to eat even if they are not hungry. Medication is written into the activity schedule to increase compliance and ensure that it is taken right around the same time each day. Quiet time to relax is also scheduled into the day. Late-night phone calls or projects are discouraged, and high-risk situations avoided. The activity schedule provides corrective data that lets clients know when they are problematically pushing limits or doing too much. It provides them a scheduled plan to adhere to, which is designed to sustain wellness.

COGNITIVE RESTRUCTURING

Getting clients mobilized through behavioral activation typically provides the energy and data needed for more advanced cognitive work to take place. Setting the foundation for this more advanced work is crucial because cognitive restructuring is the cornerstone of CBT for depression. Addressing clients' negatively biased thoughts, assumptions, and beliefs is critical in reducing depressive symptoms and preventing relapse.

Keep in mind that during behavioral activation, cognitive restructuring was already taking place when clients were asked to reframe give-up thoughts into go-to ones. Although clients with functional impairment and more severe symptoms often require behavioral work for an extended period before cognitive work can begin, others will simultaneously be able to do both. Clients with significant hopelessness require immediate cognitive intervention to reduce their vulnerability and potential suicide risk.

Although the focus of this section is on cognitive restructuring for unipolar depression, addressing biased thoughts, assumptions, and beliefs is also key in reducing manic symptoms and preventing relapse in bipolar disorder. Whereas negatively biased thinking is the problem in depression, overly positive thinking is the problem in mania. In particular, when clients with bipolar disorder are in the manic phase of the disorder, they have an inflated view of themselves, the future, and their experiences. In particular, they tend to overestimate their capabilities, rely excessively on luck, underestimate risk, minimize their problems, and overvalue immediate gratification. Therefore, when clients are manic, treatment should seek to address and replace these risky thinking patterns by engaging in careful planning, weighing the pros and cons, and reviewing past experiences (Newman et al., 2001).

Depression

Eliciting Automatic Thoughts

When you understand clients' thinking, you get a road map to their inner world. However, eliciting clients' thoughts, assumptions, and beliefs is a multistep process, which involves identifying their situation-specific automatic thoughts and then linking these thoughts to their rules, guiding assumptions, and self-imposed doubt beliefs. Situation-specific automatic thoughts have to do with how a client perceives or interprets an event. For example, they might include thoughts such as these: "My boyfriend is late because he is blowing me off," "My grade is so bad that the teacher didn't tell me my score," or "She didn't call me back because she's mad." These thoughts tend to be easily accessible in clients with depression, but not always. Eliciting these thoughts provides us with an understanding of the client's distress. Here are some potential strategies to bring out these thoughts in session:

1. When you notice a shift in a client's affect in session, ask them what they are thinking or what thoughts are connected to what they are feeling. For example, if you notice that a client is tearing up, you might ask, "What are you thinking?" or "What thought connects to those tears?"

2. Have clients think about a recent distressing situation or time, and ask them what they were thinking at that time.

3. Consider having clients use imagery to relive a specific situation or time in detail as if it were happening right now, and ask what they are thinking.

4. Try doing a role-play of a previous distressing situation or a potentially upsetting situation, and ask clients what they are thinking throughout the role-play.

5. You might try being paradoxical by offering the opposite of what clients are likely thinking. For example, if you know a client is not happy with his performance on a recent work assignment, you might ask, "Are you thinking about what an awesome job you did?" When the client does not provide an affirmative response, you can follow up with, "You don't think that you did such a great job, so what were you actually thinking?"

6. For clients who always with respond with statements such as, "I am not thinking anything," or "I don't know," you might try a more drastic approach. In particular, you can tell them to take some time to think about it and then walk out of the room. After standing in the hall for a minute, return and ask them again what they were thinking.

7. Though not ideal, you might provide examples of what you imagine the client might be thinking in order to "prime the pump."

Even with the use of these elicitation techniques, it is still likely that clients will want to tell a story about the specific situation in question, rather than discussing their associated thoughts or feelings. You can use that to your advantage by guiding the story and evoking the information you need to understand your clients and their problem. For example, imagine that a client begins to tell you what happened when her husband returned home from a business trip. As she starts to tell you all the details of what he said and did, consider the following options of how you might respond:

Option 1: You patiently listen, allowing her to spend the first half of the session telling you all the details of the story.

Option 2: You interrupt her story with probing questions. For example, "When he asked you why you didn't go to the store, what were you feeling? What were you thinking? And when he asked you why you didn't go to the school function, what did you think? Feel? And what did you do?"

The goal of treatment is to reduce distress and improve functionality, and you can see how the first option results in a non-goal-directed conversation that can delay that process. In contrast, eliciting the thoughts and behaviors associated with the client's distress allows for immediate goal-directed work. Therefore, the next time your clients begin to tell you a story behind a distressing situation, try option two by interrupting them and eliciting the thoughts and behaviors connected to their distress.

Downward Arrow Tool

When probing clients for situation-specific automatic thoughts, the first thought elicited is often not the most important. The initial automatic thought often represents what is going on at the surface, but you want to get at the underlying doubt labels, rules, and assumptions that are driving this thought. Therefore, you want to elicit *all* the distressing thoughts and beliefs associated with that event. For example, if the client's initial automatic thought is, "I did a poor job on that sales call," then you want to probe deeper to determine what is driving this thought. For example, the client's assumption might be, "If I performed badly, then I am failing at my job," and the doubt label might be, "I am a failure."

To elicit this deeper meaning, the downward arrow is a technique you can use, which involves asking probing questions to get to the root of the client's automatic thoughts. The following is a list of potential downward arrow questions:

- "What does that mean?"
- "If that's true, what's so bad about . . . ?"
- "What about that . . . bothers you?"
- "What about that . . . is a problem for you?"
- "What's the worst part about . . . ?"
- "So, what if . . . ?"
- "What does that . . . mean about you?"
- "What does that . . . mean to you?"

To illustrate the downward arrow technique, consider the following example. A husband returns home from a business trip to find that his wife, Amy, has been struggling and hasn't done many of the things that she said she would do in his absence. In turn, he jumps in with solutions. Upon seeing her therapist, Amy is distressed because she thinks her husband doesn't believe she is trying hard enough. The therapist might engage in the following dialogue to uncover the deeper doubt labels and underlying assumptions driving this belief.

Amy: "He thinks I am not trying hard enough."
Therapist: "What does it mean to you that he thinks you're not trying hard enough?"
Amy: "It means that I'm giving in."
Therapist: "What does it mean about you if you are giving in?"
Amy: "That I don't care."
Therapist: "What does it mean if you don't care?"
Amy: "That I'm lazy."
Therapist: "What does it mean about you if you are lazy?"
Amy: "That I'm damaged."
Therapist: "What does it mean that you are damaged?"

Amy:	"That I'll never succeed."
Therapist:	"What does it mean about you if you will never succeed?"
Amy:	"I am a failure."

In addition to the downward arrow technique, identifying doubt labels can be aided by collaboratively working with clients to identify the main theme behind their automatic thoughts. Does the theme involve a concern about their capability, desirability, or both? In the previous example, some of the wife's thoughts were, "I'm lazy" and "I'll never succeed," which indicate concerns about capability. Ascertaining whether the client's concerns revolve around achievement, social interactions, or both can help guide the discussion. If we know which theme is of greatest concern to the client, then we know to look for doubt labels relevant to that theme. Achievement concerns are associated with beliefs about incompetence or helplessness, while social concerns are associated with beliefs about perceived undesirability and unlovability. Especially when clients are psychologically naive or not in touch with their self-doubt, helping them recognize what they value and the likely theme for their self-doubt can uncover their personalized doubt label. Identifying this personalized doubt label is critical, as this label is at the root of the client's vulnerability to psychological distress.

Potential Pitfalls

When using the downward arrow technique, keep some potential pitfalls in mind. First, clinicians often have automatic thoughts of their own about continuing to ask probing questions to clients. In particular, they believe that clients will feel annoyed or irritated with the repeated querying. However, the opposite is true, as giving clients undivided attention typically results in their feeling listened to and understood. Therefore, don't be concerned about asking probing questions. It's better to err on the side of asking what seems like too many questions than not asking enough questions.

Second, there is the possibility of client obstruction, as some clients may tell you, "I don't know what that means." For some clients, it may very well be true that they don't know the answer. In that case, try asking a different downward arrow question, such as, "Why does that bother you?" or "Why is that a problem for you?" You can also abort the questioning and try again at a later time, or you can consider providing them with more guided probes, such as, "Is it possible that it means something about your capability or desirability?" On the other hand, it may be that clients don't want to tell you or are avoiding talking about it because it evokes distress. In that case, it's important to validate how difficult this process may be while helping clients see that processing through their distress will ultimately lead to recovery.

Evaluating Automatic Thoughts

Guided Discovery with Socratic Questioning

A critical concept in cognitive restructuring is that automatic thoughts are not necessarily false or biased; they may reflect truth or partial truth. That is why, as clinicians, we never challenge thoughts but examine and evaluate them for both validity and utility. Instead of telling clients how to think or what to conclude, effective therapeutic change comes from helping clients see new perspectives through the process of guided discovery. By using Socratic questioning, we allow clients to be scientists, look at the facts, consider alternative viewpoints, and draw more accurate, less negatively biased conclusions for themselves. The process of guided discovery is the art of CBT in that the more proficient you get at examining thoughts, the more creative you can be with this process. The following is a list of possible guided discovery questions:

- "Are these thoughts necessarily true? What is the evidence that supports and doesn't support this idea?"
- "What are some other possible explanations?"
- "Is there a different way to think about it?"
- "What are some alternative possibilities?"
- "How might someone else think about this situation? Is there another perspective to consider?"
- "What might you say to someone else in this same situation?"
- "Are these thoughts helpful? What is the effect of believing this thought?"
- "What's the worst that could realistically happen? Could you survive it?"
- "What's the best-case scenario?"
- "What's the most realistic possibility?"
- "If you could beam yourself into the future—a day, month, or year later—what might you think about this same situation?"
- "Is there something you can do about it?"
- "What is a more reasonable or helpful way to look at this situation?"
- "What is your overall conclusion?"
- "Does this conclusion impact the way you see yourself?"

Although this list represents potential questions you can ask clients directly to help them evaluate their thinking, you can design your own individually tailored Socratic questions to guide clients toward a more accurate and realistic perspective. You can ask clients to examine the evidence for and against a thought, or to look at an alternative way of seeing the situation, but this may not yield helpful answers. Keep in mind that clients with depression have a negatively biased view of the past and present, so they are likely to blindly accept their distorted viewpoint. Your role as the therapist is to help them understand the whole picture and look at all the relevant data so they can evaluate the accuracy and helpfulness of their thinking.

For example, consider the previous example of Amy, whose automatic thought regarding her husband was, "He thinks I am not trying hard enough." Asking her to look at the evidence for and against this thought may inadvertently result in confirmation of this idea when it may not be true. Instead, the following are some questions that you might ask to help her examine the validity of this thought:

- "Has he told you that he thinks you are not trying hard enough?"
- "Does he see how hard it is for you to do things and how much distress you are experiencing?"
- "Do you tell him how hard it is?"
- "Does he ever acknowledge or tell you positive things about your effort?"

Similarly, if you ask, "Is there an alternative reason why your husband may have been questioning you upon returning home?" and that again fails to provide a helpful response, more guided questions may be warranted. The following are some more pointed questions that you might ask the client to help her consider an alternative perspective:

Depression

- "What does your husband do professionally?"
- "Does he spend his time working on solving problems?"
- "Is that his go-to strategy, to fix the problem?"
- "Why does he want to fix problems?"
- "Do you think he sees your situation as another problem?"
- "Why might he be invested in solving your problems?"
- "Could his questioning be his way of trying to solve the problem rather than judging what you have or haven't done?"

Although we often have lots of information about a client's case (which can help guide the client to see the facts or consider alternatives), we don't know the answers to these questions ahead of time. Therefore, the most important thing is to make meaning out of the data collected. It is not enough to gather a pile of evidence that contradicts your client's thought if you don't link that evidence to a new conclusion. In the previous example, the evidence suggests that Amy's husband does understand that she is trying her hardest. Therefore, you can help Amy see that when her husband was bombarding her with questions, that was his way of trying to fix the problem, given that problem solving is a strong skill for him and is thus his modus operandi.

Thinking Errors

When working with clients to evaluate their negative automatic thoughts, it is necessary to identify common thinking errors (or cognitive distortions) that are contributing to their distress. The goal is not to label the thinking error for each specific automatic thought, but to learn to identify and replace a *pattern* of thinking errors with more valid viewpoints. Some typical thinking errors that clients with depression experience include the following: extreme thinking, depending on your emotions, negative self-labeling, and zooming in on the negative.

Extreme thinking involves seeing everything in all-or-nothing terms. The world is black or white with no shades of gray in between. Things are either "good" or "bad," or a "success" or "failure." Extreme thinking prevents clients from seeing the bigger picture, which leads them to jump to more negative conclusions than are warranted. For example, Jordyn got a B+ on her science test and viewed herself as a failure since she didn't get a perfect score. To help clients overcome extreme thinking, they need to learn how to focus on the big picture, taking into account all the pluses and giving more appropriate weight to the minuses.

Depending on your emotions involves drawing conclusions about a situation based on emotions rather than facts. When clients are subject to this thinking error, they ignore the facts of a situation and view their emotions as truths instead. Statements such as, "I feel guilty, so I must have messed up," "Everything feels overwhelming, so there's no point in trying," and "I feel incompetent, so I must have done a bad job" are all examples of depending on your emotions. Although emotions are valid and helpful sources of information, they can lead to biased and unhelpful conclusions when they are used independently of facts. Helping clients overcome this thinking error involves teaching them to look beyond their feelings and examine the facts of a situation.

Negative self-labeling involves using a negative self-definition to describe yourself. Clients with depression tend to use negative self-labeling when they fall short of their expectations, or they may call themselves negative self-labels simply because they are struggling with depression. For example, clients who make a mistake may label themselves as "stupid," or they may view themselves as a "loser" if they aren't the top pick for their school's sports team. An important part of overcoming negative self-labeling is helping clients recognize how unhelpful it is to beat themselves up and to stop letting one mistake or shortcoming define who they are.

Zooming in on the negative involves focusing exclusively on the negatives and discounting the positives of a situation. For example, Jordyn received one critical comment from her teacher after giving a class presentation, and she took this to mean that her teacher thought the presentation was a disaster, despite the fact that her teacher gave her lots of positive comments and praised the presentation overall. Helping clients with depression see the big picture is critical. Identifying positive, negative, and neutral information can help them remove the negative bias and more accurately view their world. Without acknowledging the positives in ourselves and our situations, it is impossible to take credit and feel good.

You can use a thought register with your clients to help them begin the process of identifying and modifying any unhelpful or inaccurate automatic thoughts.

Thought Register

A thought register (also called a thought record) is the therapist's and client's road map to collecting, evaluating, and restructuring biased and inaccurate thoughts. The main components of a thought register are all the same, regardless of which version you choose to use. The first component involves documenting the **activating situation**, which is the event or stimulus that triggered the distress. This trigger may be external in nature, such as hearing bad news, or internal, such as experiencing a strong body sensation, emotion, thought, or image.

The next three components involve documenting the **body responses**, **automatic thoughts**, and **emotions** associated with this triggering event. That is, what sensations did clients experience in their body, what thoughts were going through their mind, and what emotions were elicited as a result of the activating situation? Clients also rate the intensity of these emotions on a 10-point scale (0 = no distress, 10 = highest distress possible).

The fifth and sixth components of the thought register involve identifying the **thinking errors** and **doubt label** associated with their automatic thought. Remember that doubt labels are the negative names that clients call themselves when their self-doubt is activated. You can elicit this negative core belief by using the downward arrow techniques described earlier.

The next component is developing an alternative viewpoint of the situation by asking guided questions that help clients gather and evaluate the **facts**. This is the raw data from which clients can come to a new conclusion or reframe the original upsetting thought or image. Finally, the last component is known as "**go time**," which involves summarizing the new, objective conclusion (rethink), re-rating the emotions about the situation (relax), and planning an effective behavioral strategy (response).

The sample thought register on the following page shows what Amy concluded about her husband. In particular, after reviewing the facts, she was able to recognize that jumping in and problem solving is her husband's way of handling stress, including his own. When she considers this alternative point of view, the unsolicited solutions that her husband provided to her now seem typical, and she realizes that her reaction to the situation was disproportionate.

Sample Worksheet

THOUGHT REGISTER:
AMY

Activating Situation	Body Response	Thinking Errors	Doubt Label	Facts	Go Time: Rethink, Relax, Respond
My husband returned home from a business trip and found out I hadn't done many of the things I said I'd do while he was gone. In turn, he jumped in by trying to offer a bunch of solutions.	Heaviness in body, lethargic, crying **Automatic Thoughts** He thinks I'm not trying hard enough. **Emotions (0-10)** Sad, hurt (7)	Extreme thinking; depending on your emotions	I'm not good enough.	He never told me, "You're not good enough." My husband's job is to problem solve all day at work. In fact, the reason he flew out of town is because there was a big problem he needed to fix. He came home and saw me struggling, and that's why he jumped in with solutions. There is no evidence that he thinks I am not trying hard enough.	**Rethink:** My thought that my husband thinks I'm not trying hard enough is not true. He did notice several of the things I got done and was happy about that. I have to remember that this is the way he is and what makes him good at his job. It was my doubt that was getting in the way. **Relax:** I notice that I am less upset and hurt. **Respond:** Give myself credit for what I was able to accomplish and use some of his suggestions to put a better and more realistic plan in place for tomorrow.

Copyright © 2019 Leslie Sokol & Marci G. Fox, *The Comprehensive Clinician's Guide to Cognitive Behavioral Therapy*. All Rights Reserved

Before you ask clients to complete a thought register, it's helpful for you to first practice doing one on yourself. One option is to complete the record whenever you notice a change in your body response or your emotions, and to see if you can determine what the activating situation for these changes was. You can also fill out the thought register whenever you experience a situation that you recognize was particularly challenging or distressing. Once you get the hang of completing the thought register on yourself, you can try it out with your clients using the worksheet on the following page. Make sure to practice the thought register together in session first, and then ask clients to continue on their own outside of session.

Client Worksheet

THOUGHT REGISTER

∙∙∙∙∙∙∙

The thought register can help you identify your thinking errors and reframe your thinking in a more accurate and objective way so you can take charge of feeling better and doing the things you want to accomplish. When you experience emotional or physical distress, take note of the situation and record your accompanying body responses, automatic thoughts, and emotions. Next, try to identify the thinking error(s) driving your distress, but don't be concerned if you cannot identify the error. Then, see if you can identify the doubt label that was activated. Finally, consider the data by recording the facts, and rethink a more accurate conclusion. Relax by noticing the decrease in the intensity of your distress, and now respond by specifying a new and more effective action.

Activating Situation	Body Response	Thinking Errors	Doubt Label	Facts	Go Time: Rethink, Relax, Respond
					Rethink:
	Automatic Thoughts				
					Relax:
	Emotions (0-10)				
					Respond:

Copyright © 2019 Leslie Sokol & Marci G. Fox, *The Comprehensive Clinician's Guide to Cognitive Behavioral Therapy*. All Rights Reserved

Alternatives to the Thought Register

Pie Chart

Although the thought register is an important tool to help clients use facts to reframe their negative automatic thoughts, it is not the only tool available to do cognitive restructuring. A responsibility pie chart is another valuable tool when the goal is to help clients consider all the factors when making conclusions. Often, clients with depression take full responsibility for negative events or outcomes. The pie chart can help them see the bigger picture.

Consider a mother whose child is misbehaving at school and who believes that she is fully responsible for the situation. The pie chart asks her to consider what other factors could be contributing to her child's behavior, and to then assign percentages to those factors to help her realize that it is not possible for her to be 100 percent responsible. For example, although the mother plays a significant role in shaping her child's behavior, so do various other factors in the child's life (e.g., other adults, peers, relatives, or siblings; the classroom environment; the child's temperament; learning issues; boredom; or the influence of media, such as music, internet, television, and movies). The list can be endless.

Similarly, consider a client with depression, who has been inactive for some time and has gained significant weight, and who now concludes that he is undesirable or a failure. The pie chart can help him see that no one is defined solely by their shape or size. By taking into account all the factors that define him (e.g., other physical attributes, personality, aptitudes, interests, experiences, intellect, education, personality), the client can come to a more balanced conclusion that he is much more than his shape or size.

Use the pie chart on the following page to help your clients reframe their negative automatic thoughts and come to more balanced conclusions.

Client Worksheet

PIE CHART

• • • • • •

Think of a situation where you made the conclusion that you were solely responsible for the outcome. Are you taking full responsibility for a situation in which you are only one of many factors involved? Make a list of all the factors that could have contributed to this outcome, and put all of these factors on the pie chart below. Then, ask yourself if it's possible that you are not fully responsible for this outcome, and try to determine what percentage you would hold yourself accountable when considering all of the factors at play.

Event or situation: _____

Factors that could be contributing to this outcome:

_____

_____

_____

Put the factors on the pie below, and assign percentages to those factors:

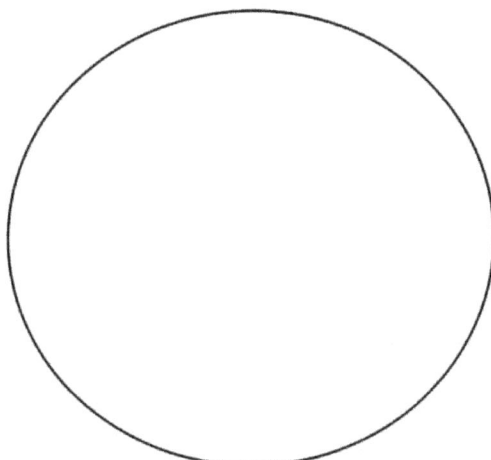

Now, ask yourself if you are 100% responsible or if your conclusion is based on one factor. What is a more reasonable percentage? _____%

Collages or Pictures

Many clients are reluctant to complete thought registers for various reasons, such as difficulties with literacy, language barriers, or outright unwillingness. In this case, the use of a collage is a viable alternative. Magazines and newspapers provide pictures that can symbolically represent clients' automatic thoughts and potential reframes to these thoughts. Either in session or on their own at home, have clients cut out pictures that represent their automatic thoughts, assumptions, and beliefs about the situation, as well as pictures that represent an alternative reframe.

For example, consider a woman with depression who had the task of making cupcakes for her daughter's sports game but believed that she was useless and weak, leading her to think, "It's too much for me. I can't do it. No one wants me there." She made a collage of pictures that showed a woman who was impaired, holding her head in pain, falling down, walking with assistance, and sitting alone. Together in session, we created an alternative collage of a woman teaching a class, presenting a cake, surrounded by children as she read a book to them, walking up a steep set of stairs, and working out with weights in her hands. She then took a black marker and put a giant "X" on the collage that represented her negative thoughts and beliefs, and she spent the week looking at the alternative collage and trying to find more pictures in support of the non-depressed viewpoint.

Similarly, in working with clients who have literacy or developmental delays, pictures are an alternative way to examine thoughts. Take the case of an adult client who had the intellectual capacity of a second grader. She had recently lost her father to heart disease and now believed she couldn't function or be happy unless a relative was by her side. Looking at family pictures that her mother provided, we were able to make a case that it was possible for the client to be happy and function without her mother or one of her siblings by her side. Finding pictures that showed her having a good time doing her favorite things, such as dancing and bowling, unaccompanied by family helped make this point.

Cost-Benefit Analysis

The cost-benefit analysis is another tool to help clients restructure their thoughts. It is particularly helpful when clients are struggling with a decision (e.g., "Should I end the relationship, take the job, move?") or when they are caught in a pattern of thinking that is unhelpful, even if the thoughts are true (e.g., "What purpose does it serve to continue to talk about this? What use is there in continuing to call myself that nasty name?"). By considering the pros and cons of continuing the action versus not continuing the action, clients can come to a more balanced conclusion.

For example, Niki constantly dwelled on her past and insisted on making it the focus of every conversation, and she blamed her family for her current problems. Significant time in therapy had been spent on helping her accept that the past couldn't be changed, that it is possible she was making conclusions not based on facts, and that her memory might actually paint a more negative picture than the truth. However, she only wanted to focus on every injustice she remembered. By considering the pros and cons of continuing to focus on her past, and the pros and cons of *not* continuing to focus on her past, Niki realized that nothing was to be gained from the conversation. Focusing on the past prevented her from living in the now, interfered with her ability to experience joy, and only served to fuel anger toward her family and disconnect her from the family she wanted to be a part of.

As another example, consider the case of Zeke, who called himself a loser whenever he didn't perform up to his standards, whether it came to work, sports, or playing cards. Although he sometimes really did lose at something, he mostly performed quite well and actually exceeded others' expectations. However, in his mind, anything less than his ideal made him a loser. By completing a cost-benefit analysis of calling himself a loser, Zeke was able to recognize that there was no upside to calling himself this nasty name. Rather all it did was make him feel defeated, and instead of pushing him on, it made him want to quit. In order to help your clients consider the pros and cons of thinking a certain way—or of deciding to take a certain action—use the cost-benefit analysis worksheet on the following page.

Client Worksheet

COST-BENEFIT ANALYSIS

• • • • • •

Specify a thought that is causing you distress and, regardless of whether the thought is true or false, try looking at the pros and cons of dwelling on this thought. Or, if you are deliberating whether to take a certain course of action, write the pros and cons of doing so, and see what the exercise helps you conclude.

Advantages of Thinking or Taking a Specific Action	**Disadvantages of Thinking or Taking a Specific Action**
_____ _____ _____ _____	_____ _____ _____ _____
Advantages of <u>Not</u> Thinking or Taking a Specific Action	**Disadvantages of <u>Not</u> Thinking or Taking a Specific Action**
_____ _____ _____ _____	_____ _____ _____ _____

Conclusion: _____

_____

_____

Cognitive Continuum Analysis

Looking at data on a continuum is another way to help clients put things in perspective. Instead of seeing their actions (or themselves) in the worst possible way, a cognitive continuum analysis puts it in a more objective view. For example, Brandon thinks he is the worst employee ever, as he is sometimes late with deadlines, makes minor errors, and gets nervous when people ask him questions. When Brandon is asked what the best employees do, he says, "They always meet deadlines, never make errors, don't get nervous, do stellar work, never complain, show up every day, and give it their all." By completing a continuum analysis, he is able to realize that he does good work most of the time, rarely complains, shows up every day, and gives it his all. In turn, he concludes that he has a lot in common with his definition of a good employee.

In addition, when he thinks about all the characteristics of bad employees (e.g., those who lie, call in sick all the time to avoid work, never do the work at all rather than it being late, try to get others to do the work for them), he decides that he is not the worst employee ever. In fact, he is still learning and is willing to ask and accept help to continue to improve, which only validates the good employee that he actually is. Help your clients put their viewpoints into a more balanced perspective by using the cognitive continuum analysis on the following page.

Client Worksheet Example

CONTINUUM ANALYSIS
......

Recall a time when you made "a worst-case scenario" conclusion about yourself or the situation at hand. Create a continuum from the worst to the best of what you have concluded about yourself or the situation. A sample continuum analysis is provided below, followed by a blank one for you to fill out regarding your own situation.

Example: It was the worst dinner party ever.

Worst Dinner Party | Best Dinner Party

Food Poisoning   Food Burned   **(Food Mediocre)**   Food Adequate   Food Pretty Good   Food Awesome

Injuries   Fighting   Yelling   Heated Conversation   Limited Conversation   Mostly Positive Conversation   **(Great Conversation)**

Complaints   Some Negative Feedback   Neutral Feedback   Some Positive Feedback   **(Mostly Good Feedback)**   Rave Review

State your new conclusion: It was far from being the worst dinner party ever. In fact, everyone had a good time despite the disappointing food.

Client Worksheet

CONTINUUM ANALYSIS
· · · · · ·

State the label or event: _____

Worst _____ **Best**

(Most Negative) _____ (Less Negative) _____ (Somewhat Negative) _____ (Somewhat Positive) _____ (More Positive) _____ (Most Positive)

(Most Negative) _____ (Less Negative) _____ (Somewhat Negative) _____ (Somewhat Positive) _____ (More Positive) _____ (Most Positive)

(Most Negative) _____ (Less Negative) _____ (Somewhat Negative) _____ (Somewhat Positive) _____ (More Positive) _____ (Most Positive)

State your new conclusion: _____
_____
_____

No Judgment

Often, clients with depression will allow a negative situation to mean more than it does. For example, they will often ascribe personal meaning to the situation or assume that things will never get better, which only serves to breed hopelessness, fear, and self-doubt. One way to help clients get out of this pattern of negative thinking is to help them cultivate a nonjudgmental attitude of acceptance. The ability to acknowledge negative information without judgment is what underlies the notion of acceptance. Acceptance requires acknowledging things as they are without letting doubt, uncertainty, or judgment get in the way.

Clients can practice cultivating a nonjudgmental attitude by using the triple A's of effectiveness: acknowledging, accepting, and taking appropriate action. In particular, they can learn to **acknowledge** (e.g., record the facts of the situation), **accept** (e.g., reserve judgment and draw accurate conclusions based solely on the facts), and **take appropriate action** (e.g., choose a course of action most effective and appropriate for the situation). For example, if a client receives an abnormal mammogram, that doesn't mean she has cancer, that there is no treatment, and that she will die. However, if the client lets herself believe this, then she might stop taking care of herself and avoid treatment. Instead, the client can practice the triple A's of effectiveness by acknowledging, accepting and taking appropriate action. In particular, she can acknowledge the abnormal result, accept the data as it is now by reserving judgment until she has the facts (which means considering the various explanations for her abnormal test results, many of which are benign), and take appropriate action by following up on the recommended next steps. This cognitive tool can be used to address automatic thoughts and beliefs across a multitude of situations.

Client Worksheet

TRIPLE A'S

• • • • • •

The next time you are feeling distressed, use the triple A's of effectiveness to reduce your distress: **A**cknowledge the facts, practice **A**cceptance by reminding yourself not to give unnecessary meaning or judgment to the situation, and take appropriate **A**ction.

Acknowledge the Facts

Record the specifics of the situation, including your feelings and body response.

What are the facts of the situation? _____

_____

Accept

See the situation objectively. Don't judge, give exaggerated personal meaning, or make future predictions.

What do the facts tell me? _____

_____

Act Appropriately

Instead of using ineffective strategies (e.g., avoidance, ineffective communication, self-harm), take effective and appropriate action (e.g., face the situation, effectively communicate, self-soothe).

What are some appropriate actions I can take? _____

_____

Depression

Reframing the Doubt Label

Once you start to gain traction in helping clients discard, modify, and reframe any inaccurate or distorted thoughts into more realistic viewpoints, then you can move on to reframing the doubt label. Clients are able to gain a new perspective by reframing their negative automatic thoughts, which allows them to draw new conclusions that can be used to modify the underlying doubt label. For example, if clients are able to conclude that they succeeded in a specific situation, then the doubt label of being a failure no longer fits.

Given that doubt labels negatively impact the ways clients with depression perceive themselves and the world around them, reframing the doubt label is important to recovery and prevention of relapse. To do so, collect current and historical data that help the client examine evidence for and against the doubt label. This data should focus on objective, observable facts—rather than the client's thoughts, feelings, imagined worries, or biased past reflections. Don't let the focus be on any one piece of data but, rather, look at the big picture of what does or does not support their doubt label.

Often, clients will try to discount what they consider "small" pieces of data that provide evidence against their doubt label. Make sure they take credit for every piece of action and progress, regardless of how small, so that the evidence against the doubt label piles up. It can also be helpful to look at the available data from another person's viewpoint to consider any supporting evidence that the client may have missed. If in the process of collecting this data, any new derogatory labels come up, make sure to address those at a later point too. However, only address one doubt label at a time.

Once you have gathered all the available evidence, ask clients how much they believe the evidence in support of their doubt label and how much they believe the evidence against their doubt label on a scale from 0 to 100 percent. You want to make sure you have gathered sufficient data so that there is more evidence against the doubt label than for it. Returning again to Amy's situation, she was able to come up with 11 total pieces of evidence: four in support of her belief that she is "not good enough," which she believed at 40 percent intensity, and seven against the belief, which she believed at 60 percent intensity. Thus, the evidence against her doubt was more believable. It is not the number of items in each column per se but, rather, how strongly the client believes these items to be true.

Evidence for "I'm not good enough"	Evidence against "I'm not good enough"
I am doing less than I should be doing.	I made the dean's list in college.
My husband is always giving me solutions.	I have an advanced degree.
I can't get over this depression.	I make a mean meal.
I am not the size I want to be.	I am good at taking care of others.
	I have a successful marriage.
	I have friends.
	I manage all the household responsibilities.
How strongly do you believe this evidence (0–100%)? __40__ %	How strongly do you believe this evidence (0–100%)? __60__ %

Once you have collected all the available data, go back and look at each piece of information in the first column (e.g., in support of the doubt label) and help clients consider an alternative conclusion. Ask them to reframe each piece of evidence by coming up with a new, more realistic way of thinking. This serves to shrink the believability in the doubt label. The following table provides a continuation of Amy's example:

Evidence for "I'm not good enough"	Reframe
• I am doing less than I should be doing.	• I am depressed and that makes it hard to do anything. The fact that I am doing anything is an accomplishment.
• My husband is always giving me solutions.	• My husband is not trying to insult me; he is just trying to help in the way he knows how.
• I can't get over this depression.	• Even if my depression is getting the best of me, that is not a reflection of my character or my fault. Struggling with depression is the definition of being depressed.
• I am not the size I want to be.	• Just because I have gained weight doesn't mean I am less than as a person. I wish I hadn't gained weight, but I have lots of other qualities to feel good about that make me who I am.

After working with clients to reframe each piece of evidence, have them look over their responses in the first table and re-rate how strongly they believe the evidence for and against the doubt belief. The reframes they completed in the second table should have diminished the believability of the doubt label. For example, after reviewing the evidence, Amy believed the evidence in support of her doubt label at only 10 percent, whereas she believed the evidence against the doubt label at 90 percent.

Finally, ask clients to come up with a new, realistic overall conclusion. Note that this new conclusion may be the complete opposite, a variation, or a less extreme perspective of the initial doubt label. For example, instead of "I am not good enough," the client may state, "I am acceptable," "I am sufficient," or "I am adequate." Returning to Amy's example, she was able to come to the following new, realistic conclusion: "I am good enough just the way I am. I'm just depressed and that makes me self-critical."

On the following page is a worksheet you can use with clients to help them modify their doubt label and reframe it into a more realistic, helpful belief.

Client Worksheet

MODIFY THE DOUBT

• • • • • •

Reframing your doubt label is an important part of recovery and preventing relapse. Write your doubt label on the following line, and over the next week, record evidence for and against your doubt label.

What is the doubt label? _____

Now find some evidence for and against this belief.

Evidence for Doubt Label	Evidence against Doubt Label

Now, look at the evidence in each column and rate how strongly you believe the evidence in support of and against the doubt label (0–100%).

_____%: Evidence in support of the doubt label

_____%: Evidence against the doubt label

Once you have examined the evidence, go back and look at the data in the right column (e.g., evidence in support of the doubt label) and consider an alternative conclusion for each piece of evidence.

Evidence for Doubt Label	Reframe

Now, re-rate your percentages from the first table. How strongly do you believe the evidence for and against the doubt label (0–100%)?

_____%: Evidence in support of the doubt label

_____%: Evidence against the doubt label

What is a new, realistic, overall conclusion? Consider a new belief.

_____

_____

_____

Identifying and Evaluating Conditional Assumptions

As discussed in Chapter 2, conditional assumptions are the intermediate beliefs between the doubt label and our compensatory coping strategies. They are the "if, then" statements that guide how individuals operate in this world. Although it is not necessary to break these assumptions down into negative versus positive assumptions, doing so can be helpful because negative assumptions activate the doubt label, whereas positive assumptions reflect protective strategies that clients use in an attempt to deactivate the doubt label.

For example, Amy's negative assumption may be, "If people give me feedback or suggestions, then I'm not good enough." As a result, any time that someone gives her advice (e.g., her husband, family member, employer, colleague, friend, or stranger), she is at risk of activating the doubt label that she is "not good enough." When this occurs, she is likely to blow the situation out of proportion, experience intense emotional or physical symptoms of discomfort, and experience worsening mood. To compensate, her positive conditional assumption may be, "If I am perfect and do everything right, then people won't find out I'm not good enough." Since it is impossible to get everything done all the time, let alone perfectly, she continues to make herself vulnerable.

Conditional assumptions are testable. We can often look at examples in our clients' personal lives to test their ideas. For instance, how many times did Amy fail to do something "perfectly" from her perspective, and yet no one else noticed? Data from other people's examples can also be helpful to test the assumption. Does Amy know anyone who she thinks is good enough but who doesn't get everything done or doesn't do things perfectly? Often, testing assumptions requires setting up experiments to test the conditional hypothesis. For example, Amy could run an experiment at work by purposely putting some minor errors in a memo she distributes (e.g., grammatical or spelling errors) and see if anyone notices. If anyone does notice, then she can see what the consequences are and if she can survive them (assuming there are any actual consequences). Like any good experiment, it is important to obtain Amy's predictions and match them with the observed data so her hypothesis can be modified.

Remember, faulty assumptions can be modified through the use of Socratic questioning and guided discovery to help clients draw more accurate and realistic conclusions for themselves. For Amy, reframing her conditional assumptions may involve creating a realistic plan of what she can get accomplished, putting forth effort into the things she can get done, and accepting feedback as helpful.

Considering Bipolar Disorder

For clients with a diagnosis of bipolar disorder, doubt labels are often associated with the meaning they give to their diagnosis or the medication they are prescribed. For example, they may believe they are impaired, not good enough, undesirable, or incompetent because of their diagnosis. Similarly, they may consider themselves flawed, weak, or defective if they have to take medication. Therapy helps clients with bipolar disorder define themselves beyond the confines of their diagnosis (e.g., through their interests, skills, aptitudes, values, personality), which helps them defeat their self-doubt. They can also make peace with taking medication when they recognize that medication compliance is a sign of strength and wisdom, rather than a reflection of weakness and disability.

SUSTAINING AND GROWING CONFIDENCE THROUGH ACTION

Battling depression is a multistep process. Putting all the steps in place—**rethink, relax, respond**—is vital to success. Ideally, with all these pieces in place, clients experience recovery from depression and stay that way. The first step—**rethink** thoughts, assumptions, and beliefs—is the key to reducing distress and maintaining those gains. At the situational level, Amy learned to see that her husband's feedback was intended to be helpful and was not meant as a criticism. In addition, Amy replaced her assumption about needing to be perfect and doing everything right with a more reasonable assumption that involved having realistic expectations and recognizing that error is acceptable. Most importantly, her doubt label of "I'm not good enough" was modified into a more accurate and positive view of herself: "I am good enough just the way I am."

The second step, **relax**, is the easy part. Once clients are able to modify their thinking and develop more realistic, helpful beliefs, it is likely that positive emotions will follow. However, it doesn't hurt to help propel these emotions along. You can help clients quiet their body by providing them with practical techniques that promote relaxation, such as self-soothing techniques, slow diaphragmatic breathing, progressive relaxation, and meditation.

The final step, **respond**, not only involves putting together a behavioral strategy that clients can implement immediately, but it also involves developing strategies that clients put into place well into the future. Depression steals energy and motivation, and it robs people of their ability to take effective action. Negatively biased thoughts convince people to quit, avoid, escape, isolate, withdrawal, and shut down. Therefore, although mobilizing clients toward initial action is key, it is critical to help them maintain these gains in the long run in order to build and sustain their self-confidence. The following are some ideas to help clients reinforce their new, more positive view of themselves and grow their self-confidence:

- Have clients reconnect with others by saying "yes" to invitations and opportunities.

- Tell clients to stand up for themselves by saying "no" when it is warranted.

- Ask clients to pay attention to data that confirms their new positive self-view and to record it daily. For example, provide clients with a daily record they can use to track the messages they receive that make them feel good about themselves. Ask them to review it at the end of every day.

- Instruct clients to come up with at least three daily affirmations about themselves that are consistent with their new self-view. Have them rehearse these affirmations on a daily basis and add new ones as their confident self-concept grows.

- When information comes up that makes clients doubt themselves, ask them to consider the facts and see if a more reasonable conclusion is warranted.

- Direct clients to plan an activity that aligns with their more positive self-view.

- Invite clients to take on challenges and do things that push themselves out of their comfort zone.

- Provide clients with coping cards they can carry, either electronically or on paper, that remind them of the new, more realistic conclusions they've drawn about themselves.

6

ANXIETY

THE COGNITIVE MODEL OF ANXIETY

Anxiety is an adaptive biological response that arises when we are facing dangerous situations. It equips us to face difficult and challenging conditions and prevents harm. In other words, it is nature's internal alarm system. When we perceive danger, this internal alarm activates our sympathetic nervous system, which releases a rush of adrenaline and triggers the fight, flight, or freeze response. This physiological activation serves to rapidly increase heart rate and pump more blood through the body, slow down digestion, metabolize fats and sugars to energize the body, and release chemicals that clot the blood more rapidly.

When we believe we are in harm's way and become physiologically activated in this manner, our behavioral inclination is to survive by fighting against the threat, fleeing from it, or hiding from it. For example, if we are faced with the real threat of a fire and lack the necessary resources to put that fire out (e.g., no firefighter on-site or hose on hand), then the anxiety we experience is adaptive because it cues us to run out of the building. Anxiety only becomes a problem when our perceptions of threat and available resources are inaccurate, but our body still responds as if the danger is real. When this occurs, our behavioral inclination to fight, flee, or freeze becomes maladaptive.

According to the cognitive model of anxiety, anxiety disorders are all associated with an exaggerated perception of threat and an undervaluation of resources. Therefore, the cognitive model is a theory of appraisal, risk, and resources (Beck & Emery, 2005). When a client faces a stimulus—either external (e.g., sound, smell, event) or internal (e.g., bodily sensation, thought, feeling, image)—the brain makes two appraisals. The first is an appraisal of threat. That is, how dangerous is the situation being faced? Clients with anxiety exaggerate this danger because they overestimate the probability of the threat and its potential consequences. The second appraisal is one of resources or ability to cope with the situation. Clients with anxiety underestimate the resources they have available because they fail to see external sources at hand (e.g., friends, colleagues, professionals, first responders) and discount their ability to cope.

When these two appraisals indicate that a threat exists (whether real or imaginary) and resources are believed to be limited, then anxiety is activated. For example, consider a man with social phobia, who arrives at a physician's office after months of waiting for an appointment for a serious medical concern. As he sits down in the waiting room, he looks around and thinks that everyone is looking at him, judging him, and criticizing him (exaggerated perception of probability). To him, being judged is intolerable (exaggerated perception of consequence), and he believes he is not strong enough to bear this scrutiny (underestimation of ability to cope). In turn, he flees the office and misses his sought-after appointment, thus compromising his health.

In this example, the man's perceptions of threat are exaggerated, as most people sitting around in waiting rooms are not paying attention to anyone else; rather, they are typically absorbed in their phone, watching TV, reading, or napping. The odds that they are looking at him are low, and the likelihood that they are negatively judging him is even lower, though not impossible. However, the opinion of one random stranger is not going to affect his life in any way. It won't impact how the doctor treats him, compromise the quality of his healthcare, or affect how significant others in his life feel about him. Simply put, it won't greatly impact his life. Additionally, as unpleasant as it might be to think that someone doesn't like us, the truth is we can survive criticism.

As this example illustrates, individuals with anxiety experience unnecessary activation of their internal alarm system, which leads to inappropriate and ineffective behavioral action. According to the cognitive model of anxiety, the anxiety disorders share this common bias in cognitive processing, which is why the assessment and treatment of anxiety is similar across anxiety disorders and can be readily adapted to target specific symptom profiles (Clark & Beck, 2010). What differentiates the anxiety disorders is the specific content of the fears underlying the anxiety and the ensuing strategies that individuals use to cope. Thus, the key to understanding the anxious client is to identify the content of their fears, as well as the ineffective behavioral strategies they use to cope.

To illustrate this point, consider a man who has a fear of flying and refuses to fly in a plane. In the case of a specific phobia, the content of his fear may be that the plane will crash and he doesn't want to die. However, specific phobias can be more complicated than that. Perhaps the client's fear of flying is not about the plane crashing at all. Maybe he is afraid he will die, and his fiancée won't be okay without him, or perhaps he questions whether he has done enough good deeds to have a good afterlife.

On the other hand, imagine that this client has social phobia. In this case, his fear of flying is related to worries about social humiliation, such as the potential that there will be a foul odor on the plane and everyone will think it came from him. In turn, he believes that the subsequent embarrassment would be unbearable. Finally, imagine that the client is diagnosed with obsessive-compulsive disorder (OCD). In this situation, his fear may be that he will be seated in the emergency exit row, and he knows he will experience an urge to open the emergency door and fling himself out of the plane. He is worried about acting on this unwanted, intrusive thought, even though there is no evidence to suggest that he actually would.

Across each of these scenarios, the underlying mechanism driving the client's anxiety is the same (e.g., exaggerated perception of threat and undervaluation of resources), but his specific fear differed as a function of the disorder (Beck & Emery, 2005). Different fears give rise to different symptom presentations, so identifying the specific content of a client's fear is an important component of treatment. For example, clients with specific phobia are characterized by an irrational fear of specific situations or objects, and their coping strategy is to avoid exposure to the feared stimulus at all costs. In contrast, those with generalized anxiety disorder (GAD) experience more free-floating anxiety that spans across multiple situations, which causes them to be hypervigilant and chronically worry about everyday life events.

For clients with panic disorder, the fear is bodily harm. They misinterpret bodily sensations as significantly more dangerous than they actually are and engage in a variety of avoidance behaviors to minimize the occurrence of any physical symptoms. When these symptoms do arise—which they inevitably do—clients with panic disorder believe these symptoms are life-threatening and seek urgent medical help, typically at the nearest emergency room. Illness anxiety disorder (or what is typically known as health anxiety) is similar to panic disorder, but the fear is that a medical problem or catastrophe will happen *at some point*. Clients with illness anxiety live on guard, are hypervigilant to any sign of a medical problem, and excessively seek reassurance from medical providers. Instead of heading to the nearest emergency room, they are at the specialist's office.

In social phobia, clients exhibit a fear of being judged and negatively evaluated by others in the context of social or performance situations, so their coping strategy is to avoid these situations altogether. In OCD, the fear is associated with intrusive thoughts and urges (e.g., obsessions). Clients with OCD exaggerate the power and importance of their obsessions, which causes them to try and suppress these thoughts or engage in a variety of compulsive behaviors as a means of neutralizing their anxiety. Finally, post-traumatic stress disorder (PTSD) can be conceptualized as an anxiety problem wherein the content of the fear is reexperiencing the horror of a trauma. Clients with PTSD attempt to suppress trauma memories by avoiding any reminders (e.g., people, places, events, feelings) associated with the trauma.

As the previous examples illustrate, not only do the anxiety disorders share a common cognitive bias that results in overestimation of threat and underestimation of resources, they also share a similar coping strategy: avoidance. In particular, clients with anxiety will either directly avoid the situations that cause them anxiety or engage in a variety of safety behaviors that neutralize any feelings of anxiety. For example, clients with illness anxiety may excessively seek reassurance from medical providers, and those with panic disorder may ensure that a hospital is nearby when venturing out in public. Similarly, clients with social phobia may go to extreme measures to prevent the world from seeing them blush, such as wearing a turtleneck, applying excessive makeup, and wearing their hair so it covers their face.

Avoidance is a dysfunctional coping strategy because it is a consequence of inaccurate perceptions. What clients believe will keep them safe actually prevents their recovery. Avoidance does just that. Avoidance prevents new learning from taking place and reinforces their imaginary perceptions. It keeps clients from finding out the truth and prevents them from developing a new, more accurate perspective. Although clients think they are securing safety or avoiding danger, they are actually contributing to the persistence of anxiety because avoidance prevents them from discrediting their inaccurate perception of threat (Clark & Beck, 2010; Salkovskis, 1996).

It is difficult for clients to give up avoidance behaviors because they are under the misguided assumption that anxiety is dangerous and that the goal should be to extinguish it. Adjusting expectations is important. The truth is that anxiety is adaptive, as it signals the presence of a dangerous threat. If we were to disconnect nature's alarm system, then we would fail to respond appropriately to real threats and be doomed to death. *The problem is not the anxiety itself; rather, it is clients' fears surrounding the anxiety.* Therefore, the goal of treatment is to help clients learn that anxiety is not dangerous, so they can stop engaging in avoidance, face their fears, more accurately appraise threat and resources, and turn off the false alarms while keeping nature's alarm system intact.

In this chapter, we explore the two components of CBT for anxiety disorders: cognitive restructuring and exposure therapy. Cognitive restructuring represents the first phase of treatment, in which clients learn to identify and modify the irrational thinking patterns that are contributing to their anxiety. Once clients have developed the sufficient cognitive skills to manage their anxiety, they can move on to the second phase of treatment, which involves the use of exposure-based techniques to confront the very things they fear. In conjunction, these two techniques work to treat anxiety by addressing clients' tendency to overestimate threat and underestimate their ability to cope.

COGNITIVE RESTRUCTURING

Cognitive restructuring has been well established in the treatment of various anxiety disorders, including panic disorder, social phobia, GAD, OCD, and PTSD (Clark & Beck, 2010). Similar to cognitive restructuring for depression, treatment for anxiety aims to identify and modify inaccurate or unhelpful thoughts that are contributing to clients' distress. For this reason, the available cognitive restructuring strategies discussed in Chapter 5 also apply to the treatment of anxiety. For clients with anxiety, though, the specific focus of cognitive restructuring involves addressing clients' tendency to overestimate the likelihood ("the probability error") and severity of negative outcomes ("the catastrophic error"), as well as their tendency to underestimate their ability to cope or use internal and external resources ("the resource error"). The following sections discuss each of these three errors in further detail.

The Probability Error

Clients with anxiety tend to misjudge the probability that a negative outcome will occur. Regardless of whether an event is possible, probable, or given, the client with anxiety misperceives that the worst-case scenario will happen. For example, a client with OCD who experiences harm obsessions regarding her husband may believe that simply having intrusive thoughts increases the probability that she will follow through with them. Or, a client with panic disorder may falsely believe that every time he has chest discomfort a heart attack will result. Similarly, a client with a phobia of cats may believe that any exposure to cats will result in an unprovoked cat attack where she is mauled.

Counteracting the probability error is accomplished by helping clients examine the evidence for and against their distorted belief. Returning to the example of the client with OCD who experiences harm obsessions, she is giving the thought as much weight as actually acting on the thought itself. Indeed, clients typically give thoughts more value than they deserve. They allow intrusive thoughts to hold more meaning than they should and allow such thoughts to define their character (e.g., "I am a bad person for having this thought"). To address the probability error, you can try running a behavioral experiment to test the validity of their hypothesis. For example, you could ask the client with OCD to buy a lottery ticket and think to herself, "I am going to win the lottery" to see if thinking this makes it more likely to happen. Helping clients understand that thoughts are not as powerful or meaningful as they think serves to counteract the probability error and allows them to draw new, realistic conclusions about their intrusive thoughts.

For the client with panic disorder, you can counter the probability error by asking guided questions that help him examine the probability of having a heart attack as a result of experiencing a racing heart and sweating. It's important to note that simply asking, "What is the evidence for and against your hypothesis?" is not usually effective, as clients typically only see evidence to support their biased view. Rather, a skilled therapist uses Socratic questioning to guide clients to a new, accurate conclusion, such as the following: "How many times have you had these symptoms of panic? How many times have you had a heart attack? How many times have you died? Have you had these symptoms checked out? Did they run any tests? What were the results: normal, abnormal, low risk, high risk? Did they give you any medication? What kind, an anxiolytic? Did it work? It did? An anti-anxiety pill effectively made your symptoms go away? Could it have prevented a heart attack? No? What does that tell you about the likelihood of having a heart attack?" In this case, examining the evidence helps the client consider that having a heart attack as a result of experiencing panic symptoms is extremely unlikely. The new conclusion is that the probability of having a heart attack as a result of a racing heart and sweating is extremely unlikely.

The challenge in addressing the probability error is when clients' avoidance of the feared symptom, object, or experience prevents them from testing their probability hypothesis. For example, consider the case of the cat phobic, who takes extreme measures to avoid cats. She asks her husband to scan the yard before she enters the house and avoids all potential venues where cats might be found, including her backyard, outdoor showers, open air restaurants, pet stores, and the home of any friends or family who have cats. This prevents her from testing out her fear hypothesis that a cat will attack her, which leaves the probability error unchallenged. When clients avoid, data disconfirming their fear hypothesis is unavailable and their probability error cannot be modified.

The Catastrophic Error

Not only do clients with anxiety overestimate the probability of negative outcomes occurring, they also overestimate how bad those outcomes will be. Typically, they make catastrophic assumptions and believe that the worst-case scenario will happen. For example, a client with GAD may overestimate the probability of missing a flight and believe that missing this flight would be the end of the world. In fact, however, that client may still have an hour to make the flight, and another flight may be readily available an hour later (as well as five more later in the day). There is a possibility that missing the flight may have real consequences, but your role as the therapist is to help the client see that those consequences, although unpleasant, may not be as catastrophic as imagined.

To help clients examine their catastrophic thinking, the following are some useful questions you can use to guide the conversation:

- "Are these thoughts necessarily true?"
- "Are these thoughts consistent with the evidence?"

- "What is the worst, best, and most likely outcome?"
- "Could you survive the worst outcome, and would it actually be a problem?"
- "Are there other ways to think about this situation?"
- "Are these thoughts helpful?"
- "What might you say to a friend or another person in this situation?"
- "What resources do you have within and outside of yourself that are there to help you face this situation?"

To illustrate how this conversation might look, imagine a woman with social phobia, who believes that it would be the end of the world if someone doesn't like her or thinks poorly about her. Your first line of questioning would help the client examine the validity of her anxious thoughts. For example, you might ask, "If someone doesn't like you or thinks poorly of you, how would that person treat you? What evidence do you have that this person is treating you like that? What evidence do you have that this person is not treating you like that? How might an objective observer describe how this person treats you?" Then, you can help the client consider what she would do *even if* this feared outcome turned out to be true. For example, you might ask, "How would it actually impact your life if this one person doesn't like you? Does it mean that all 7,655,957,369 people on earth do not like you?" By helping this client see that the opinion of one single individual is inconsequential in the grand scheme of things, she learns that she *can* cope if someone doesn't like her or judges her negatively. Instead of fearing this outcome, she can learn to accept it as a possibility and recognize that it doesn't necessarily have to be a problem.

A part of coping with anxiety is recognizing that there is rarely complete certainty in life and that anomalies or flukes can happen. Clients cannot always be totally reassured that something bad won't happen. When the probability of something bad happening is high, then addressing how to cope with those consequences is warranted. However, it is not helpful to address catastrophic thinking when the probability of the threat is nonexistent or minuscule. Problem solving for every remote possibility of threat means that clients cannot be present, experience joy, achieve goals, or be connected to others. Preparing to cope with a bird attack at a playground, an outbreak of the bubonic plague, or a tsunami in a landlocked state makes no sense.

The Resource Error

Clients with anxiety underestimate the available resources they have within and outside of themselves to cope with threats as they arise. Therapy involves helping clients see what resources they already have at their disposal, as well as building additional internal and external resources. For example, a client with social anxiety may need to develop skills in communication or assertiveness, whereas a client with a driving phobia may need driving education and practice with an instructor before facing the actual road. When it comes to internal resources, many clients already have the necessary skills at hand or simply need additional training to develop them further. Some examples of these internal resources include intellect, street smarts, aptitude, spirituality, coping skills, talents, knowledge, personality, sense of humor, physical strength, resiliency, and—most importantly—self-confidence.

Self-confidence is perhaps the most important internal resource to work on within the context of therapy because anxious clients believe they are helpless to do anything about their anxiety, which only exemplifies their self-doubt. The truth is no one is helpless. We all have abilities, skills, knowledge, and strengths that equip us to face life. (And even if clients do lack specific life or therapeutic skills, therapy can help them gain those skills!) The key is helping clients see that. By helping clients develop self-confidence, you bolster their ability to view themselves as capable and desired, instead of questioning their competency or social desirability (Sokol & Fox, 2009). Clients who are confident in their capabilities understand that they don't have to be "perfect" and can make mistakes, and they recognize that asking for help or obtaining more training does not negate their competency. Similarly, clients who are confident in their social desirability no longer fear rejection (e.g., someone not liking them or being upset with them) because they know that those actions do not define their value. Self-confidence is the key to eliminating unfounded anxiety. Therefore, clearly articulating and recording the client's strengths and resources, both within and outside of themselves, is an important part of treatment for anxiety. Without self-doubt, anxiety cannot exist.

In addition to internal resources, addressing the resource error involves helping clients recognize the available external resources that they already have access to. It can also involve building additional sources of support for clients who may be more socially isolated. External resources can include a variety of individuals in the community at large, including friends, family, neighbors, good Samaritans, police, firefighters, electricians, plumbers, mental health professionals, medical doctors, lawyers, accountants, construction workers, and first responders. For example, a lecturer who is afraid of being unable to answer questions can learn to recognize that other audience members or presenters may know the answer. Similarly, a client going into a business negotiation has a team of lawyers, accountants, and sales executives who have the expertise to address any issues that may come up.

When clients are able to recognize the internal and external resources they have at their disposal, this minimizes their perceived sense of risk and arms them with the necessary tools to move forward to the next face of treatment: exposure therapy.

EXPOSURE-BASED STRATEGIES

In order to prepare your client for exposure-based strategies, first explain the cognitive model of anxiety in the context of their specific fears. What exactly are they afraid of? You want to elicit the fears regarding the likelihood that this feared outcome will occur (probability), the imagined consequences of this feared outcome (severity), and the perceived resources they have to deal with this outcome. Then, use the principles of cognitive restructuring to help clients see their exaggerated perceptions of threat and underevaluation of internal and external resources.

Once clients understand the cognitive model of anxiety and are equipped with knowledge through cognitive restructuring and behavioral experiments, they are ready to begin the process of exposure therapy. Exposure is an opportunity for clients to test their fear hypothesis. It is a powerful tool in modifying inaccurate and distorted thinking, as it provides concrete factual data to contradict their fear hypothesis.

You can use a number of exposure-based modalities with clients, including in vivo, imaginal, interoceptive, and virtual reality exposure. **In vivo exposure** involves having clients directly confront their fear in real life. For example, asking clients to touch an object that elicits fear (e.g., a snake), having them intentionally spill coffee down their shirt and walk around in public, or asking them to eat alone in a restaurant are all examples of in vivo exposure.

According to Clark and Beck (2010), most therapists recommend the use of in vivo exposure whenever possible, but it is sometimes simply not feasible to do so. For example, in certain situations in vivo exposure would be dangerous, impractical, or unethical. In these cases, **imaginal exposure** can be effective, in which clients are asked to face their fears in their imagination. For example, you can have clients imagine driving their car over a large bridge, dropping their grocery bag and its contents on the floor, or having a panic attack in front of their child. Imaginal exposure is particularly appropriate when the client's fear involves a thought, image, or idea. It can also help acclimate clients during the initial stages of exposure therapy, particularly for those clients who refuse to start with real-life exposures.

Interoceptive exposure is another type of exposure therapy used for the treatment of panic disorder, which involves intentionally inducing feared bodily sensations, such as dizziness, sweating, chest palpitations, and breathlessness. For example, you might ask clients to hyperventilate on purpose, breathe through a narrow straw with a pinched nose, spin in a chair, run in place, or stare at a herringbone pattern. The key to interoceptive exposure is to produce the feared bodily symptom. Finally, **virtual reality exposure** involves the use of technology to create a virtual simulation of the feared stimulus. Virtual reality equipment can be used to provide a realistic replication of a variety of feared situations, including being on a high ledge, in an airplane, or in front of an audience.

Key Components of Exposure Interventions

Before beginning any type of exposure therapy, it's important to provide clients with a rationale for doing so. You want clients to understand that facing their fears is a necessary component of recovery. If they continue engaging in avoidance behaviors, they will always be held captive to their fears, which will continue to compromise their opportunities, goals, and interests. Avoidance doesn't allow clients to test their fear hypothesis and prevents new learning from taking place. Help them see that exposure is the opposite of avoidance and the mechanism through which the fear hypothesis can be put to rest.

In exposure therapy, the key is to have clients draw new, more accurate conclusions about their feared predictions and consequences. For this learning to happen, you must first specify the feared outcome, have clients do the exposure, and then discuss the results. The actual "doing" of the exposure is where this success lies. A successful exposure is defined by whether clients face their feared outcome—and not by how they feel before, during, or after the exposure. In fact, if clients experience high anxiety during an exposure, this can provide them with even more convincing information against their fear hypothesis. In particular, if clients believe that they cannot function while anxious, then their hypothesis is negated when they see that they *were* able to function and get through the exposure despite their high anxiety. For example, a client who is able to ride in an elevator in spite of his anxiety learns that he will not suffocate and die. The fact that he rode in the elevator is the success in itself.

Like any good experiment, reliability comes from replication. Exposures need to be frequently replicated so clients can objectively draw more accurate conclusions about their predictions. A one-time success might seem like a fluke, but success across repeated exposures is sound evidence. In addition, the duration of the exposure itself must be long enough for emotional learning to take place. Exposures that are too brief in nature do not allow this learning to take place, as no processing of information occurs. If clients end the exposure prematurely, then they don't learn that they can tolerate their anxiety and that they will eventually habituate to their feared outcome. Therefore, always encourage clients to stay in the exposure longer than they believe they can so their fear hypothesis is fully tested. For in vivo exposure, a duration of 20 minutes is often recommended, while other forms of exposure may not require such a long duration. For example, with interoceptive exposures, clients are typically asked to hyperventilate for one minute and to repeat this breathing exercise multiple times.

Although making sure that exposures are of sufficient duration is an essential part of treatment, the question of intensity is not as clear-cut. In general, subjective levels of distress that fall in the range of 30 to 40 percent are considered a good place to start, but new findings suggest that learning can take place regardless of the intensity. On the one hand, having a heightened state of anxiety is preferable because it allows clients to disconfirm their fear hypothesis and experience new learning. It allows clients to see that they can confront their fears and that they can tolerate the uncomfortable feelings associated with anxiety.

On the other hand, though, if anxiety becomes too intense, then clients may require some anxiety management (e.g., deep breathing, relaxation techniques) to encourage prolonged and repeated exposure (Clark & Beck, 2010). Anxiety management techniques present a slippery slope because clients may begin to use these techniques as an avoidance strategy, which prevents new learning from taking place. This is especially true in panic disorder, where clients may use relaxation or breathing strategies as a means of avoiding feared bodily symptoms. When this occurs, clients are unable to learn that their bodily symptoms are not as dangerous as they believe, which prevents them from seeing that their fear is unfounded.

Asking clients to confront the very things they fear can be a difficult sell, so it's important to work collaboratively with clients to decide how slowly or expediently they want to approach exposures. For many clients, it can be helpful to develop a fear hierarchy on which they rank their fears from those that are least distressing to those that are the most anxiety-provoking. You can then ask clients to start with exposures that cause them the least distress and have them move up the hierarchy as they gain confidence. Although using a hierarchy typically means a slower course of therapy, it can increase client cooperation and make them less likely to drop out of treatment prematurely.

Once you begin exposure therapy, it's important for clients to continue engaging in exposures until their level of functioning increases and their fear hypothesis is negated. Have clients repeat the exposures every day, and even multiple times a day, until the desired learning is accomplished. As clients gradually confront their fears and disconfirm their fear hypothesis, exposures will become effortless and no longer needed.

Potential Pitfalls

When clients engage in safety behaviors, this can compromise exposures because it inhibits learning. For example, a client with panic disorder who fears fainting may hold onto a desk whenever she feels dizzy, which prevents her from testing whether she will actually faint. Similarly, a client with PTSD may dissociate whenever he must recount the trauma narrative, which prevents him from learning that he can cope with the distress associated with the trauma memory. Or, a client who fears driving over bridges may insist on always driving in the instructor's car (where the instructor has access to his steering wheel and brake), which prevents him from learning that he can safely drive over the bridge. Pay attention to whether your clients are engaging in any of these safety behaviors, as these behaviors need to be eliminated if you want clients to gain anything from the exposures.

In addition to safety behaviors, another potential pitfall of exposure therapy is having clients confront a situation that is too high on their fear hierarchy, which will result in dysregulation and prevent any new learning from taking place. If this happens, you can review the cognitive conclusions you have previously collected regarding their perceptions of danger and resources, reduce the duration of the exposure, back down to a situation lower on the fear hierarchy, or use calming techniques to help them engage in the experience.

Finally, one of the most challenging obstacles in exposure therapy is the client's refusal to practice the exposure. To help clients become more comfortable with exposures, it's preferable to have them initially practice the exposure in session so they feel more prepared doing it on their own outside of session. Although in-session practice is easier if the exposure work is imaginal, interoceptive, or virtual reality-based in nature, some in vivo exposures can still be conducted in session. In addition, it can be useful to enlist the help of family members, friends, or significant others who can assist clients in facing the exposure trials. Finally, you can help clients overcome their reluctance by reminding them of the reasons they decided to engage in exposure work, as well as how continuing to engage in avoidance will impede recovery.

SUMMARY: EIGHT STEPS TO EXPOSURE

1. Identify what clients are avoiding and what they fear.
2. Discuss the rationale for exposure therapy and how avoidance prevents recovery.
3. Remind clients that a successful exposure is facing the fear itself—not how they feel before, during, or after an exposure.
4. Decide which type of exposure is most appropriate. It is possible that multiple types of exposure can be used.
5. Make clear predictions before asking your client to begin exposures.
6. Have your client start doing exposures. If necessary, develop a hierarchy and have clients work from the bottom up.
7. Discuss the outcome of each exposure so that clear conclusions and learning can take place.
8. Practice, practice, practice!

INTERVENTIONS FOR SPECIFIC ANXIETY DISORDERS

As discussed, the anxiety disorders share a common thread in that they all involve an exaggerated perception of threat and an undervaluation of resources (Beck & Emery, 1985). Therefore, the overall goal of treatment is the same in that it involves teaching clients how to more realistically appraise risk and resources. However, the critical treatment components used to achieve this goal are varied based on the specific content of the client's fear. The sections that follow discuss specific interventions for a variety of common anxiety disorders, including GAD, social anxiety, panic disorder, specific phobia, illness anxiety disorder, OCD, and PTSD. In particular, we discuss the symptoms of each disorder, and also present specific cognitive and behavioral interventions that can be used with each disorder.

Generalized Anxiety Disorder

Generalized anxiety disorder (GAD) involves excessive and ongoing anxiety across a variety of life domains (e.g., health, family, work, finances). The main feature of GAD involves a persistent worry that something "bad" will happen and a desire to control that event. Although occasional worry is a normal part of life, individuals with GAD experience worry that is disproportionate in nature, as they tend to anticipate disaster despite a lack of evidence. In addition, the worry that characterizes GAD is chronic and pervasive. The worry does not involve a single concern about a potential problem that might occur; rather, it involves obsessive and ruminative thoughts that take control (APA, 2013).

Cognitive Interventions

A primary component of cognitive restructuring in GAD involves helping clients see that worry is maladaptive and serves no purpose. Clients with GAD often believe that their worries are helpful in some way, so it is important to point out its various disadvantages. For example, worry causes them stress, interferes with concentration and learning, impedes their ability to experience pleasure, and prevents them from fully participating in the present. Even in the face of these disadvantages, some clients with GAD will still continue to hold positive beliefs about worry because they mistakenly believe that worrying is a way to gain certainty. The key is to help clients learn to tolerate uncertainty and accept their powerlessness. Bad things do happen, but worrying is not a way to prevent those things from happening or to help them cope. Helping clients accept this powerlessness and uncertainty is a crucial step.

In addition, clients need to understand that problem solving is not the same as worrying. Problem solving leads to solutions, whereas worrying just involves going over the problem repeatedly without taking action. Therefore, instead of worrying, the goal is to teach clients to appraise danger more accurately and to problem solve and take appropriate action only if a threat is a real possibility. Clients with GAD actually tend to be good problem solvers, and when faced with real emergencies, they tend to shine. To help clients see that they do possess these problem-solving abilities, you can ask them to recall past experiences where they have successfully faced and overcome challenges. It can also be valuable to use imagery and ask clients to imagine various possible outcomes regarding a feared scenario, as well as to consider all the ways they could cope.

The following coping card can be used to help clients with GAD learn to tolerate uncertainty, become better problem solvers, and break out of the cycle of worry. On the page that follows is a handout that clients can use to evaluate the utility of their worries.

Coping Card

WORRY FREE

- Worry is a disorder of thinking in itself. It steals energy, fatigues me, distracts me, and otherwise tortures me. It interferes with my ability to be present and prevents joy. My goal is NOT TO WORRY.

- Instead of worrying, I can tell myself: "There is nothing I can do at this moment to tackle this issue. When I am ready, or it is necessary, I will figure it out and tackle it then. For now, table it."

- I am a good problem solver, so when I am ready, or it is necessary to face the problem, I have the skills to face it.

- I don't need to figure out everything ahead of time. It's okay to not have it all figured out.

Client Worksheet

EVALUATE YOUR WORRIES

• • • • •

When you find yourself worrying, **STOP** and go over the following steps:

1. Ask yourself: What are my concerns? Is the concern likely to happen, a remote possibility, or an impossibility?

   _____

   _____

2. Ask yourself: If it did happen, what would be the worst thing that could happen? The best? The most likely?

   _____

   _____

3. If what you are concerned about could happen or is likely to happen (*and* it would be a problem if it did happen), then proceed to question 4. However, if what you are concerned about is not possible or likely to happen (and even if it did happen, it would *not* present a problem), then it doesn't make sense to spend your energy thinking about it.

   _____

   _____

4. If it is likely to happen and a problem, is there something you can do about it?

   _____

   _____

5. If so, what are your options? Evaluate the pros and cons of each option, and choose a course of action. If your options cannot take place until later, then accept the wait. If you have no personal options to take, accept your powerlessness and let the universe rule!

   _____

   _____

Copyright © 2019 Leslie Sokol & Marci G. Fox, *The Comprehensive Clinician's Guide to Cognitive Behavioral Therapy*. All Rights Reserved

Behavioral Interventions

Given that clients with GAD are in a state of constant tension, it is also helpful to incorporate interventions that decrease their level of automatic arousal. Behavioral interventions that promote relaxation—such as deep breathing, progressive muscle relaxation, mindfulness, yoga, and exercise—can all serve to reduce tension and make clients less reactive. These interventions can be especially helpful before taking more direct interventions (e.g., cognitive restructuring or behavioral exposure) when unusually intense somatic anxiety exists (Clark & Beck, 2010). Not only do these interventions calm the body, but they also have the secondary effect of reducing worry. In particular, interventions such as yoga and mindfulness can help clients turn off their ruminative mind and tune into their body instead. However, if clients fear the anxiety itself, then cognitive restructuring must first work to address the fear surrounding the anxiety before you give clients the tools to reduce their subjective experience of it. Otherwise, relaxation techniques can become a form of avoidance in themselves.

Another helpful behavioral tool involves having clients schedule an intentional "worry time" each day. Clients with GAD are consumed by worry throughout the day, repeatedly going over their problems and failing to reach any resolution. By scheduling a predetermined worry time, clients learn how to postpone their worries and continue on with their day. In order to implement this intervention, first ask clients to identify a 20-minute period during the day where they can set aside time to worry. Then, whenever they find themselves worrying throughout the day, ask them to jot down those concerns and table them until the next worry time. Often, clients report that they are unable to worry at the allocated worry time, as they find that the anticipated problem did not occur or wasn't such a big deal, thus negating the need to worry so much. In turn, clients learn that when they worry, they make problems bigger than they are, which leads to anxiety and gets in the way of rational thinking.

GAD: TYPICAL HOMEWORK SUGGESTIONS

Ask clients to:

1. Practice relaxation techniques.
2. Schedule a set worry time and delay any worries until that time.
3. Read their coping cards.
4. Problem solve instead of worry.
5. Practice tolerating uncertainty.
6. Imagine alternative outcomes to their fears.
7. Remind themselves of all the times they handled difficult situations.
8. Focus on their strengths and record them to grow a positive self-image.

Social Anxiety Disorder

Social anxiety is characterized by a fear of judgment in social or performance-related situations. Individuals with social anxiety fear the possibility of social humiliation or rejection, and they are terrified of embarrassment. They are hyperattentive to internal processes (e.g., anxious feelings, distorted automatic thoughts, physiological arousal), and they ruminate about how their perceived social deficiencies will cause them to "mess up" in some way. As a result, individuals with social anxiety tend to avoid social situations, which inhibits their ability to socialize, date, travel, work, go to school, and otherwise function in life (APA, 2013).

Cognitive Interventions

Clients with social anxiety overestimate the probability that people are paying attention to them and experience acute distress if they perceive that they are being judged or rejected in some way. Because they are overly focused on internal cues—and use these cues as a gauge for their perceived social incompetency—this interferes with their ability to make objective assessments of actual social cues. Therefore, a primary component of treatment involves helping clients examine the real data instead of relying on these internal cues. Work with them to evaluate their hypothetical fears by having them observe cues from the external world and teaching them to question their distorted probability appraisals.

For example, consider a prepubescent older adolescent who fears that everyone notices his lack of development. He claims that, "Everyone thinks I look like a little kid. No one is going to take me seriously. No one is going to want to hang around a kid. I am going to feel humiliated." These fears lead him to refuse to attend school, and without disconfirming evidence, his fears continue to grow. Cognitive restructuring can help him evaluate his automatic thoughts so a more appropriate course of action can occur. While it's true that his growth is delayed, it does not mean that the world is negatively judging him. At his summer job, no one treated him any differently than anyone else. Customers didn't ask to be helped by an older employee, and no one made fun of his stature or lack of facial hair. His friends still treat him like they always have, still sharing their secrets, hanging out, and even driving with him in his car with his newly obtained license. The reality is that everyone sees him as "one of them" and not some prepubescent younger kid. Helping the client realize this enables him to return to school, where his fears are further disconfirmed.

As another example, take the woman who sweats profusely. She imagines that others take notice of her excessive sweating and are bothered by it, and she assumes that they make a variety of horrible conclusions about her as a result. Her fear of judgment leads her to avoid people and decline invitations, which further disconnects her from the world and reinforces her fears. In this situation, the goal of therapy is not to reduce her sweating, although reducing her fear of sweating would likely reduce its intensity. Rather, it is to help her see that her thoughts are characterized by exaggerated perceptions of rejection. The truth is that she does sweat more than the average person, but most of the world does not judge her as harshly as she judges herself. In fact, much of the world is oblivious to it. While there is a possibility that someone might find her sweating unpleasant or negative in some way, this still doesn't necessitate the feared consequence she imagines. For example, her sweating has not prevented her from being happily married, having friends and children that adore her, or holding down a successful job. It is the imagined consequences of sweating, rather than reality, that cripples her. Even if someone out there found her sweating disgusting, so what? Would it affect any of the things that matter to her? Cognitive restructuring can help her to realize that she is not her sweat; rather, she is a complex package of assets, talents, interests, and experiences that make her a desirable and capable person.

Finally, individuals with social anxiety tend to ruminate on their perceived mistakes when reflecting on any kind of interaction involving other people. For example, consider a client who believes that he is socially awkward and did poorly on a recent job interview. He reportedly remembers not making eye contact, profusely sweating, taking too long to answer the questions, and not sounding smart. Instead of allowing his imagination to reign, cognitive restructuring can help him more objectively evaluate his perceptions and reframe any faulty conclusions. One way to accomplish this is to have the client relive the experience through imagery or recorded data. For example, you can ask the client to report what the prospective employer actually asked him and have him recount his answers to you. In doing so, it becomes evident that his responses during the interview were right on target.

To help clients realize that the social anxiety they are experiencing is disproportionate to the situation at hand, use the following coping card to remind them that their anxiety is driven by overestimations of threat and underestimations of resources.

Coping Card

AVOIDING FEAR OF SOCIAL JUDGMENT

- Any one individual's negative opinion of me doesn't have to define me.

- Any one individual's negative opinion of me doesn't need to impact me at all.

- The world is not paying attention to me; everyone is too preoccupied.

- Being perfect isn't a requirement of being successful or loved. I can embrace my shortcomings.

- I can put myself out there. I am not going to let my fear of social judgment stop me from going after what I want and doing the things I enjoy.

- I can get out of my head and look at the world around me. It's probably not the monster I think it is.

Behavioral Interventions

When treating social anxiety within a CBT framework, build on the cognitive reframe by collecting behavioral data within the context of exposures. Exposures provide clients with an opportunity to test their feared predictions and disconfirm their faulty perceptions. For example, returning to the example of the prepubescent student, the only way that he can learn that he is not going to be rejected or isolated is to return to school. Similarly, the woman who sweats profusely can only overcome her fear by facing the world as her sweaty self. Instead of hiding her sweat with bulky clothing or rushing to the bathroom to mop her face, she must learn to face the world, sweat and all, so she can become confident in who she is and realize that she is not defined by her sweat.

However, sometimes clients with social anxiety have been engaging in avoidance for so long that their social skills have, in fact, become compromised. Indeed, it is understandable that clients may struggle with small talk if they haven't had any practice. In these situations, it can be helpful to provide clients with social skills training. For example, you can help clients practice making small talk by identifying topics of interest (e.g., favorite television shows, movies, books, sports, music) and then role-play having a conversation about these topics. The goal is for clients to practice sharing their opinions, asking questions of others, and tolerating silence during a conversation. Conversation is a two-way street, so they are not solely responsible for it to flow.

For clients who passively keep their opinions and needs to themselves, assertiveness skills training might also be warranted. To do so, you can teach clients the basic skills involved in being assertive (e.g., stating the facts, letting others know how they feel, acknowledging the other person's point of view, and expressing what they desire) and then role-play using those skills in session. Once clients have gained practice with you in session, they can begin using assertiveness skills with people they perceive as "safe" (e.g., family, close friends) and gradually branch out from there. Although being assertive will likely feel uncomfortable at first, it will come more naturally over time.

SOCIAL ANXIETY: TYPICAL HOMEWORK SUGGESTIONS

Ask clients to:

1. Review coping cards to remind them that their anxiety is caused by overestimations of threat and underestimations of resources.

2. Collect actual data in social or performance situations by focusing on external cues (instead of internal cues).

3. Face their fear of rejection so they can prove to themselves that they can survive the experience. This may involve purposely putting themselves in a situation where rejection is guaranteed.

4. Focus on their strengths and record them to grow a positive self-image.

5. Face situations they have been avoiding.

6. Put themselves in situations that exceed their worst fears.

The following page contains a handout you can give to clients to remind them of the general principles that should guide exposure-based strategies when they are working to face their fears.

Client Handout

FACE YOUR FEARS

• • • • • •

- Face the situations you are afraid of and see if your feared predictions come true.

- Push yourself to face the most uncomfortable of challenges so you can put your fear to rest.

- Be careful not to let subtle avoidance keep you from being free. Let the world see you as you are. Walk around when you are blushing or sweaty, have coffee stains on your shirt, or lipstick on your teeth—and know those shortcomings do not define you.

- Acquire social skills if you lack them. It is possible that your avoidance has caused your communication or assertiveness skills to become rusty. Make it easy to start. For example, practice conversing with others by making small talk with your family, asking where to find something in a store, or initiating a conversation with a neighbor. Practice being assertive with something minor, like modifying a menu item, declining an invitation, or saying no to an unreasonable request. Work your way to speaking up to let others know how you feel and what you prefer.

- It's okay to practice, especially if you are new at it. Practice leads to comfort and skill. For example, make a daily plan to strike up a conversation, assert yourself, or put yourself in an uncomfortable situation.

- Use your social support. No one says you always have to do it alone.

Panic Disorder

Clients with panic disorder experience recurrent and unexpected panic attacks, and they are overly preoccupied with the fear of having future panic attacks. As a result of this anticipatory anxiety, these clients become hypersensitive to physical sensations and often seek immediate medical assistance whenever these symptoms arise. They may engage in a variety of avoidance behaviors in an attempt to minimize the likelihood of a panic attack, such as restricting physical activity or limiting activities that they believe may induce panic. Often, this avoidance can lead to agoraphobia, in which clients avoid leaving home because of the fear that they will become trapped and unable to escape if they develop panic symptoms (APA, 2013).

Cognitive Interventions

Clients with panic disorder make catastrophic misinterpretations about the bodily sensations they experience during a panic attack (e.g., they fear that they are having a heart attack or "going crazy"), which leads them to fear future panic attacks. Therefore, targeting this catastrophic misinterpretation is a critical intervention point (Clark & Beck, 2010). The first step is to identify each individual's panic cycle to determine the dysfunctional beliefs, triggers, appraisals, and catastrophic misinterpretations driving the panic. The following figure illustrates the cognitive model that underlies this basic panic cycle.

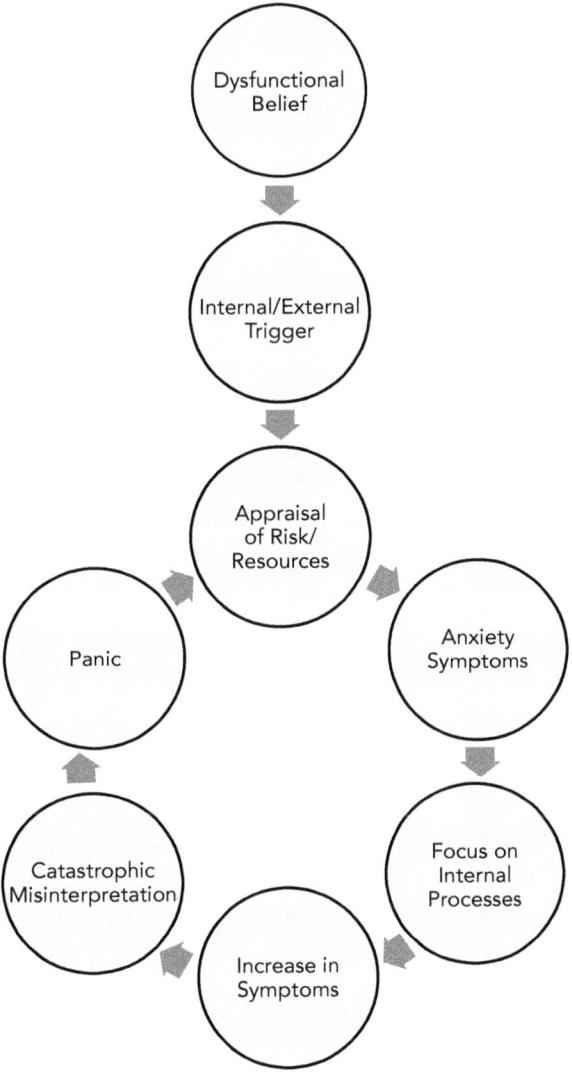

Adapted from Clark (1986)

For example, consider a 60-year-old woman who holds the doubt label, "I am damaged" (*dysfunctional belief*). On her way to work, she realizes she has forgotten something at home (*trigger*) and thinks to herself, "This is a sign of trouble with my memory. I cannot handle this" (*appraisal of risk/resources*). In turn, she begins to feel squirmy and experiences a tingling sensation in her body (*anxiety symptoms*). She continues to focus on these bodily sensations and hyperventilates by trying to take deep breaths (*focus on internal processes*). As a result, she begins to feel hot, experiences tightness in her chest, an increased heart rate, and an upset stomach (*increase in symptoms*). She thinks, "I am going crazy. I am going to lose my memory forever" (*catastrophic misinterpretation*), and she immediately begins to *panic*. In turn, she thinks, "I'm never going to get better. I'll be stuck like this forever" (*appraisal of risk/resources*), and her symptoms of anxiety are perpetuated.

Each point in the panic cycle is a point of understanding and a point of intervention. The most powerful point of intervention lies in addressing the catastrophic misinterpretation. In particular, guided Socratic questioning can help clients evaluate their misinterpretation and consider an alternative conclusion: that their symptoms, although unpleasant, are not medically dangerous. In the previous example, the client fears that she is going crazy and will lose her memory. This is particularly upsetting, because her mother is dying, and she fears not only the loss of her mother but a more global loss if her memory disappears as well. Cognitive restructuring can help the client see that "going crazy" and developing a psychotic disorder at the age of 60 is very unlikely, and that memory loss and forgetfulness are normal signs of aging. In addition, you can help the client realize that her panic symptoms disappear when she is distracted or when she takes her anti-anxiety medication, which supports the hypothesis that these symptoms are a result of anxiety and not an underlying medical disease.

Although cognitive restructuring represents one treatment component of CBT for panic disorder, it is typically not enough. Many clients with panic disorder have had numerous tests and seen many doctors and regardless of all the disconfirming data, they still believe they are in medical danger. Therefore, addressing their catastrophic misinterpretations through behavioral interventions is another key component of treatment, and it is especially important when agoraphobic avoidance is prominent.

Behavioral Interventions

Interoceptive Exposure

The primary behavioral intervention for panic disorder is interoceptive exposure, which involves intentionally exposing clients to feared bodily sensations. The goal of interoceptive exposure is to elicit these feared bodily sensations, activate any unhelpful beliefs, maintain the feared bodily sensations without distraction or avoidance, and allow new learning about the bodily sensations to take place. It is most helpful to elicit the particular physical symptoms that clients fear most, though this may require moving up a hierarchy and starting with the least feared symptoms first.

These body sensations can be elicited in a variety of ways, depending on the particular symptoms that clients fear most. For example, a client who has a fear of increased heart rate may run in place or do jumping jacks for one minute, whereas a client who fears being dizzy and fainting may spin in a chair. The point is to purposely try to induce a panic attack or mirror the panic symptoms in as great a detail as possible. The "Interoceptive Exposure Exercises" handout on page 131 describes more specific exercises that you can use to induce specific symptoms of panic.

Before beginning interoceptive exposures, start by asking clients for a general rating regarding their subjective unit of distress. This rating will provide you with a baseline measure of their anxiety so that you can gauge the extent to which the exposure intensifies their feelings of anxiety. Then, review the specific anxiety symptoms that clients experience during panic attacks and identify their specific fear hypothesis. Doing so helps you determine whether the exposure is successful in eliciting their feared outcome. Finally, begin to intentionally induce their feared symptoms through interoceptive exposure. **The Interoceptive Exposure Guidelines** on page 133 provide you with the specific steps involved in this process, including how to process the exposure and help clients develop new, more accurate conclusions regarding their symptoms of panic.

Clinician Handout

INTEROCEPTIVE EXPOSURE EXERCISES

• • • • • •

Rationale

Interoceptive exposure exercises attempt to simulate feared bodily sensations to evaluate clients' danger hypotheses. Various interoceptive exercises can be tried to produce the feared symptom(s) and test the danger prediction. Inductions using more than one interoceptive exercise at a time are feasible and can help to activate fear. The more diverse the symptoms, the more generalized the learning. Therefore, exercises that produce symptoms the client doesn't typically experience can be helpful as well. The duration of the exposure is flexible, as the goal is for clients to do it long enough to experience their feared symptoms, test their fear hypothesis, and stay in the exposure longer than they believe they can handle. Allowing clients to quit the exposure only reinforces their fear, as it validates their hypothesis that if they had continued with the exposure, then a bad result would have likely happened.

Practice

Interoceptive exposures should first be done in the office followed by independent daily practice. Many clients find it helpful to vary the exposure exercise when practicing on their own in order to fully fortify themselves against their exaggerated and inappropriate fear of bodily harm.

Some Ideas

Dizziness, lightheadedness, tingling, nausea, sweating

- ☐ Hyperventilate/overbreathe (e.g., shallow breaths through the mouth and nose at a quick rate of 100–120 breaths per minute) for approximately one minute.

- ☐ Spin in a chair a few times.

- ☐ Stand up quickly from a sitting position.

- ☐ For sweating, turn a space heater on while practicing the above.

Breathlessness or smothering feelings

- ☐ Breathe through a stir straw with a round opening with the nose pinched for approximately 45 seconds.

- ☐ Hold breath for 30 seconds.

- ☐ Sit with a heavy blanket or coat covering the head.

Racing heart

- ☐ Run in place for two minutes.

- ☐ Do jumping jacks for two minutes.

- ☐ Run up and down the stairs for one minute.

Derealization/feelings of unreality

- ☐ Stare at self in the mirror for three minutes.

- ☐ Look at a florescent light and then try to read something.

- ☐ Stare at a small dot (e.g., the size of a dime) posted on the wall for three minutes.

- ☐ Stare at a herringbone pattern for three minutes.

Clinician Handout

INTEROCEPTIVE EXPOSURE GUIDELINES

• • • • •

1. Let clients know that you would like to do a diagnostic experiment with them to better understand their panic and help them cope.

2. If you have not done so already, review the specific anxiety symptoms they experience during a panic attack and identify their specific fear hypothesis.

3. Before starting the exposure, get a baseline measure of their distress by asking clients to rate their anxiety on a scale of 0 to 10.

4. Then, begin the exposure. Depending on the client's specific fears, you can start with any of the exercises on the **Interoceptive Exposure Exercises** handout. Remember, you are purposely trying to induce a panic attack. If it helps, you can practice the exercise along with them and coach them to continue. If the specific exercise you have chosen does not simulate their feared symptoms, then consider an alternative interoceptive exposure (e.g., holding their breath for 30 seconds, spinning in a chair, running in place, breathing through a small straw).

5. During the exposure, ask clients:
   - What physical symptoms are you experiencing?
   - How anxious are you on a scale of 0 to 10?
   - Are any thoughts racing through your head and, if so, what are these thoughts? What is your worst fear?

6. Once clients have finished the exposure, ask them to re-rate their anxiety on a 0 to 10 scale. Depending on the intensity of their anxiety and their ability to process the exposure, choose one of the following two options:
   - **Option 1:** Begin processing the experience (skip to step 7).
   - **Option 2:** If the client is experiencing overwhelming levels of anxiety that would interfere with the ability to meaningfully process the exposure, try one of the following anxiety management techniques first. However, remember that the goal is for clients to eventually confront their feared symptoms, so you don't want them using these techniques to control panic in the long run.
     - Use distraction for a few minutes and talk about something relevant and benign to the client, such as a TV show or movie.

- Ask clients to practice diaphragmatic breathing. Have them close their mouth and breathe in and out through their nose as slowly as possible for three breaths. A six- to 12-second breath is recommended.
- Ask clients to quietly read a paragraph backward to themselves or to describe a picture on your wall.
- Have clients name all of the states in the United States.

7. Ask clients how similar or different the exposure was compared to their actual experience of a panic attack. Have them rate the similarity on a scale of 0 to 10.

8. Ask clients about their conclusions following the exercise. For example, what catastrophic thoughts did they have during the exposure? Did any of these come true? If the anxiety-reducing techniques in option 2 were used, what does that say about the medical seriousness or dangerousness of their symptoms? Remember, you are guiding the client to a new hypothesis: The symptoms are not dangerous. If clients conclude that they can control their symptoms, then they can realize that they are not dangerous.

9. To help clients realize that they play a part in bringing on their panic attacks, point out how they play a role in exacerbating their symptoms by overly focusing attention to their feared thoughts or by overbreathing. For example, try to have clients bring on the symptoms simply by breathing rapidly in and out of their nose, and they will see it is impossible to produce the symptoms. Experiments that demonstrate the ability to manipulate the symptoms validate the hypothesis that these symptoms are not to be feared.

10. Work with clients to collaboratively develop a coping card that summarizes their conclusions. The coping card should include a statement that reflects a new (and accurate) hypothesis regarding their feared symptoms, the data substantiating that new hypothesis, appropriate action (if warranted), and a clear statement specifying that the symptoms—no matter how uncomfortable—are not dangerous and will eventually go away without any intervention. For example, "I thought I was going to _____ [have a heart attack, pass out, suffocate, etc.] but it wasn't true. These symptoms may be unpleasant, but they will not hurt me. They are driven by my scary thoughts and by overly focusing attention on my body. By breathing normally, I can make these symptoms go away. That tells me that these symptoms are not dangerous." The sample coping card on the next page illustrates the new conclusions that the previous 60-year-old woman gained from interoceptive exposures. This coping card combines the work from cognitive restructuring and exposure.

11. Once clients have completed interoceptive exposures in session, make sure they continue practicing them for homework so that new learning can continue between and across sessions. After every exposure, have clients continue writing conclusions and encourage them to read them regularly. You can also have them complete the **Panic Log** worksheet to see how their reactions to panic change over time with continued interoceptive exposure practice.

Sample Coping Card

- These symptoms are not going to make me go crazy. If I were going crazy, it would have happened well before now. Even though anxiety feels awful, it cannot hurt me, and it cannot cause me to go crazy or experience physical harm.
- I know this because of these reasons:
  - Hyperventilating brought on an anxiety attack, but changing my breathing took the panic feelings away. If anxiety was a sign of something physically dangerous, that couldn't happen.
  - Anxiety is controllable. I make it worse by focusing internally and by overbreathing. The fact that I can control my symptoms means they are not dangerous.
  - Anxiety is just stress showing itself. It is *not* something serious.
  - Anxiety is distressing, but it is not harmful.
  - I have had anxiety many times, but I have never gone crazy or lost my memory. Every time, regardless of how I respond, the symptoms do eventually disappear.
- **The conclusion:** Anxiety can't hurt me, and it will go away!

Client Worksheet

PANIC COPING CARD

• • • • • •

Create a coping card that details your new, accurately modified hypothesis, the data substantiating that new hypothesis, appropriate action (if warranted), and a clear statement specifying that the symptoms—no matter how uncomfortable—are not dangerous and will eventually go away without any intervention.

_____

_____

_____

_____

_____

_____

_____

_____

_____

Client Worksheet

PANIC LOG
• • • • • •

The panic log can help you see if your reactions to panic and high anxiety change over time. Record instances of panic and high anxiety, the situation in which it occurred, the symptoms you experienced, your interpretation of sensations, your response to the panic, and whether it escalated into a full-blown panic attack.

Date, time, and duration of panic	Situation in which panic occurred and its severity (0–10)	Description of panic symptoms	Interpretation of sensations	Your response to the panic. What did you do? Note any medications taken and dosage.

Was this a full-blown panic attack? If not, explain why. _____
_____
_____

Copyright © 2019 Leslie Sokol & Marci G. Fox, *The Comprehensive Clinician's Guide to Cognitive Behavioral Therapy*. All Rights Reserved

Short-Term Anxiety Management

During interoceptive exposures, the goal is for clients to use cognitive restructuring to talk back to their panic symptoms and maintain their feared bodily sensations without distraction or avoidance. However, as we mentioned in the "Interoceptive Exposure Guidelines," it is sometimes necessary to teach clients short-term anxiety management techniques, such as distraction, refocusing, and deep breathing, to reduce their physical symptoms. In the short run, using these techniques can encourage clients to stay in anxiety-provoking situations and minimize phobic avoidance. These techniques also keep clients from using addictive short-acting anxiolytic medication.

The use of short-term anxiety management techniques does not have to prevent new learning if you are clear in helping clients understand that the fact that these tools work is evidence that their symptoms cannot be medically serious or dangerous. In addition, it is important to gradually reduce use of these strategies over time. Eventually, the goal is for clients to face their symptoms solely with the use of their cognitive reframe or coping card. The following are two coping cards you can give clients to help them overcome the desire to continue long-term use of distraction techniques and anxiolytic medication.

Coping Card

I DON'T NEED DISTRACTION

In the short run, distraction is great to help me continue to practice exposures to my fears. However, in the long run, I have to face my feared thoughts that I am going to _____ [have a heart attack, pass out, suffocate, etc.] by simply talking back to these thoughts and continuing to practice exposures.

Coping Card

I DON'T NEED ANXIETY MEDICATION

I don't need medication to block the anxiety. Anxiety is just my body's normal alarm system. It is a human response to life. I can reduce anxiety by deep breathing, and I can keep away panic by reminding myself that there is no danger. I have to keep working on talking my way through the anxiety.

Phobic Avoidance

Once you have addressed clients' fear of bodily harm through the use of interoceptive exposures, then clients are ready to tackle their phobic avoidance. Whether their phobic avoidance is limited or severe, the preceding cognitive and behavioral work has armed them with knowledge that makes this next step of exposure work less threatening. To help clients overcome their agoraphobia, you will be asking them to intentionally induce panic symptoms in the situations or settings they fear most (e.g., being outside the home, going to public places, being in a crowd, etc.). For example, a man with a fear of having a heart attack may go running alone and purposely overbreathe to the point of discomfort, or a woman who fears passing out may go to a crowded mall and spin around in circles.

For some clients, gradual exposure is unnecessary, and they are ready to face their previously feared situations and intentionally bring on panic symptoms without much prompting. For clients with more severe avoidance, though, this exposure may need to be more gradual and graded. For example, you may have to develop a hierarchy of feared situations and ask clients to slowly work their way up to inducing panic symptoms across these settings.

Eventually, the therapeutic work can go back to what triggered the client's initial apprehension. It is irrelevant what triggered the bodily sensations themselves, as any stimulus can potentially trigger a bodily response; rather, it is important to examine the underlying core belief, or doubt label, that made clients vulnerable to panic. Do they see themselves as weak, vulnerable, incompetent, or defective? If so, as long as they embrace that doubt label, they are at risk to experience a relapse in their panic symptoms. Continuing cognitive work and behavioral experiments can help clients compile the evidence needed to push back against their doubt labels and overcome their panic disorder.

PANIC DISORDER: TYPICAL HOMEWORK SUGGESTIONS

Ask clients to:

1. Review coping cards that remind them that their symptoms are unpleasant but not dangerous.
2. Intentionally and regularly bring on feared physical sensations by practicing interoceptive exposures at home. Consider trying out different types of exposures.
3. Confront the feared situations they have previously avoided.
4. Intentionally and regularly practice interoceptive exposures in these feared situations.
5. Keep a panic log to see if their reactions to their panic change over time.
6. Focus on their strengths and record them to increase their self-confidence.
7. Reframe any anxiety-provoking automatic thoughts that disconfirm their doubt label.
8. Look for triggers that make them apprehensive and examine the accuracy of their perceptions of threat and resources.

Specific Phobia

Specific phobia is characterized by an excessive and irrational fear regarding specific objects or situations. These phobias can involve a variety of stimuli, including animals or insects (e.g., spiders, dogs), the natural environment (e.g., heights, darkness), situations (e.g., flying, driving), blood-injection injury (e.g., needles, seeing blood), or other nonspecific factors (e.g., vomiting, loud sounds, clowns). For clients with a specific phobia, simply thinking about the feared stimulus can cause anxiety. In addition, the fear or anxiety elicited by the stimulus results in an attempt to avoid places, situations, and objects associated with the stimulus (APA, 2013).

Cognitive Interventions

In the case of specific phobias, the data suggest that simply doing cognitive restructuring is rarely enough to put these fears in remission (Clark & Beck, 2010). However, in preparing the client to face their feared objects, it can be helpful to identify the inaccurate danger hypothesis that is contributing to their fear and to collect data to the contrary. For example, a client with a phobia of cats may believe that all domestic cats will attack her and claw her eyes out. You can help prepare this client for exposures by discussing the size of domestic cats, emphasizing their skittish nature, and pointing out how many people of all ages (even young children) have cats as pets or come across them in everyday situations without harm.

Although in vivo exposure is most often used in the treatment of specific phobias, it is sometimes not necessary, especially in cases where the feared object is deemed particularly disgusting by people in general (e.g., graphic images of vomit), which is likely to produce a visceral response in anyone and makes direct exposure unnecessary. In these cases, cognitive restructuring without exposure to the object itself may be enough.

Behavioral Interventions

In vivo exposure is the treatment of choice for specific phobia, and it is usually necessary to test out the fear hypothesis and extinguish the fear (Clark & Beck, 2010). Like any good exposure, first identify the client's feared prediction, run a behavioral experiment using exposures, and then discuss the client's observations from an objective standpoint—as if the client were a trained scientist—to make new, realistic conclusions. If the client exhibits particularly severe phobic avoidance, then it may be necessary to conduct these exposures at a slower pace by gradually moving up a fear hierarchy. For example, returning to the client with a phobia of cats, you might start by having her look at videos of cats until she habituates to the anxiety elicited by this exposure and experiences new learning. Then, she can gradually work her way to being in the same room as a cat and ultimately petting a cat.

Constructing a fear hierarchy requires first establishing anchor points for fear-provoking stimuli, typically in the form of subjective units of distress (SUDs) that range from 0 to 100. Next, feared objects, animals, activities, or situations are identified and ranked from least to most anxiety-provoking on the hierarchy. Clients then prepare to face these feared stimuli by conducting an accurate evaluation of the perceived threat, as well as their resources to deal with the perceived threat. Fortified with the knowledge that they are not being asked to face real danger and are armed with resources, clients are then ready to begin the exposure work.

No matter the speed in which you move up clients' fear hierarchy, it is vital that exposures are repeated often so that false expectations continue to be disconfirmed. For example, you may ask the client with a cat phobia to visit a friend who has a pet cat. Even if she experiences intense anxiety upon entering her friend's house, by staying in the exposure she will learn that she is able to tolerate the anxiety and that eventually her distress will subside. Furthermore, if she is able to see that her friend's cat initially runs away when she enters the room, that it gently rubs itself against her leg upon returning, and that her friend has both eyes perfectly intact—this evidence disconfirms her fear hypothesis (e.g., that all domestic cats will attack her and claw her eyes out).

The more that the exposures are varied, the more generalized the learning. It is critical for clients to stop avoiding what they are afraid of or their irrational fear will continue disrupting their life. Facing their fears is the only way to allow new learning to take place and to realize that there is no threat.

SPECIFIC PHOBIA: TYPICAL HOMEWORK SUGGESTIONS

Ask clients to do the following homework:

1. Regularly and repeatedly face their feared object, animal, activity, or situation.
2. Review coping cards that remind them that their perceived danger is exaggerated and unfounded.
3. Focus on their strengths and record them to grow their self-confidence.
4. Face the situations they have been avoiding, regardless of the chance that their feared object may be there.

Illness Anxiety Disorder

Illness anxiety disorder, which is also referred to as hypochondria or health anxiety disorder, is associated with excessive preoccupation about becoming seriously ill even after medical tests rule out any underlying health problems. Clients with illness anxiety disorder do not exhibit any physical symptoms to support their concerns, but they still fear that medical catastrophe will happen at some point. Thus, they are hypervigilant to bodily cues—often misinterpreting physical symptoms that reflect normal body sensations or body discomfort that is not reflective of a more serious medical condition—and compulsively seek medical assurance against illness (APA, 2013).

Cognitive Interventions

Clients with illness anxiety disorder are preoccupied with internal stimuli (e.g., stomach pain, discoloration of the skin, pressure in their head) and base their distorted health beliefs on faulty observations that convince them that these beliefs are true. For example, they often search the internet for information and seek reassurance from individuals in their life to support their false hypotheses. In addition, they are hypervigilant of symptoms that represent normal bodily functions, which further maintains their health concerns. For example, a client with bowel discomfort may fear losing control of her bowels, which leads to more stomach tightening and discomfort. Similarly, consider a client who fears throat cancer and experiences tightness in his throat after eating a heavy meal. In turn, he repeatedly swallows to ensure that he does not have difficulty doing so, which only causes him to experience further throat discomfort and reinforces the belief that he has cancer.

The anxiety these clients experience does not stem from the physical symptoms themselves but from their anxiety about the meaning behind these symptoms. Therefore, cognitive restructuring can work to help clients understand that they have based their conclusions on particular observations, and that it is possible that other alternative explanations may be valid. For example, the client who believes he has throat cancer can be asked to consider other possible causes for his symptoms. Did he overeat? Eat too quickly? Eat food that was spicy or greasy? Did he consume too much alcohol or caffeine? Is he under more stress than usual? By examining this evidence, the client can test out alternative explanations and consider the possibility that his symptoms were a result of indigestion or acid reflux.

When you work with clients to consider alternative evidence for their symptoms, this evidence should not be gleaned by having clients seek out additional medical tests, providing them with reassurance, or engaging in a lengthy discussion of the symptoms. Rather, you want clients to consider alternative explanations for their symptoms and, at the same time, to tolerate the uncertainty that they may develop a serious medical concern one day. Regardless of what clients do (or don't do), it is still possible that a serious medical problem might present itself in the future; however, worrying about that is not going to prevent it from happening. By helping clients accept their powerlessness, you empower them to take control and live their lives instead of worrying.

Behavioral Interventions

The most important behavioral intervention for illness anxiety disorder is to help clients reduce the behaviors that are perpetuating their fears, which include health-related behaviors (e.g., scanning their body for signs of illness) and reassurance seeking. If clients are constantly touching something that concerns them, this only serves to increase swelling, redness, and discomfort. Similarly, although body scanning and reassurance seeking result in a temporary reduction of anxiety, these behaviors increase anxiety in the long run because they perpetuate health-related concerns. Reassurance seeking can also be counterproductive because it is not uncommon for clients to misinterpret the reassurance by selectively attending to information that confirms their feared outcome.

Therefore, once you have worked with clients to tolerate uncertainty and consider alternative explanations for their symptoms, it is important for them to practice resisting the urge to seek out medical information or reassurance from others. For example, consider a young client whose family calls her the nervous chicken because she interprets any bodily symptom as a sign of an oncoming horrible medical calamity. In her mind, any possible medical issue is going to happen, and it will be catastrophic in nature. After working with her to develop some cognitive reframes, direct her to practice resisting the urge to act on any health-related compulsions. For example, every time she gets a piece of ambiguous medical information, she could practice thinking, "It probably isn't a horrible thing, don't catastrophize," instead of researching information on the internet. Or, if she finds a lump on her body, she can run an experiment to see if it goes away in a few days, instead of rushing to the doctor as she would have in the past. Or, if she is out of town and starts to get a runny nose, she can tell herself, "The probability that this is a cold is much more likely. Think of how many people get colds and how many get pneumonia," instead of rushing home early. Finally, instead of underestimating herself, you can help her consider the idea, "I can handle it." Have her remind herself that if she were ever really in medical trouble, there would be plenty of outside help and quality medical care in good facilities with qualified professionals.

ILLNESS ANXIETY DISORDER: TYPICAL HOMEWORK SUGGESTIONS

Ask clients to:

1. Consider alternative explanations for their bodily symptoms.
2. Accept living with uncertainty and think of all the ways uncertainty has led to positive things.
3. Resist the urge to seek reassurance.
4. Resist getting more medical tests.
5. Run experiments where they don't focus on their symptoms and see what happens.
6. Practice relaxation or distraction strategies when their anxiety drives them to research their symptoms.

Obsessive Compulsive Disorder

Although OCD was removed from the anxiety disorders category in the fifth edition of the *Diagnostic and Statistical Manual of Mental Disorders* (*DSM-5*) and reclassified under the new diagnostic category of "obsessive-compulsive related disorders" (APA, 2013), OCD still shares the same underlying mechanism inherent to all anxiety disorders (e.g., exaggeration of threat and undervaluation of resources). Therefore, many clinicians still consider OCD an anxiety disorder and treat it as such.

Clients with OCD experience recurrent and uncontrollable intrusive thoughts (e.g., obsessions) that are time-consuming and interfere with daily functioning. The content of the obsessions can vary widely and involve fears of contamination, unwanted sexual thoughts, losing control, religious obsessions, harm obsessions, or a preoccupation with symmetry or things being "just right." Clients with OCD view these intrusive thoughts as more dangerous and important than they are, which causes extreme anxiety and distress. In turn, they try to suppress these thoughts or engage in a variety of ritualistic behaviors (e.g., compulsions) to neutralize the distress and prevent their feared outcome (APA, 2013).

Cognitive Interventions

The standard of treatment for clients with OCD is exposure and response prevention (ERP), which involves (1) exposing clients to the thoughts, situations, or objects that trigger their obsessions and (2) engaging in response prevention to refrain from engaging in ritualistic behaviors in response to the obsessions. However, before jumping right into exposures, help clients with OCD reframe the cognitive belief systems that surround their obsessions. Clients with OCD believe that ordinary intrusive thoughts are stimuli to be feared. By helping clients see that everyone has intrusive thoughts, you can move them closer to a point where they no longer fear these thoughts and, in turn, no longer need to engage in efforts to neutralize or avoid the thoughts. Sharing a list of intrusive thoughts and urges that have been reported by ordinary people can be useful in providing them with this needed insight (e.g., the impulse to hit or harm someone, thought of an accident occurring to a loved one, desire to fling oneself off a balcony).

In addition, chain analysis can help clients understand how their OCD perpetuates itself and where there are options for interventions. Here is the typical path:

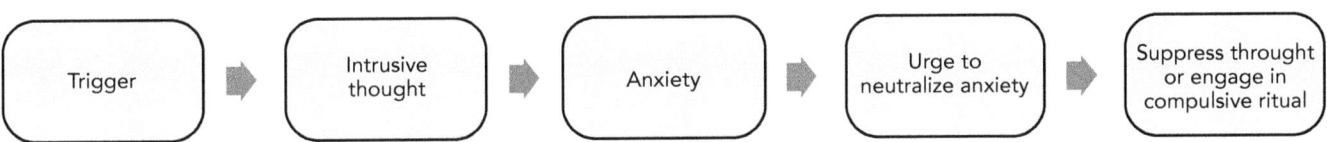

For example, consider the case of Skyler, a high school student whose OCD rituals are preventing her from participating in social opportunities, making her late for school, and disrupting her sleep. She sees a black shirt in her closet and thinks she may have touched it (*trigger*). In turn, she experiences the following thought, "I touched the black shirt, and now something socially bad will happen" (*intrusive thought*). Her *anxiety* soars, and she thinks to herself, "If I do my ritual, then I can feel better and keep the bad thing from happening" (*urge to neutralize anxiety*). As a result, she begins her ritual, which involves putting her room in order and repeating this process seven times (*compulsive ritual*).

The first point in the intervention plan is to help clients develop the motivation or buy-in to participate in treatment by examining the pros and cons of ritualizing or thought suppression. For Skyler, you can help her see that ritualizing has several downsides. For example, it makes her chronically late and prevents her from participating in things she wants to accomplish or be a part of. In addition, although ritualizing may help reduce some short-term anxiety, no amount of ritualizing fully eliminates the anxiety. It is also ineffective in the long run because the anxiety continues to perpetuate itself. Work with clients to develop this understanding so that you are both on the same page, and have them develop a coping card that reiterates why it makes sense for them to stop ritualizing. A sample coping card for Skyler could look as follows:

> Skyler's Coping Card
>
> **RITUAL PREVENTION**
>
> The goal is to stop ritualizing. Why? It is time-consuming, exhausting, and keeps me from going to bed. By stopping the rituals, I can learn not to be bothered by anxious feelings and overcome my fear of feelings. I will also stop annoying and worrying my parents, and I will feel better about myself, gain independence, get to hang out with my friends, not miss sleepovers, and regain control over my life.

Second, you must work to make the experience of anxiety less disturbing by reducing the client's fear of it. To do this, you need to first identify what about the anxiety or discomfort is unbearable or scary. For Skyler, her anxiety is connected to doubts about her social desirability, as she believes that if she is anxious, then she will say something inappropriate in social situations and be rejected. Similarly, a software engineer might think, "If I don't alleviate the anxiety, then I will make a mistake and lose my job." Notice that in both these examples, the fear or anxiety is directly linked to underlying self-doubt. Addressing this fear means using cognitive restructuring to modify the doubt label and bolster self-confidence. Skyler can learn that she is socially desirable and what people think of her is not determined by one comment. The engineer can learn that he is actually quite competent, and even if he performs at a standard that is less than ideal, he is still way ahead of the curve.

It can also be helpful to have clients practice interoceptive exposures to demonstrate that the physical symptoms of anxiety are nothing to be feared. However, unlike panic disorder (which typically requires repeated exposures), a one-time interoceptive exposure is usually effective in demonstrating to clients with OCD that anxiety is not dangerous. Once you have worked with clients to reduce their fear of anxiety, have them develop a coping card that summarizes this understanding.

> Coping Card
>
> **COPING WITH ANXIETY**
>
> Anxiety is not dangerous. It cannot hurt me. I don't need to make it go away. Instead, I can acknowledge it by telling myself, "I feel anxious, so what!" Just because I am anxious does not mean I have to act on it. Leave it alone; it will pass.

The next step in the intervention is the most critical, which involves addressing the intrusive thought itself. Clients with OCD exhibit "thought-action fusion," which involves the mistaken belief that simply having a thought makes it more probable that the thought will come true. This thinking error leads clients to confuse thought with action, causing them to believe that having a thought makes it more likely to happen, that having a thought is as bad as acting on it, and that these thoughts are a reflection of their poor character. You can teach clients that thoughts aren't as important or dangerous as they seem with a simple exposure induction. For example, ask clients to think, "It is raining," "I will win the lottery," or "I desire to hit you," and see if any of those things happen. The truth is any of these things could happen, but not because they thought it or felt it.

You can also use a more challenging experiment, such as asking them to write down that you or someone else in the office is going to die in the next two minutes. Flooding can be especially useful here, wherein you ask them to think about the statement or write it not once, but over and over. Doing so will make clients anxious, and they will want to neutralize the anxiety by crossing the statement out or tearing up the paper, but help them resist the urge to do so. The truth is that someone may die, but it will not be because of a thought or a written statement. You want clients to learn that intrusive thoughts and urges are merely an expression of anxiety talking to them and that they are a normal, everyday occurrence of the human psyche.

In addition, be careful not to spend too much time evaluating the validity of their intrusive thoughts and urges, as this promotes more obsessing. However, the first time you discuss an intrusive thought it is not unreasonable to evaluate the merit of the concern. Once you establish that the thought is just OCD talking, the key is to not allow it to have any power or importance. You can then ask clients to develop a coping card that reminds them of the thinking error behind thought-action fusion.

Coping Card

COPING WITH INTRUSIVE THOUGHTS

Rationally, I know that this thinking is not right. This is a ridiculous, erroneous thought. There is no connection between what I think and what happens. There is no thought-action connection. This is OCD talking and not reality talking.

Behavioral Interventions

Effective treatment for OCD does not only involve helping clients understand that their intrusive thoughts are not as dangerous or important as they seem. In fact, many clients recognize the irrational nature of their obsessions, but they feel compelled to ritualize in response to them anyway as a means of neutralizing anxiety. Therefore, a critical component of treatment for OCD is response prevention, in which clients refrain from engaging in thought suppression or compulsive rituals in response to their obsessions. It is usually too challenging for clients to stop their compulsions altogether without first setting up a graded hierarchy in which they do fewer rituals over time. You can start by delaying rituals and then eliminate certain types of rituals first. Other options are to initially eliminate rituals at certain times of day or at certain locations. Clients can also do something that gets in the way of the compulsion, such as the use of distraction if it delays acting on the urge. Eventually the goal is not to ritualize at all.

Sometimes, an opportunity may also come up where clients are exposed to something that triggers their obsession, but something gets in the way of their ability to ritualize. For example, clients with contamination fears may accidentally touch something "dirty" but be nowhere in the vicinity of a bathroom, which forces them to delay washing their hands or prevents them from washing their hands altogether. Use this as a learning experience to help clients see that although the response prevention was forced in this instance, it was an opportunity to test their fears.

The following is a sample coping card that clients can use to resist the urge to engage in compulsions as they begin ERP, followed by a sample exposure and response prevention plan that Skyler put into place in order to give up her compulsive rituals.

> Coping Card
> # RESIST THE URGE
>
> I can take it in small steps. I have to face my fear to overcome it. When I resist the urge to neutralize the anxiety, I do feel worse temporarily, but it makes me stronger in the long run. Let the obsessive thoughts be, and remember not to make them mean what they don't. Confidence comes from resisting the urge, and confidence makes it easier to face my OCD.

> ## SAMPLE EXPOSURE AND RESPONSE PREVENTION PLAN: SKYLER
>
> 1. Become comfortable with the anxiety. I can tolerate anxious feelings. Anxiety is nothing to fear; it is controllable and can be manipulated. It is just a symptom and cannot hurt me.
>
> 2. In order to confront my anxiety and get rid of OCD once and for all, I am going to work my way up my exposure hierarchy:
>   - Look at a black shirt.
>   - Smell a black shirt.
>   - Touch a black shirt directly.
>   - Drape a black shirt over my shoulder.
>   - Wear a shirt that was next to a black shirt.
>   - Wear a black shirt.
>
> 3. In order to prove that I can tolerate anxiety and am not afraid of anxiety, I am going to start disrupting my nighttime ritual. I will try doing only one round of lotion, and I will close my door and flip the light switch off only once. I will do the pillow fluffing and 1-2-3 flip out of order. I will try switching the order of the room check.
>
> 4. I will not give in! I can get comfortable not doing the rituals. I can practice not ritualizing every day. I can become comfortable not doing the ritual if I do not give in. I do not have to do these rituals at all.
>
> 5. Keep reminding myself every day: There is no connection between ritualizing or making one choice (versus another choice) and something bad happening. This connection feels true, but objectively it is not true.
>
> 6. When an intrusive thought pops up in my head, I can remind myself: This is just an intrusive thought. Ordinary people get these same intrusive thoughts. What makes it OCD is the fear of the thought. If I try and suppress the thought, it will get louder, stronger, and more vivid. Just face it, flood it.
>
> 7. Regularly remind myself: My tendency is to get anxious, so stress is going to push my OCD button.
>
> 8. Most importantly, remind myself: I am a socially desirable, fun, caring person, and nothing I do or say in any given moment will have the power to negate a lifetime of data.

> **OCD: TYPICAL HOMEWORK SUGGESTIONS**
>
> Ask clients to:
>
> 1. Make a list of all the disadvantages and advantages of continuing to ritualize versus resisting the urge to ritualize. Draw an overall conclusion.
>
> 2. Flood themselves with intrusive thoughts (either verbally, in writing, or to themselves) while resisting the urge to ritualize or suppress thoughts.
>
> 3. Read the coping cards they have created in therapy.
>
> 4. Stand up to anxiety instead of trying to make it go away.
>
> 5. Focus on their strengths and record them to reinforce a positive self-image.

Post-Traumatic Stress Disorder

Although PTSD was reclassified as a trauma and stressor-related disorder in the *DSM-5* (APA, 2013), it still makes theoretical sense to treat it under the umbrella of anxiety, as PTSD involves a fear of re-experiencing the horror of a trauma. Clients with PTSD often experience recurrent and intrusive memories or nightmares associated with the trauma, and any triggers that remind them of the trauma elicit extreme distress. As a result, they attempt to avoid internal cues (e.g., memories, thoughts, feelings) and external cues (e.g., people, places, situations) associated with the trauma narrative. PTSD can be conceptualized as a "normal" reaction to abnormal circumstances, extending in time and scope beyond its usefulness. In particular, clients who experience PTSD experience an overactive and prolonged fight-or-flight response, which is repeatedly activated despite there being no real stressor or threat present.

Cognitive Interventions

The key elements in treating PTSD—regardless of which protocol you follow (e.g., prolonged exposure, cognitive processing therapy, or CBT)—are cognitive restructuring and exposure (Clark & Beck, 2010). Typically, formal treatment should not begin until clients' symptoms have been causing them distress and interfering with their daily functioning for three months. Although this is not a rigid guideline, pushing clients to work on their trauma narrative prematurely can be harmful. Keep in mind that most people recover from a trauma without any formal intervention, and early symptoms may actually be medical in nature (e.g., brain injury, side effect of medication, physical pain). In addition, PTSD work is contraindicated if clients are still in a relationship with their assailant, exhibit severe dissociation, have an inadequate memory of the trauma, or are using substances and are unable to attend therapy sober (Foa, Hembree, & Rothbaum, 2007).

Like all anxiety disorders, the goal of treatment for PTSD is to correct negative appraisals of the trauma and its sequelae. However, treating PTSD is particularly challenging work, as individuals with PTSD often exhibit poor autobiographical recall of the trauma (frequently remembering the events of the trauma out of sequence) and heightened perceptual priming of trauma-related triggers (causing them to be easily triggered and re-experience the trauma as if they were still there) (Clark & Ehlers, 2004).

In addition, while avoidance is an obstacle in the treatment of any anxiety disorder, it is a particular problem in PTSD. Most clients do not want to think about, talk about, or relive what happened, which can significantly limit your ability to do PTSD work. Therefore, help clients recognize the merit in no longer avoiding the trauma narrative and its associated stimuli. Avoidance allows the trauma memory to stay in charge and disrupt their life—and it will likely continue to make their symptoms worse. Work with clients to help them understand that by revisiting the trauma narrative, they give themselves a chance to work through the memories, lessen their impact, and think about them in a more helpful and accurate manner. The following is an example of a coping card that clients can use to gain the courage to stop avoiding the trauma narrative.

Coping Card

OVERCOMING AVOIDANCE

I can't run away if I want to get better. Avoidance prevents recovery. If I keep running away, then the memory will stay in charge. As scary as it sounds, if I face the memory, then I can overcome it. I can stand up to it. I can be free.

Once clients are amenable to working on their trauma narrative, the goal is for clients to learn how to tolerate and process the complex and conflicting thoughts and emotions associated with the trauma. Clients who have experienced trauma exhibit a variety of thinking errors that cause them to maintain a negative view of themselves, the world, and the future, which serve to perpetuate misinterpretations of external threats (e.g., "The world is a dangerous place") and internal threats (e.g., "I'm damaged," "I cannot take care of myself," "I'm dead inside," "I'm weak"). By using Socratic dialogue (e.g., examining alternative viewpoints and perspectives, analyzing implications of beliefs), you can help clients alter their beliefs about themselves and the world. In particular, cognitive restructuring can help address cognitions embedded within the trauma memory—including those based in fear (e.g., "I am going to die"), anger (e.g., "They are deliberately hurting me"), guilt (e.g., "It's my fault"), and shame (e.g., "They are embarrassing me")—as well as cognitions that continue to occur following the trauma (e.g., "I have to be on guard all the time," "I will never feel okay," "I deserve to be punished").

For example, consider a robbery victim, who believes it's her fault that she was in a bad neighborhood at the time of the assault and that bad things happen to bad people. Cognitive restructuring can help this client learn that although bad things do happen, it is not a given that they will always happen. In addition, bad things can happen to anyone. In turn, she can learn to accept that the robbery was neither her fault nor a reflection of her merit but, rather, a random event. Instead of thinking that no one can be trusted, she can accept that there are people who would never hurt her, who care about her, and who can be trusted.

Behavioral Interventions

In addition to cognitive restructuring, the treatment of PTSD involves the use of exposure-based strategies, including imaginal exposure (e.g., reliving the trauma through imagination) and in vivo exposure (e.g., approaching trauma-related situations in real life), the latter of which is usually done for homework and in between sessions. Exposures are an important component of treatment because they allow clients to modify any unhelpful cognitions surrounding the trauma and help clients make sense of the bad memories. Exposure-based strategies are necessary to help uncover the trauma cognitions and provide information for new, more accurate perceptions to reign. Sometimes, clients remember the event differently than it happened, which results in feelings of guilt or shame about something that was not their fault. As the therapist, you can help clients more realistically look back at these memories.

In addition, exposures allow clients to confront previously avoided situations and learn that these situations are safe, which modifies their cognitions about the danger. For example, a client who has been in a horrific multivehicle accident involving multiple fatalities may purposely avoid the part of the road where the accident happened. Ideally, revisiting that part of the road and spending time observing cars go by can alter the client's misperception that a current threat still exists and that there will always be an accident there. If necessary, driving that part of the road—first as a passenger and eventually on their own—will help reinforce the new learning that just because a tragedy happened there doesn't mean that it is still happening or going to happen again.

Typically, before beginning exposures, it is helpful to teach clients some form of relaxation to facilitate their compliance, as well as to dampen any overengagement with the trauma narrative. When recounting the trauma memory, overengaged clients may become too close to the trauma narrative, causing them to relive the trauma as if it were happening all over again. When this occurs, clients may decompensate by dissociating, exhibiting regressed behaviors (e.g., urinary or fecal incontinence), or uncontrollably sobbing. In these cases, the use of relaxation techniques can be used in order to reground clients and remind them that they are safe. When restarting the exposure, try modifying the procedures to decrease engagement by asking clients to talk in the past tense, keep their eyes open, or write the trauma narrative instead of talking about it. On the other hand, if the client is underengaged, ask them to talk in the first person, close their eyes, and use their senses to get in better touch with the event.

Consider the case of the female college student who blamed herself for a date rape experience. She could not return to her apartment where the rape took place and could not tolerate being in her family home, as she believed that her parents also blamed her for what happened, and the thought of facing their perceived anger was unbearable. She avoided her friends and was skipping her summer job out of fear that she would have an emotional breakdown or face questions she did not want to answer. When she first sought treatment, she did not want to talk about the rape, so therapy began by addressing the issue of avoidance in general and helping her set goals for reclaiming her life. Eventually, she was able to recount the trauma narrative, although reliving it was a painful and difficult task. After recounting the trauma memory only one time, she immediately recognized that her original conclusions of self-blame were unsound. She concluded: "I felt like I let it happen, so I was mad at myself. I now know there was nothing I could have done. I didn't let it happen. He bullied me. He outpowered me. A monster attacked me. I blame him, the person who did it. IT CLICKED! I now have the power. What he did was wrong. I am still whole. I can heal. He got nothing. Avoiding means that I am giving him the power to take things from me. I am not going to let that happen."

Once she recognized that the blame was on him, she could face her parents and realize that their anger was directed toward him and not her. She was able to face the situations and people she had been avoiding, which led her to disclose her story to others. The reaction she got in recounting her story was more positive than she had ever imagined, and it even resulted in her being designated risk manager for her sorority, which guaranteed that she would fearlessly relive her story in the hope of protecting others.

PTSD: TYPICAL HOMEWORK SUGGESTIONS

Ask clients to:

1. Recount the trauma memory by listening to or reading their narrative. It can also be done by telling their story to others.
2. Practice relaxation techniques.
3. Face situations they have been avoiding.
4. Remind themselves of the new conclusions they have gained from evaluating the trauma narrative and continue collecting evidence in support of their new viewpoints.
5. Focus on their strengths instead of letting PTSD feed into their self-doubt.
6. Reclaim their life and engage in activities that they have been avoiding.

Summary: Anxiety Disorders

Clients with anxiety disorders tend to overestimate the likelihood and severity of negative events, and they underestimate their ability to cope. The use of cognitive restructuring in conjunction with exposures is a powerful way to address and modify these distorted beliefs. Exposures represent behavioral experiments that allow clients to test the validity of their fear hypothesis. In particular, exposures allow clients to determine whether their feared outcome actually happened (and, if so, whether the outcome was as bad as they thought it would be) and, most importantly, whether they had the necessary resources to cope. Clearly, if they are in your office talking about the exposure after the fact, then they do possess these resources.

ANGER

THE COGNITIVE MODEL OF ANGER

Anger can be an important warning sign that signals the need to act and protect ourselves from harm. More often though, anger comes from misguided perceptions that cause us unnecessary distress, lead us to take inappropriate actions, and make us regret our words and actions later. It comes from unfulfilled or violated expectations that are typically expressed in the form of "shoulds," "musts," "ought to's," and "have to's" (Beck, 1999). Anger lurks right on the surface, driving us to dwell on the injustice, compromising our ability to objectively evaluate the situation, and giving us ill-advised permission to act out.

The treatment of anger, like anxiety, is not to eliminate the emotion of anger but to help clients recognize when it is a result of erroneous thinking. When clients assume that others "should" or "ought to" fulfill some request, they are assuming they have control over others and the world around them. Learning to let go of this anger involves teaching clients that we, as humans, have no power over what others think, feel, or do—nor do we have control of the external world. In addition, although we don't have complete control over the emotions we feel or the thoughts that pop into our head, we *do* have control over how we choose to act in response to these thoughts or feelings.

By helping clients learn to accept their powerlessness over others and the world, they can learn to replace their unrealistic demands with more reasonable requests (e.g., "It would be nice if," "I would prefer," "I would like," or "I wish"). Replacing the demand with a request dampens the anger and allows clients to dig deeper for the specific thoughts about the situation that are bothering them. The meaning behind the unmet expectation is often linked to underlying feelings of fear or hurt. Asking clients what the unfulfilled demand means to them, or what it means about them, can uncover these automatic thoughts so they can be further evaluated. Often, the automatic thoughts that clients have regarding these unmet expectations are untrue or exaggerated. One way to help clients identify and modify any distortions in their thinking is to ask them to imagine putting themselves in the other person's shoes. Encourage clients to imagine what the other person might have been thinking and feeling, or what circumstances may have driven that person to react the way he or she did. You can also ask clients to think about how they would want to be treated in a similar situation and to consider that action toward the individual who made them angry.

For example, consider Alex, who was rushing home from work to make dinner for her family and planned on making a quick stop at the grocery store to buy the necessary ingredients for dinner. Hardly believing her luck, she saw a parking spot right in front of the store, but before she had a chance to pull into the spot, another woman took it. She became enraged that someone else would take the spot she had been waiting for, so she rolled down her window and began to verbally berate the woman. "How dare you! You shouldn't have stolen my spot! You're an awful person!" She continued to yell at the other woman as she drove away to find another parking spot. When the two women crossed paths again in the store, Alex again attacked the woman, yelling, "You purposely stole my spot! You are just one more person trying to take advantage of me!"

In this example, Alex's anger stemmed from the belief that the other woman stole her spot, and it was this belief that led Alex to experience so much distress, causing her to perseverate on the perceived injustice and leading her to lash out inappropriately. By teaching Alex the cognitive skills to identify and drill beneath her thoughts, she can recognize that her thinking may have been distorted by a variety of thinking errors, including a lens of demands (e.g., "She shouldn't have stolen my spot"), jumping to conclusions (e.g., "She did it on purpose"), and labeling (e.g., "She is an awful person").

In addition, the goal of anger management is to help Alex evaluate the meaning she gave to the perceived injustice, as the specific automatic thoughts she experienced were linked to the assumption that people were taking advantage of her, which activated the underlying belief that she was powerless. The role of the therapist is to help Alex evaluate these automatic thoughts, gather data for and against these thoughts, and consider alternative explanations for the woman's behavior (e.g., perhaps the woman didn't realize that Alex was waiting for the spot). Alex can also develop a more logical overall conclusion about the situation by putting herself in the other woman's shoes and considering whether this incident is as big of a deal as she is making it.

Additionally, therapy can help Alex consider how *even if* the woman did purposely steal her spot (which is possible), that she was powerless to control the other woman's actions. Sometimes, people do things that are unfair to us, but it's not up to us to control their actions. Moreover, although the woman's actions were offensive, they were not necessarily personally directed toward Alex. The therapist can help Alex practice acceptance that all of us are powerless to control everything in the environment, but we can manage how we respond to it and learn to say, "So what!"

The following pages contain various handouts, worksheets, and coping cards you can give clients to determine the extent to which unfulfilled expectations or demands (e.g., "shoulds," "musts," "ought to's," "have to's") are driving the anger in their life, as well as to help them reframe these demands into more reasonable preference statements.

Client Handout

KEY WORDS TO ATTEND TO

When we have expectations that other people "should," "must," "ought to," or "have to" do something, this can cause us to experience anger if these expectations don't get fulfilled. One way to help reduce feelings of anger is to reframe these demands into a more reasonable preference (e.g., "It would be nice if," "I would prefer," "I would like," or "I wish"). The following are some examples.

Instead of: ➡ **Think:**

- "You should …"
- "You have to …"
- "You must …"
- "You ought to …"

- "I wish you …"
- "I would like it if you …"
- "I would prefer it if you …"
- "It would be nice if you …"

- "You should have called me last night."
- "You have to do me this favor."
- "You must stop working so late."
- "You ought to drive more slowly."

- "I wish you would have called me last night."
- "I would like it if you could do me this favor."
- "I would prefer it if you stopped working so late."
- "It would be nice if you drove more slowly."

Copyright © 2019 Leslie Sokol & Marci G. Fox, *The Comprehensive Clinician's Guide to Cognitive Behavioral Therapy*. All Rights Reserved

Client Worksheet

REFRAME THE EXPECTATION

• • • • •

In this exercise, you will look at two hypothetical scenarios to see how you could reword a demanding "should" statement into a more reasonable preference statement, reframe the meaning of the unfulfilled demands, and consider more appropriate actions. A sample scenario is provided below, followed by two blank scenarios for you to fill in yourself.

Sample Scenario: You are going to the store to pick up some necessities and are in a rush to get home. As you are waiting in the checkout line, the cashier starts to engage in a conversation with the customer in front of you, causing a slight holdup in the line.

Demanding Statement

The cashier should stop talking so much and move on to the next customer.

Ascribed Meaning

He is purposely going to make me late. He is so inconsiderate.

Possible Actions

Stand there tapping your foot, exasperated that it is taking so long. Give the cashier the evil eye.

Reframe

I wish the cashier would stop talking and hurry up.

He is probably just trying to be friendly. Maybe he doesn't want to be impolite and cut off the person talking to him. Being friendly is not indicative of being inconsiderate. He doesn't know I am in a hurry.

Assertively and politely ask the cashier if he could speed things up as you are in a hurry. Patiently wait, knowing you chose to run an errand on a tight schedule.

Scenario 1: You are driving home from work and approaching an intersection. You notice that the traffic light has just turned yellow, so you speed up and try to make the light. However, the woman in the car in front of you slams on her brakes, causing you to slam on your brakes too.

Demanding Statement What in the heck are you doing lady? You shouldn't be so stupid to slam on your brakes at a yellow light. You should have gone.	**Reframe** _____ _____ _____ _____ _____
⬇	⬇
Ascribed Meaning She has no consideration for others and could have caused a major pileup. She doesn't belong on the road, how irresponsible of her to do that.	_____ _____ _____ _____ _____ _____ _____ _____ _____
⬇	⬇
Possible Actions Honk your horn repeatedly for her to go. Give her the finger or yell out the window at her.	_____ _____ _____ _____ _____

Scenario 2: It's your birthday today, and you have been waiting for your son to call you all day long. Although he sent you a Facebook message and a text, he still hasn't picked up the phone to call you, and the day is almost over.

Demanding Statement	**Reframe**
It is ridiculous that my son didn't take a minute to call me on my birthday because he should have called. My son should have called me on my birthday.	

⬇

Ascribed Meaning

He doesn't care about me. I am not important enough for him to make my birthday a priority.

⬇

Possible Actions

Act annoyed with him the next time he calls. Avoid him for a while.

Coping Card
FREE YOURSELF FROM ANGER

- Don't let anger trap you. Look out for anger that comes from making a demand.
- Identify the demanding statement (should, ought, need, have to, must).
- Don't should on yourself.
- Don't should on others.
- Replace the demand with a preference statement (wish, like, prefer, would be nice).
- Remember: You have no control over what other people think, say, or do.
- Beware of giving unmet expectations inaccurate meaning.
- Accept your powerlessness in controlling others and the world.

Client Sample Worksheet

ANGER LOG

Whenever you find yourself getting angry, use this log to look for the hurt or fear underlying your anger, as well as the thoughts that drive those feelings. Examine the validity of those thoughts and ask yourself if you are making the situation more personal or giving it more meaning than it deserves. Try to consider all the alternative explanations and possibilities for what happened, and let the facts help you draw more accurate conclusions. A sample log is provided below, followed by a blank log for you to use.

The Facts (What you or another person said or did: what happened)	Your Expectation (Demand)	Your Interpretation (Meaning)	Replace the Demand (Wish, prefer)	Question the Meaning (Alternative view)
Husband left a pile of dirty clothing on the floor	He should put his dirty clothing in the laundry. **Feelings:** Angry, frustrated	He did it purposely to get me upset. **Feelings:** Hurt	I wish he would put his dirty clothes in the laundry.	It's not that he doesn't care. Being messy is just the way he has always been. He is not going to change, so there is no benefit in demanding that he does so. I have to accept the negative side of who he is, while also reminding myself that the positive side is a lot bigger. He is smart, kind, a good friend, responsible, reliable, and attractive.

Copyright © 2019 Leslie Sokol & Marci G. Fox, *The Comprehensive Clinician's Guide to Cognitive Behavioral Therapy*. All Rights Reserved

ANGER LOG

The Facts (What you or another person said or did: what happened)	Your Expectation (Demand)	Your Interpretation (Meaning)	Replace the Demand (Wish, prefer)	Question the Meaning (Alternative view)
	Feelings:	Feelings:		

ANGER AROUSAL

Dwelling on anger-driven thoughts (e.g., "How dare she!") only increases autonomic arousal, which further escalates physical and emotional symptoms. Muscles tense, anxiety climbs, and clients' ability to objectively evaluate the situation becomes compromised. In turn, they act on misguided assumptions (e.g., "She deserves it. I have to make my point!"), which mobilizes them toward ineffective action. For example, clients who are angry will lash out and act aggressively or impulsively, instead of asserting their needs in a more appropriate manner.

In cases where anger has fueled intense emotions, it is helpful to ask clients to check the intensity of their affect using a 10-point scale. If their emotional thermometer is at an 8 or higher, this is a cue for them to take a "time-out" from the situation and use relaxation or distraction strategies to dampen the arousal. After practicing these strategies for a specified time, they can recheck their emotional thermometer and return to the situation when they are less reactive and can think more clearly. To help your clients get into the habit of managing their anger arousal, provide them with the following coping card, as well as the handout on the next page.

Coping Card

MANAGING ANGER AROUSAL

People do not always listen to me. They don't always do what I want, they don't always think like me, and they don't always value what I do. I cannot control their actions. I can accept that people will sometimes ignore my wishes. Although I wish it was different, I can accept reality. When I am angry, I can calm down by practicing deep breathing, taking a walk, or using some other relaxation technique.

Client Handout

DAMPEN THE AROUSAL

When emotions are in charge, it is hard to think clearly and behave responsibly. If you find that your anger is getting the best of you, take a moment to step back and rate how intense your feelings of anger are using the following scale.

0	1	2	3	4	5	6	7	8	9	10
Not irritated		Mildly irritated		Somewhat Frustrated		Very Irritated		Angry		Enraged

If you find that your anger is at an 8 or higher, that is a signal for you to take a break and get your emotions in check. Calm your body by using some of the following relaxation or distraction techniques. Return to the situation once your anger has subsided to a manageable level and you can think more clearly, and then use the energy from your anger toward constructive action. It's also helpful for you to practice these techniques even when you are not emotionally aroused, as doing so will raise your emotional threshold and help keep your emotions in check.

- Practice diaphragmatic breathing
- Count to 20
- Try progressive muscle relaxation techniques
- Take a walk
- Exercise
- Visualize a relaxing scene
- Look at a picture of a stop sign
- Watch television
- Listen to music

ASSERTIVE COMMUNICATION

Assertive communication maximizes our effectiveness in being heard and increases the chance that we will get our needs met. Being assertive means clearly and directly expressing our thoughts, feelings, and desired course of action. It involves getting our point across clearly and expressing ourselves in a calm, conversational tone. Assertiveness is in contrast to extreme passivity and aggression, which are less effective forms of communication. These forms of communication fall along a continuum, ranging from passive to aggressive, with assertiveness falling in the middle:

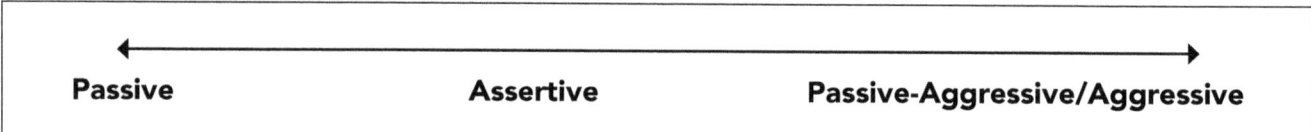

Passive communication involves essentially not communicating, either by not expressing ourselves, hoping that people will read our mind, or expressing our needs in an unclear and watered-down manner. On the other end of the continuum is aggressive communication, which involves being threatening, making demands, or pressuring others. Aggressive communication is designed to intimidate or antagonize others, and it can be viewed as hostile, destructive, and forceful. Aggressive communication can also involve being aggressive in a passive manner. Instead of outright expressing ourselves, saying "no," or voicing an option, passive-aggressiveness involves acquiescing with the intent to be defiant. For example, someone may purposely "forget" to perform an important task that someone asks of them, as opposed to directly telling the other person that they are unable to do it. Another form of passive-aggressive communication involves the use of sarcasm or jabs.

The following chart provides some examples of each type of communication:

Passive Communication	Assertive Communication	Aggressive Communication	
		Passive-Aggressive Communication	Aggressive Communication
"I hope someone comes to my aid on this project."	"I would really appreciate your help on the project."	"I'll get right on it." (But they won't.)	"You must do this right now."
"I know you're probably busy and don't have time to talk, so you can call me back if you want."	"I'm not available to help today, but I can help you tomorrow."	"I would have told you about the meeting if you had called."	"How can you be so stupid and have forgotten?"
"I wish I could give the opinion in my head, but I am going to just agree with everything they say."	"I felt sad when you canceled our plans. Let's set another date right now."	"Oops, I must have forgotten to give you that important message from your boss."	"I demand that you stop what you are doing and do what I want now."

Client Handout

ASSERTIVE COMMUNICATION

• • • • • •

Assertive communication maximizes the possibility that you will get what you want. Instead of demanding, yelling, or threatening, being assertive means explicitly asking for what you would like. When you shout, your voice is heard, but your message is not. In order to be assertive, avoid asking "why" questions, as this elicits defensiveness and piles of excuses—but it doesn't get you results. Instead, use a clear and quiet voice to assertively communicate your needs. Let others know what they did (or didn't do), what they said (or didn't say), and how it made you feel. Then, express what you would like. Be willing to acknowledge others and hear what they have to say, and work toward compromise if warranted.

Assertive Communication Steps

1. **State the facts:** What happened (or didn't happen) or what was said (or not said).

2. **Express how you feel:** Describe your emotions about the situation.

3. **State what you would like:** No demands! State what you would like, prefer, or wish.

4. **Acknowledge the other person:** Use active listening and hear them out.

5. **Consider a compromise:** Find a place on the continuum that makes sense for both of you.

Beware: No yelling, no "whys," no passively waiting for the other person to read your mind, no demanding "shoulds."

EFFECTIVE RESTRAINT

Effective restraint involves the ability to resist acting on aggressive urges, even in the face of anger. One way to help clients develop better self-control is to have them engage in a cost-benefit analysis of acting on their angry urges. In particular, you want them to consider both the advantages and disadvantages of lashing out. As the therapist, these disadvantages are likely readily apparent to you. However, when completing this cost-benefit analysis, you want to acknowledge that lashing out has its benefits (e.g., it gets people's attention, it may get clients what they want), as well as its downsides (e.g., it actually results in negative attention, causes clients to lose credibility, and compromises their relationships or opportunities).

Keep in mind that although clients may identify some advantages of acting out, these advantages are likely more perceived than they are real. Therefore, the use of guided questions can help clients develop a longer and more effective list of cons of acting out. Here are some examples of guided questions to help move clients toward this conclusion:

- "Imagine how you would feel _____ (minutes, days, weeks, months, years) after taking that action."
- "If a friend described that same situation and told you that she would take that specific action, what would you say?"
- "How will that impact the relationship when you are no longer upset?"
- "How would you feel and what would you think if someone responded to you that way?"
- "If someone you cared about was treated this way, what would you say to that person?"
- "How might other people think of you after you take that action? What overall consequences may there be?"

For all clients, this list of negative consequences may include the acknowledgment that acting on their anger could cause them to say things they regret, get them arrested, ruin relationships, isolate them, negatively affect their mood, reinforce the negative opinions that others have about them, alienate them, and prevent new opportunities. If clients are able to recognize that acting out is not the right path, then those angry, permission-giving beliefs won't misguide them.

Use the worksheet on the following page to have clients do a cost-benefit analysis the next time they are feeling angry and considering taking an aggressive or problematic action.

Client Worksheet

COST-BENEFIT ANALYSIS OF ACTING ON ANGER

• • • • • •

Sometimes, we let our emotions get the best of us, which makes us reactive. Use this worksheet to examine the costs and benefits of lashing out versus using an alternative strategy. Consider questioning your data with the following guided questions: Does the evidence suggest a new conclusion? Is there a bigger price to consider? Then, draw an overall conclusion so you can be effective instead of reactive.

Advantages of Lashing Out	**Disadvantages of Lashing Out**
_____	_____
_____	_____
_____	_____
_____	_____
Advantages of Using an Alternative Strategy (Doing nothing, being assertive)	**Disadvantages of Using an Alternative Strategy**
_____	_____
_____	_____
_____	_____
_____	_____

Conclusion: _____

PUTTING IT ALL TOGETHER: DIVERTING ANGER

The following example illustrates how the principles discussed in this chapter can divert the path of anger and put your clients on a more effective path that allows them to objectively evaluate the situation and take appropriate action.

The Situation:
Will is cleaning his friend John's house when another friend shows up to use the computer.

The Demand:
"He should know not to come in while I am cleaning. Doesn't he see my car? He should be more considerate."

Reframe:
"I don't have control over the rest of the world. It would be nice if the world followed my rules, but I cannot demand that he see the world the way I do. My expectations and rules are not the same as his, so he doesn't even know he is breaking my rule."

New Meaning:
"He is a nervous guy who is driven by his anxiety. All he is trying to do is manage his agitation by getting on the computer. His emotions are in charge and not his brain. He did not set out to inconvenience me. He didn't know I would d be here, and he probably doesn't even realize I don't want him here. I could be sympathetic, and even gracious, knowing he is not doing anything intentionally to me."

Ascribed Meaning:
"The audacity! Am I supposed to accommodate him? This is so inconsiderate. My time doesn't matter. He thinks the world revolves around him."

Cost-Benefit Analysis:
Will considers some of the pros of lashing out (e.g., the friend would probably leave and he could finish cleaning) and some of the cons (e.g., he'd feel guilty, John might be upset with him and ask him to never clean his house ever again). He realizes that lashing out is not in his best interest.

Appropriate Action:
Will allows the friend to use the computer and finishes cleaning as soon as the friend leaves.

Urge Toward Inappropriate Action:
"Will experiences the urge to strike out and tell the friend, "You need to leave right now!"

Manage Anger Arousal:
Will realizes that his anger has escalated to a 9, so he decides to go to another room and practice some deep breathing. After a few minutes, his anger subsides to a manageable level.

End Result:
Will's feeling of anger and annoyance subside. He feels good about himself for not letting his anger get the best of him. He realizes he is not powerless and actually in control when he doesn't let his anger get the best of him. He plans to put these tools into practice at work, on the road and in his personal life.

SELF-CONFIDENCE

As previously discussed, the meaning clients give to their unfulfilled demands is usually driven by underlying feelings of hurt or fear, and this hurt and fear is often linked to core beliefs that involve self-doubt. In particular, when clients make judgments that they "should," "ought," or "need to" meet some expectation, then their self-doubt can become activated if they fall short of these expectations. In turn, they become angry with themselves, resulting in a cycle of further judgment, criticism, and anger.

For example, take the case of a business executive who is angry at herself when her sales numbers are not as high as she thought they should be. She thinks to herself, "I should be able to do better. I should be more organized, efficient, and successful." The meaning behind this unmet expectation is driven by her underlying doubt label: "I am a failure. I am lazy." As a result, she starts to second-guess herself and questions if she has what it takes to succeed, which causes her stress, anger, frustration, and depression to escalate.

Part of overcoming this client's anger involves examining the many other plausible explanations for why her sales numbers are lower than expected. For example, her business is a tough road, developing a list of clients takes time, and she is still new. She is steadily growing her list of clients, and her boss is happy with her progress. She puts in long work hours, and she has the intelligence and experience needed for the job. All of this evidence demonstrates that regardless of how many sales she makes, she is not lazy or a failure. If she were lazy, she wouldn't bother to show up, make calls, or send any emails. If she were a failure, she wouldn't try and wouldn't have accrued any clients. In truth, she puts in an excessive amount of effort, works too many hours, and makes many personal compromises for work. Although her sales numbers are not as high as she would like, they are more than enough to be held in high regard by her employer.

When self-doubt is lurking, any opportunities that provide clients with evidence of "failure" only further fuel their self-doubt and anger. One way to help clients push back against their unrealistic demands and gain self-confidence is to have them pay attention to their strengths and take credit for their accomplishments. In doing so, clients can learn that their self-imposed demands are likely unreasonable. To help clients develop this alternative perspective, provide them with the following coping card and accompanying worksheet on the next page.

Coping Card

BEATING THE SELF-DOUBT

I can overcome my self-doubt by doing the following:

1. Not calling myself nasty labels I do not deserve.

2. Looking at all I can do, have done, and am doing.

3. Taking credit for both my efforts and successes.

4. Considering that the demands I place on myself may be unreasonable.

5. Reminding myself that even when I don't live up to my expectations, that doesn't mean I am falling short.

6. Focusing on my strengths and staying on the path to what I want.

Client Worksheet

COLLECT DATA TO SUPPORT SELF-CONFIDENCE

• • • • • •

Sometimes, we can feel angry with ourselves when we believe we have not lived up to our own expectations. To overcome that anger, we need to beat up the self-doubt by paying attention to our strengths and our accomplishments. Use this worksheet to collect some data that supports your self-confidence. Write five or more specific, positive, and effective actions that you took so far today, and then describe what those actions mean about you.

For example:

1. I paid someone a genuine compliment.
2. I got to work on time even when I didn't want to go.
3. I returned a phone call that was on my list to do.
4. I finished a work project.
5. I called a friend going through a rough patch to let her know I care.

Meaning: I'm a good person who overall does good things.

Now it's your turn:

1. _____
2. _____
3. _____
4. _____
5. _____

Meaning: _____

8

SUBSTANCE USE DISORDERS

Similar to many other psychological issues, substance abuse can be understood from a lens in which problems in thinking and dysfunctional behavioral patterns lead clients to give into problematic urges. According to the cognitive model of relapse (Beck, Wright, Newman, & Liese, 1993), when clients with addiction experience a triggering stimulus (e.g., coming home from a stressful day at work or heading to a restaurant for a meal), this activates their underlying drug-related beliefs (e.g., "Drinking is the only way to manage my stress"), which influences the development of substance-biased automatic thoughts (e.g., "I need it to relax. I need a drink"). These automatic thoughts, in turn, lead to an increase in urges and cravings, which facilitate permission-giving beliefs (e.g., "I'll stop drinking tomorrow," "I'll just finish this bottle," "I'll just have one") that rationalize their desire to use. Clients will then engage in instrumental strategies to obtain access to their desired drug of choice, which results in continued use or relapse.

This chapter explores the cognitive model in greater detail as it applies to substance use and discusses points of intervention along the way. However, before you can begin implementing these therapeutic strategies, it's necessary to first tackle what is perhaps the most important issue when working with clients who are struggling with addiction: getting clients to buy in.

MOTIVATION AND BUY-IN

Often, the biggest obstacle in treating substance use is that clients suffering from addiction do not recognize that there is a problem in the first place—and even if they do have this level of insight, they are generally not committed to working on the problem. In many cases, clients are only seeking treatment (or have been mandated to treatment) because some negative event occurred that forced them to address their addiction (e.g., DUI, arrest, divorce, job loss). Therefore, working to increase motivation and getting clients to buy in is the first step in treatment.

One way to help clients develop the willingness to engage in treatment and propel them toward recovery is to ask them to do a cost-benefit analysis of using substances, in which they consider the pros and cons of continuing to use versus giving up their addiction (Liese & Franz, 1996). Given that clients tend to focus on the benefits of using (while ignoring or minimizing its negative consequences), this analysis can help create a case for sobriety by demonstrating to clients that abstinence has far greater advantages, while continuing to use has far greater disadvantages.

For example, consider the case of Jim, who had a history of heavy alcohol use but believed that drinking was not a problem for him. Over the past several months, he was yielding to his urge to drink more and more often, causing his wife to file for divorce without warning. One night, Jim was arrested for a DUI after hitting a parked car while intoxicated. The minor car accident complicated the DUI, but luckily no one was in the parked car, and no one was injured. As a result, Jim was mandated to seek out treatment for his substance use. Initially, Jim was resistant to therapy and insisted that he didn't have a problem and didn't need therapy. He made excuses for the accident (e.g., claiming that he was exhausted while driving) and blamed his wife for quitting on their marriage.

Treatment first focused on helping Jim develop a list of pros and cons regarding his substance use, which helped him gain insight into his drinking problem and made him more receptive to treatment. A glance at his cost-benefit analysis highlights the disadvantages of continuing to drink and the advantages of sobriety. Although the cost-benefit analysis also acknowledges the advantages of drinking (and the disadvantages of sobriety), these items include an objective reframe that allows Jim to see the bigger picture regarding his problematic substance use.

Advantages of Drinking	Disadvantages of Drinking
1. It helps me relax, but it has resulted in losing my family and getting arrested. 2. It numbs feelings of shame, but now I have a mug shot and everyone knows I was arrested for a DUI. My children's friends even know. 3. It feels good in the moment, but it makes it hard to get up and go to work in the morning. 4. I like drinking, but I want to pick my wife over the bottle.	1. Death of myself or others 2. Limited contact with my children 3. Inability to work or live independently 4. Bad role model for my kids 5. Potential of another DUI 6. Alcoholism negatively affects my health
Advantages of <u>Not</u> Drinking	**Disadvantages of <u>Not</u> Drinking**
1. Be a good role model for my kids 2. Have more opportunities to be with my family 3. Maintain a job and live independently 4. Gain confidence 5. Avoid DUIs	1. I will have to tolerate bad feelings, but those feelings are temporary and will pass. 2. I will have to face the mess I've made, but then I can work on fixing it, keeping it from getting worse, and hopefully getting what I want in the long run.

Once you have worked with clients to develop a cost-benefit analysis of substance use, have them reevaluate the pros of continuing to use and the cons of abstinence. The point is for clients to see that sobriety has more advantages. Help clients draw an accurate conclusion from their cost-benefit analysis that they can use as a coping statement. For example, Jim's conclusion might be as follows: "In the short run, drinking keeps me from facing my situation and shame, but in the long term, my problems never go away and just get worse. I can overcome my shame and replace it with pride by having the courage to face my mistakes and show my children that overcoming adversity is possible. While I might have to tolerate some bad feelings to do this, becoming sober will allow me to face the mess I've created and clean it up once and for all."

On the following page is a worksheet you can use with clients to complete this cost-benefit analysis and develop a healthy conclusion about working toward sobriety.

Client Worksheet

COST-BENEFIT ANALYSIS OF SUBSTANCE USE

• • • • • •

Use this worksheet to examine the advantages and disadvantages of continuing to use substances versus abstaining from substance use. At the same time, try to see the "but" in the advantages of using (e.g., "It feels good, but . . . ") and the disadvantages of not using (e.g., "Sobriety might be hard, but . . . ").

Advantages of Using Substances	**Disadvantages of Using Substances**
_____	_____
_____	_____
_____	_____
_____	_____
Advantages of <u>Not</u> Using Substances	**Disadvantages of <u>Not</u> Using Substances**
_____	_____
_____	_____
_____	_____
_____	_____

Overall conclusion (Make sure you consider the "but" when developing this realistic, objective perspective): _____

_____

THE COGNITIVE MODEL OF RELAPSE

Triggering Stimuli

Substance use triggers can come in the form of various high-risk stimuli, which can be external or internal in nature. External triggers include people, places, or things associated with the desire to use (e.g., a stocked minibar in a hotel room, an empty wine glass on a dinner table, entering a bar, playing a musical instrument), whereas internal triggers include body sensations, images, thoughts, or feelings. The most common internal triggers involve feelings of stress, anxiety, boredom, elation, or frustration, as well as the typical body reactions that accompany these feelings.

Especially in the early stages of recovery, it is preferable for clients to avoid their triggers when possible by implementing a specific plan to remove the trigger or reduce its impact (e.g., asking the hotel to unload the stocked minibar, asking the waiter to remove the empty wine glasses, avoiding the bar). These external triggers can sometimes be avoided but not always. For example, if clients have to attend an important event where alcohol is served, they can mediate this trigger by filling their champagne glass with water, physically placing themselves on the other side of the room from where the bar is located, or going with a sober companion.

However, triggers are sometimes more difficult (if not impossible) to avoid or escape, particularly with internal triggers, which involve emotions and body sensations. In cases where avoidance is not possible, work collaboratively with clients to brainstorm ways they can reduce the impact of the trigger or cope with it. It is important for clients to learn how to stand up to their triggers despite the discomfort or fear that it may cause them. Help clients recognize that even if they do nothing, these feelings are temporary and will pass. In addition, while the feelings may be uncomfortable, that doesn't mean they have to act on them; instead, they can do nothing. Instead of tackling the discomfort, they can face it and feel empowered. For example, in the case of boredom, you can help clients overcome these feelings by reminding them that boredom is a temporary state they can tolerate, or by scheduling activities to overcome the boredom.

Similarly, consider a recovering alcoholic who is experiencing stress and frustration related to his job, which is a trigger for his alcohol use. You can reduce this client's stress by helping him normalize the stress and see it as temporary to the natural ebb and flow in his position. You can also create a pie chart of what is important in his life so he can recognize that work is a small part of what truly matters to him. In addition, you can ask him to write the benefits that he gets from his job that help him to enjoy his personal life (e.g., it allows him to own a home, go on nice vacations, hold a gym membership, interact with good friends who are also work colleagues, etc.). Treatment can also help him recognize and use the support that he and his colleagues provide one another so he can ask for help or possibly delegate at work.

Stress decreases when people believe they have the resources to face the challenge at hand. You can ask clients to practice managing stress on a daily basis by having them engage in activities that increase pleasure or accomplishment and that take the focus away from their urges. For example, they can cope with triggers by getting exercise, watching television, taking a shower or bath, walking the dog, listening to music, doing yard work, cooking, meditating, reading, smelling their favorite scent, or any other endless array of relaxing activities.

Underlying Drug-Related Beliefs

Triggers represent the first path in the cycle of substance use because they evoke underlying drug-related beliefs that perpetuate addiction. Typically, these beliefs are exaggerated or biased perceptions of the substance or behavior. They can include beliefs such as, "I can only enjoy playing my guitar when I am high," "Drinking is the only way to manage my stress," "I am more social and more desirable when I am drunk," or "I have to drink to be one of the guys." None of these beliefs are 100 percent true, and most are not true at all.

Helping clients evaluate these beliefs is another step toward recovery. Evaluating these false beliefs can be done through guided questioning, which allows clients to become aware of their thinking errors, or by having clients run a behavioral experiment to test the validity of their drug-related belief. For example, if clients believe that playing the guitar while high is the only way to enjoy making music, then ask them to test out this hypothesis by trying the opposite. They may find that not only do they enjoy playing the guitar sober, but they also like that they can remember the notes and write them down. Similarly, you can dismantle the belief "I have to drink to be one of the guys" by helping the client see all of the factors beyond drinking that connect him to his friends, such as their shared hobbies and interests (e.g., enthusiasm for sports, politics, movies, vacations). The point is to help clients develop alternative beliefs that counteract the desire to use (e.g., "I can make better music when I am sober" or "I don't need to drink for my friends to consider me one of them").

Substance-Biased Automatic Thoughts

Drug-related beliefs continue the cycle of addiction by giving rise to substance-biased automatic thoughts. These are thoughts such as, "I need a drink," "I feel like getting high," and "It would be nice to open a bottle," which escalate the urge to use. Instead of accepting these thoughts at face value, use basic questioning to have clients examine the validity of these thoughts and consider different perspectives. For example, instead of, "I need to drink to reduce my stress," a more accurate reframe might be, "I want a drink, but I don't *need* to have one. A drink means no home life, a hangover, no job, and an ugly picture of defeat." Similarly, instead of, "I earned this drink," clients can consider, "I did work hard today, but drinking is not the only way to reward myself. I can take a hot shower, schedule a relaxing massage for myself, or treat myself to a pedicure."

Increase in Urges and Cravings

When clients experience substance-biased automatic thoughts, this triggers the urge to use, and the mental image of yielding to this urge tends to fuel the cravings. For example, an alcoholic may picture a liquor bottle and imagine how good it will feel to drink it, whereas a cocaine addict may imagine smoking a pipe while laughing and feeling the pleasure of the high. In order for clients to manage these cravings, ask them to practice replacing those positive images with negative images that reflect their real past experiences. For example, alcoholics may replace the image of the liquor bottle with the memory of hanging over the toilet, covered in vomit, with their stomach wrenching in pain, their head pounding, and the smell of their family's breakfast creating waves of nausea. Similarly, instead of remembering the high associated with using crack cocaine, the addict can remember the feelings of terror and misery associated with withdrawal (e.g., escalating anxiety, wanting to crawl out of their skin, unbearable edginess, heart racing, head pounding).

Educating clients about their cravings and urges can help them recognize that these symptoms come in waves and if they do not yield to them, the urges and cravings will eventually pass. Cognitive interventions can also help clients talk back to their urges. For example, clients can develop coping cards to remind themselves that just because they have an urge does not mean they have to act on it, that it will pass, and that they will feel proud by resisting the urge. You can also try to find examples of other areas in clients' lives where they have effectively used self-control and it paid off. Finally, clients can use relaxation or distraction strategies to ride the urge until it passes (e.g., practice deep breathing, engage in other pleasurable activities, meditate, exercise, connect with a supportive friend).

Utilizing an interoceptive exposure is another way to educate clients about cravings and urges. Clients often have the misconception that the only way to make a craving diminish is to act on it, when the truth is that cravings can diminish without yielding to the urge. An overbreathing interoceptive exposure typically induces cravings in individuals who abuse substances, and the discontinuation of the exposure results in a reduction of those cravings, in turn helping the client conclude that cravings can go away without yielding to the urge.

Clinician Guidelines

INTEROCEPTIVE URGE EXPOSURE

• • • • • •

Step 1: Have the client rate the intensity of their urge to use on a scale of 0 to 10.

Step 2: Have the client overbreathe for one minute, taking deep breaths in out of their mouth.

Step 3: Ask the client to rate the intensity of their urge again using the same 10-point scale.

Step 4: Either initiate a distracting conversation about something relevant and interesting to them (e.g., movie, politics, sports) or have them close their mouth and take a few breaths in out of their nose as slowly as possible. Doing so will reduce the arousal elicited by overbreathing and typically reduce the urge.

Step 5: Ask the client to rate the intensity of their urge again using the same 10-point scale.

Step 6: Discuss the conclusions regarding their initial craving hypothesis (e.g., "I cannot tolerate the urges. The urges will only go away if I use. I have no control over them"), with the goal of developing new conclusions that support the idea that cravings can diminish without yielding to them.

Use the worksheet on the following page to track the extent of your clients' cravings, as well as how they are coping with these cravings. Ask clients to keep a record of any triggers that come up throughout the week, their ensuing thoughts and feelings, the intensity of their cravings, and their coping response. Review the log in session each week so you can identify areas in which the client is making progress, as well as any difficulties you need to work on.

Client Worksheet

DAILY RECORD OF CRAVINGS AND COPING RESPONSE

• • • • • •

Use this worksheet to record any triggers that come up daily and throughout the week. Write down difficult situations that triggered the urge to use, and identify the thoughts or feelings generating your distress. Then, record the intensity of your cravings (using the scale below) and how you coped with these cravings.

0	10	20	30	40	50	60	70	80	90	100
No craving			Some craving		Moderate craving			High craving		Extreme craving

The following example shows you how to fill out the worksheet, followed by some space for you to complete your own daily record:

Situation/Trigger: Walked into an empty home.

Thought or feeling: I was angry and upset that my wife left without warning. I felt sad as I thought, "It's over," and then told myself, "I need a drink."

Degree of craving: 60% craving

Coping response (what you did or told yourself): I told myself that I don't need a drink and that I can face this situation better without it.

Date: _____

Situation/Trigger: _____
_____

Thoughts or feelings: _____
_____

Degree of craving: _____%

Coping response (what you did or told yourself): _____

_____

Date: _____

Situation/Trigger: _____

_____

Thoughts or feelings: _____

_____

Degree of craving: _____%

Coping response (what you did or told yourself): _____

_____

Date: _____

Situation/Trigger: _____

_____

Thoughts or feelings: _____

_____

Degree of craving: _____%

Coping response (what you did or told yourself): _____

_____

Permission-Giving Beliefs

When cravings are present, clients are more likely to act on these cravings if they listen to permission-giving beliefs, which rationalize the desire to use. These are beliefs such as: "Everyone else is partying, drinking, and getting high," "I'll just have one hit. No one will know," "I deserve this," "I can get back on track tomorrow," or "What's the point? Things are so bad." These beliefs convince clients to yield to their urges. Instead of giving in, clients can learn to talk back to these beliefs with more rational and accurate reframes. For example, the truth is that not everyone is partying (and certainly most are not drunk or high). Similarly, you can remind clients that it is unrealistic for them to believe that they can have just one drink or one hit, because history tells us that one is never enough, and one is never just one. It is also irrelevant whether anyone will know they have used because the negative consequences will still be there and, more importantly, "I will know, and that will destroy what I am working toward and crush my self-esteem. Putting off sobriety for even one minute is only going to make things harder. Things are bad, but things can get worse. Don't use this as an excuse to go down the wrong track." By talking back to the permission-giving beliefs, clients gain back their power.

Instrumental Strategies

If clients listen to their permission-giving beliefs, they then use a variety of instrumental strategies to get access to their drug of choice and act on their urges. For example, they may meet friends for drinks at a bar, go to a party where there are drugs, hang out with a friend who has drug connections, head to the racetrack, or allow the minibar to remain stocked and unlocked. The key point of intervention here is to put obstacles in place that interfere with clients' ability to act on their urge or craving. Make access more challenging by having clients adapt their schedules, change routes, and enlist the help of outside resources, such as sponsors, friends, relatives, or 12-step meetings. Encourage clients to confide in and seek counsel from non-using people. Instead of meeting friends at a bar, they can go to the gym or attend a 12-step meeting. Instead of hanging out with a friend who enables their substance use, they can go to the house of a friend who doesn't party. Instead of heading to the racetrack, they can go to a movie, and instead of allowing the minibar to remain stocked, they can ask for it to be emptied or lock the door and give reception the key.

Lapses or Relapses

If clients ultimately give in to their cravings, this can represent a temporary lapse in their recovery, or it can result in a relapse that involves more prolonged use. It is not uncommon for clients with addiction to experience relapse, as between 40 and 60 percent of people who have been treated for addiction or alcoholism relapse within the first year of treatment (McLellan, Lewis, O'Brien, & Kleber, 2014). However, a lapse does not have to be a never-ending path of destruction. A lapse is a mistake that clients can use as a learning opportunity to strengthen their resolve in working toward sobriety. Work together with your clients to problem solve their setback and pinpoint the issues that facilitated the lapse. Every point on this path is a point of understanding and a point of intervention. It is never too late to intervene and change direction. There is always hope for recovery.

The Cognitive Model of Abuse

Using the cognitive model as a framework, you can map out your clients' path of abuse and identify the various points that led to their recent lapse or relapse. Mapping out this path provides you with the data necessary to intervene and put clients on a path to recovery. Remember, every point on the path is a possible point of intervention.

Returning to the earlier example regarding Jim, a map of his alcohol abuse—with accompanying points of intervention along the way—might look as follows:

1. **Triggering Stimulus:** Without warning, Jim's wife asks for a divorce. He is told that he is no longer welcome on the family vacation and asked to vacate the home.

   > **Intervention:**
   > - Reinforce Jim's ability to cope in the face of stress: "I can accept disappointment when my family doesn't include me, but I don't need to let it turn into depression by entertaining hopeless thoughts. Just because they don't want me there now doesn't mean it will always be that way. If I am sober, the data will speak."
   > - Instead of facing the emptiness of his home, increase Jim's social connectedness (e.g., he can go to the gym, go to the store, visit his mother).

2. **Drug-Related Belief:** "The only way to cope and forget about my lousy situation is to drink."

   > **Intervention:**
   > - Reframe belief: "Drinking will not make this situation go away, but it could make it worse. Staying sober means that I am coping and problem solving, which will eventually repair this situation."
   > - Practice new belief: Drinking is an escape and not an effective way to cope.

3. **Substance-Biased Automatic Thoughts:** "Poor me, I should be with my family on vacation. I shouldn't have to move out. This is so unfair. I don't deserve this."

   > **Intervention:**
   > - Reframe automatic thought: "Given how I have been acting, it is understandable that my wife had enough. I could have hurt someone or even killed someone by driving drunk. The truth is that it took all of this pain to get me to recognize I had a problem. Now that I am working on it, I believe I deserve to be part of my family, and I am going to do everything in my power to make that happen."

4. **Increase in Urges and Cravings:** Jim pictures going to a bar, having a drink, and feeling better.

   > **Intervention:**
   > - Replace positive image with negative image: Jim can picture himself in handcuffs, being dragged into the police car, and sitting alone in a jail cell with no one to call.
   > - Use relaxation or distraction strategies to delay acting on the urge, knowing the urge will pass.

5. **Permission-Giving Beliefs:** "I deserve a drink after all I've been through."

> **Intervention:**
> - Reframe belief: "The DUI has created a hardship, but I can cope. I can find housing near public transit, ride my bike places, use delivery services, and ask others for help. I do feel bad for myself, but I played a big role in creating this problem, and I can make it better or worse. I deserve to be part of my family more than I deserve a drink, and I don't want to sabotage that."

6. **Instrumental Strategies:** He gets in the car and heads to the nearest bar.

> **Intervention:**
> - Engage in alternative activities: Instead of going to the bar, Jim can hit the gym, go to a meeting, and cook a great dinner.

7. **Lapse:** At the bar, Jim orders a drink. Then he orders another drink, and another, and another. At the end of the night, he drives home drunk, where he hits a parked car and gets a DUI.

> **Intervention:**
> - Continue engaging in behaviors that facilitate recovery and affirm the goal of sobriety (e.g., stay in therapy, begin attending 12-step meetings).

You can use the clinician worksheet on the following page to map out the path of abuse for each of your clients, as well as possible intervention points at each point.

Clinician Worksheet

PATH OF ABUSE

• • • • • •

Work with your client to map their specific path for substance use. Then, at each point on the path, record any interventions that could help put your client on an alternate path.

1. Triggering Stimulus: _____

_____

> Intervention: _____
>
> _____
>
> _____

2. Drug-Related Belief: _____

_____

> Intervention: _____
>
> _____
>
> _____

3. Substance-Biased Automatic Thoughts: _____

_____

> Intervention: _____
>
> _____
>
> _____

4. Increase in Urges and Cravings: _____
_____

> **Intervention:** _____
> _____
> _____

5. Permission-Giving Beliefs: _____
_____

> **Intervention:** _____
> _____
> _____

6. Instrumental Strategies: _____
_____

> **Intervention:** _____
> _____
> _____

7. Lapse: _____
_____

> **Intervention:** _____
> _____
> _____

VULNERABILITY TO RELAPSE

Even after clients have been sober for some time, it is still not uncommon for them to be vulnerable to relapse. Some of the most common determinants of relapse include the reemergence of substance-biased automatic thoughts (e.g., thinking that occasional drug or alcohol use is okay) and being exposed to high-risk triggers (e.g., anniversary dates, acute stress, negative news, trauma, illness, interpersonal problems, work problems). It is inevitable that clients will experience thoughts or situations that trigger the urge to use, so it is important to prepare clients for these vulnerabilities ahead of time. Help clients identify and address their vulnerabilities, rather than ignoring them. The key to long-term wellness is not to let clients get discouraged and to use every misstep as an opportunity to fight harder, learn from their mistakes, and accept that they are an addict with recovery as a lifelong crusade. Putting this on a coping card reinforces the learning.

Take the case of Sami, who after almost 18 months of sobriety from crack cocaine decided that occasional crack use might be okay. She contacted a friend and sought out crack using the money she had earned from a new job. She got high, subsequently felt horrible, and immediately came into treatment reporting that she did not want to use. With treatment, she was able to see that this temporary lapse was an opportunity for fortification against substance use. In hindsight, she learned that crack addiction is a lifelong problem that she will never be able to handle. Even one drag is too much because no amount of drags is enough. By reminding herself that there are people in her life who care about her, that she wants to be there for them, and that she doesn't want to jeopardize her comfortable living situation or her rent money, she was able to develop a coping statement that reinforced her commitment to sobriety, "I can do it. I am no longer weak. I am no longer helpless."

Always be on the lookout for drug-related automatic thoughts that perpetuate relapse (e.g., "I just want to go out and be bad. I want to party"), and make sure that clients have the tools to respond to these thoughts with the voice of reason. For example, do clients actually want to be bad? Or is there something else they actually want? What is missing from their lives, and how can they work toward having it? Make sure clients know what behaviors are likely to lead them to trouble (e.g., skipping 12-step meetings, heading to the old neighborhood, attempting to contact substance-abusing friends), and encourage clients to do everything in their power to discontinue those behaviors. Remind them of the downside of their actions and the upside of taking an alternative path.

In addition, be careful not to let erroneous beliefs rule (e.g., "Everyone else is getting away with it" or "Working hard is not paying off"). Remind clients that no one ever really gets away with using because we are all accountable to ourselves. Moreover, life is not a straight line, but a curvy, bumpy road. Sometimes, clients have expectations that recovery will bring all sorts of unrealistic positive change, which leads to disappointment when this does not occur. Instead, help clients focus on the change they can bring to their own life and the changes that have already resulted in gains.

It also helps to have clients regularly examine their cost-benefit analysis of substance use and to continually update that list by adding more and more reasons to abstain. Seeing what their life is like sober versus what it is like under the influence can help solidify their commitment to sobriety. Help clients understand the extent to which sobriety is paying off. Work with them to see all the joys and all that they have accomplished (and are continuing to accomplish) while sober. By identifying all the benefits of leading a sober life, clients are reminded of what they would lose if they were to keep using. Remind clients of the person they want to become, and ask which path will help them get there. No one wants to lose what they have, but we often have to see what we have to appreciate it.

Finally, remind clients that they are not their addiction. Drug abuse is a pattern of behavior that is problematic and often self-defeating, which results in bad outcomes. However, that does not mean that individuals with addiction are intrinsically bad, immoral, or any other self-imposed negative label. Accepting addiction as a problem with (rather than a definition of) their character allows clients to form a more positive view of themselves. For example, when Sami got sober, she believed she was a different person, which caused her to feel like a fake. Therapy helped her to see there was no "old her" and "new her"—there was just her. She was able to learn that she had always been a lovable, capable woman who struggled with the hardship of an addiction. Behaving in accordance with those beliefs helped keep her on the sober path.

In order to help your clients overcome any lapses or relapses—and get them back on the path toward recovery—you can provide them with any of the following coping cards.

Coping Card

DON'T LET A LAPSE BE A RELAPSE

Don't get discouraged! Use any missteps as opportunities to fight harder. Learn from your mistakes. Accept that you are an addict with recovery as a lifelong crusade.

Coping Card

I CAN RESIST THE URGE

Triggers are everywhere. It is not enough to just avoid them, but I can go out of my way and try. When I get a desire or urge to use, I can do the following:

- Avoid the people, places, and things associated with trouble.
- Practice thinking: "I cannot use successfully under any circumstances. Thinking this way maximizes success and maximizes acceptance."
- Remind myself of times when using caused me to feel terrible (e.g., driving to work and trying not to get sick, looking in the mirror at my swollen face, having to confront my children's fear and my wife's sadness).
- Picture a great weekend being sober (e.g., eating a breakfast of pancakes and bacon, having fun with my family, holding my children, being happy).
- Remind myself that being high only feels good for a short time (10–15 minutes) but is associated with negative outcomes that last a whole lot longer (e.g., feeling like crap, unemployment, legal problems, losing family).
- Remember the ugly results of using: alone, sick, no love, no pleasure, no accomplishment, no home, no money, no nothing.

Coping Card

I CAN STAY SOBER

- I don't want to use it.
- Everything must come second to my sobriety.
- I am and have always been a good person.
- I am and have always been capable and likeable.
- I cannot give up. I have to keep working on it.
- Just because I want to use doesn't mean I have to.
- I can survive bad feelings.
- Do the program. It works.
- I cannot do it alone, and that doesn't mean I'm weak.
- Letting others help me makes me smart and strong.
- I am an addict. No excuses.
- Using takes away my power and strength.
- Resisting the urge makes me feel powerful and proud.
- I got this.

9
PERSONALITY DISORDERS, SELF-HARM, AND SUICIDALITY

THE COGNITIVE MODEL OF PERSONALITY DISORDERS

The personality disorders are characterized by an enduring and inflexible pattern of thinking, feeling, and behaving, the onset of which generally begins in adolescence or early adulthood (APA, 2013). According to the cognitive model of personality disorders, individuals with personality disorders maintain a core set of negative beliefs or doubt labels, which lead them to have distorted automatic thoughts in response to the situations that occur around them. These situation-specific automatic thoughts, in turn, activate emotional and physiological distress, and lead to dysfunctional behavior patterns (Beck, Davis, & Freeman, 2015). As a result, individuals with personality disorders exhibit impairments across a variety of occupational, social, and other life domains.

The negative beliefs that characterize the personality disorders are thought to be influenced and sustained by a genetic predisposition in combination with life experiences. In particular, temperamental characteristics observed in the growing child (e.g., clinging behavior, shyness, or rebelliousness) persist through the developmental period of childhood into late adolescence and adulthood (Kagan, 1989), and may find continued expression in specific personality disorders, such as the dependent, avoidant, or other personality (Beck et al., 2015). The continued expression of these patterns of behavior into adulthood is influenced by the fact that our innate tendencies can become accentuated or diminished by our life experiences. For example, if a child is particularly fearful and clings to the parent, then the parent may provide ongoing protection and nurturing, which fuels ideas of dependency.

Therefore, innate predispositions and environmental influences shape our belief systems and the subsequent strategies we employ, but they do not determine them. Not all children who are trepidatious will become non-risk-taking adults. The influence of the messages we receive and the life experiences we have, coupled with our interpretation of these experiences, grow or deflate our early predispositions. For example, a child who cries and clings to the parent while entering preschool might have a parent who stays and comforts them, or a parent who leaves so the child can learn that they can survive on their own. The former situation may reinforce the child's sense of helplessness, whereas the latter may reinforce a sense of independence. On the other hand, a child with a sensitivity to rejection might interpret this situation differently, concluding that they are loved when the parent stays and unloved when the parent leaves.

From a nature-nurture perspective, clients with personality disorders deviate from others in terms of cognition, affect, and motivation (Beck et al., 2015). What differentiates one personality disorder from another is the content of the core beliefs that clients have about themselves, the assumptions under which they operate, and the behavioral actions they typically use (Beck et al., 2015). For example, the key to the histrionic personality is the belief, "I am inadequate and unable to handle life on my own," which is similar to the belief held by dependent clients. However, the manner in which clients cope with that belief is what differentiates the two disorders. Clients diagnosed with dependent personality disorder make their helplessness known and wait for someone to take care of them, while those diagnosed with histrionic personality disorder are more pragmatic in that they actively seek attention and approval to get others to take care of them. The section that follows discusses negative core beliefs across personality disorders in greater detail, as well as how these beliefs lead to problematic assumptions and dysfunctional behaviors.

Personality Disorders and Core Beliefs

The *DSM-5* identifies and organizes 10 different personality disorders, which are grouped into three clusters (APA, 2013). **Cluster A**, which is known as the odd or eccentric cluster, includes schizotypal, paranoid, and schizoid personality disorders. Clients in this cluster tend to have interpersonal difficulties, as their behavior is perceived as peculiar, suspicious, or detached. For example, clients with schizotypal personality disorder exhibit magical thinking and behave in ways that appear odd or unusual, which causes them to have difficulty connecting with others. As a result, they may believe that they are defective, assume hidden motives on the part of others, and exhibit excessive social anxiety. Similarly, clients with paranoid personality disorder may believe that they are vulnerable and assume that others will take advantage of them. As a result, they are overly suspicious of other people and overreact to perceived slights. Finally, those with schizoid personality disorder view themselves as social misfits or loners. They neither want nor take pleasure in close relationships and assume they're better off alone, leading them to detach from social relationships.

Cluster B personality disorders—which include borderline, histrionic, antisocial, and narcissistic personality disorders—are characterized by dramatic and erratic behavior. Clients with these diagnoses tend to experience very intense emotions and engage in a variety of extreme behaviors in response to their dysfunctional beliefs. For example, clients with borderline personality disorder believe they are defective, helpless, vulnerable, and bad. They don't believe they can survive on their own and assume that they will be abandoned by those on whom they depend, which results in volatility in interpersonal relationships. Clients with antisocial personality disorder also believe they are vulnerable, but they assume that they will be hurt or taken advantage of if they do not act first. In turn, they lack empathy and overtly exploit others. Clients with histrionic personality disorder believe they are inadequate and assume that they must be the center of attention to win the approval and affection of others and be taken care of, which leads to a variety of attention-seeking behaviors, such as: being excessively dramatic, dressing or acting seductively, and being overly entertaining to others. Finally, clients with narcissistic personality disorder have an inflated view of themselves, believing that they are superior and special. This superiority and need to be special is validated by their aggrandizing, self-preoccupation, competitiveness, display of outward signs of status, need to be right, and solicitation of special treatment from others. However, when they fail to be superior or are not regarded as special, then underlying beliefs of inferiority and unimportance are activated.

Cluster C personality disorders—which include dependent, obsessive-compulsive, and avoidant personality disorders—are characterized by a sense of pervasive anxiety or fear. For example, clients with dependent personality disorder believe that they are helpless and assume that they will fail if they rely on themselves. In turn, they depend excessively on other people to meet their needs. In contrast, clients with obsessive-compulsive personality disorder maintain erroneous beliefs that they are competent while others are not, leading them to assume that their world will go out of control if they delegate to others or fail to meet their own self-imposed standards. As a result, they are preoccupied with orderliness, perfectionism, and control. Finally, clients with avoidant personality disorder believe that they are unlovable and inadequate. They cannot tolerate discomfort and cannot bear to be disliked or rejected. Because they assume that others will reject them if they know the "real" them, they avoid intimacy and situations that they fear would result in criticism from others.

Although the personality disorders are largely characterized by differing core beliefs, comorbidities between personality disorders are common, and clients often meet criteria for one or more additional personality disorders

(APA, 2013). In addition, because some personality disorders share similar symptoms, it is often difficult to determine the type of personality disorder without a thorough evaluation. For example, clients with histrionic and narcissistic personality disorder both desire to be the center of attention, but those who are histrionic are more willing to act subservient to maintain attention, while those who are narcissistic will sacrifice attention to maintain their sense of superiority. Similarly, clients with histrionic and borderline personality disorder both show labile and dramatic emotions, but those with borderline personality are more likely to exhibit self-destructive behaviors and extreme discomfort with strong affect.

To further illustrate how negative core beliefs, problematic assumptions, and dysfunctional behaviors arise in the context of personality disorders, consider the case of Rob, who from birth was very sensitive to the environment. He was colicky as a baby, had chronic ear infections requiring tubes, was sensitive to any noise or light when sleeping, and did not like to be left alone. Rob was in sharp contrast to his older siblings who shared none of his sensitivities, slept through anything, and were happy to be left alone to entertain themselves. Despite these differences, Rob's parents treated him no differently than his siblings, leaving him in childcare, signing him up for activities, and giving him social and academic independence. Rob struggled to maintain these expectations, leading his parents to see him as the "challenging one" and causing him to assume that he was not worthwhile because no one tried to take care of his needs.

Rob's biologically sensitive predisposition and desire to be connected to others at all times put him out of sorts with his autonomous family. As a result, his self-doubt grew, and he became convinced that he was incapable of doing things alone, further reinforcing his global sense of helplessness. Not wanting to be left alone, he passively went along with what everyone else wanted, even when doing so caused him distress. Rather than speaking up about his needs, he found ways to manipulate the situation by being late or unprepared. Rob believed that this was the only way to get his needs met, as he assumed that if he outright asked for anything then he would be rejected and denied. In this example, Rob's dependent personality was shaped by both his genetic predisposition to be connected to others and his life experiences of being part of a household that did not share his needs. His manipulative and passive strategies worked against him, fueling constant distress and compromising his ability to function.

KEY TREATMENT COMPONENTS

Although empirical research is limited, a growing body of evidence shows that CBT can be effective for personality disorders (Beck et al., 2015). The goal of treatment is to help clients reduce their distress and increase their level of functioning by modifying their exaggerated, pervasive, and negative core beliefs into more accurate self-concepts and by changing their ineffective compensatory actions into more effective behaviors. Clients with personality disorders tend to rely on the same overdeveloped compensatory behaviors, even when these strategies prove ineffective time and time again. With treatment, clients can learn to detach themselves from these overdeveloped strategies and build alternative behavioral strategies that are more effective in nature. For example, clients with histrionic personality disorder can learn self-discipline and control instead of exhibitionism, whereas those with obsessive-compulsive personality disorder can learn to increase spontaneity instead of just seeking control. Across all the personality disorders, the goal is to help clients develop close and intimate relationships, increase self-confidence, grow self-efficacy and functionality, and build a larger repertoire of effective action options.

Similar to standard CBT for depression and anxiety, CBT for personality disorders is a goal-directed treatment that uses structured techniques, with an emphasis on self-help homework and the use of evidence gathering and hypotheses testing. However, unlike traditional CBT, which emphasizes a more collaborative therapeutic relationship, the use of empathic confrontation can also be used as a vehicle for change in the treatment of personality disorders. In particular, once a therapeutic alliance and trust have been established, the therapist can use empathic confrontation to more assertively stretch clients' cognitive capacities in relation to their unhelpful beliefs. For example, consider a client with avoidant personality disorder who has been in therapy for over a year but still continues to call himself worthless and a failure despite overwhelming evidence to the contrary. Instead of guiding the client to examine the evidence, as would be characteristic of more traditional CBT, the therapist may reiterate all the data that has been collected and directly point out that the client's view of himself does not fit with the facts.

Additionally, empathic confrontation can involve using data from the therapeutic relationship itself to help modify clients' unhelpful beliefs. For example, if a client makes the claim that no one cares about her, then the therapist can point out that he is always there for her, answers her calls, finds appointment times that work, and gives her undivided attention and effort in session, which is evidence that he cares and that the client's hypothesis cannot be totally true.

In addition to the use of empathic confrontation, CBT for personality disorders also differs from traditional CBT in that it is often lengthier, and there is a greater emphasis on pertinent historical factors that affect the client and the treatment. The section that follows discusses some of the main treatment components when working with personality disorders from a CBT framework.

Establish Goals

Vague goals mean vague therapy, and this is particularly true in the treatment of personality disorders. When clients' problems become chronic, many spheres of their life may be impacted, which can make it challenging to find focus. Imagine a client with a diagnosis of narcissistic personality disorder who is depressed amid a nasty divorce, fighting for access to his children, on probation at work for his volatile behavior, struggling with finances, and living in a hotel. Without clear goals for treatment, every session can become a time to gripe about all that is going wrong in his life. Instead, prioritizing clear goals can help therapy be more productive in alleviating his distress and improving functionality. If the therapist and client collaboratively decide that keeping his job is his top priority, then the focus might be on addressing his anger and curbing his dysfunctional aggressive behavior.

In addition, clients with personality disorders often interpret situations in extreme ways, which increases the likelihood that they will turn every situation into a crisis and exhibit extreme emotional, behavioral, and physiological reactions in response. When this occurs, therapy can easily become a series of emergency sessions focused on putting out fires each time the client comes in. This is especially common when working with clients with borderline personality disorder, for whom therapy might become a conversation of each week's injustice, abuse, abandonment, or failure instead of a time to build skills and grow a healthier self-concept. Defining which issue is most pressing to the client in the hierarchy of concerns can help establish clear goals and allow for cumulative learning.

For clients with borderline personality disorder, fear of abandonment might be at the top of the problem list because this fear has allowed them to stay in an abusive relationship, has kept them isolated from potential outside support, and has reinforced their low self-concept of being unloved. Once clients have identified overcoming this fear of abandonment as a treatment goal, then the therapist can link this goal to other areas of concern (e.g., evaluating whether staying in the relationship makes sense, reducing their fears of connecting to others, and growing a more positive, reasonable view of themselves). Although it may not be possible to evoke change in one goal without working on the others, the focus in any given session is now clearly defined.

In the beginning stages of treatment, the primary focus should be on symptom reduction and improving coping skills, especially if the client presents with more acute comorbid problems, such as PTSD, depression, or anxiety. For example, a client with dependent personality disorder and comorbid PTSD may need to address any intrusive trauma memories and avoidance before addressing core beliefs of helplessness and dependency. Similarly, a client with narcissistic personality disorder and depression may need behavioral activation if he is unable to mobilize himself to go to work or participate in social activities. Or, a client with avoidant personality disorder, social anxiety, and panic disorder may need to address the fear of bodily harm before tackling issues of self-concept or social avoidance. Once clients have addressed these more acute symptoms, they can then work on more targeted CBT interventions directed at their personality disorder issues. Identifying a clear problem list and a specific set of goals ensures that therapy keeps moving along.

Given that modifying clients' negative core beliefs is necessary for sustained recovery after symptom reduction, their doubt label needs to be identified on the problem list. The next step is to make sure that clients have a clear understanding of their doubt conceptualization, which means that they know exactly what their doubt label is, the factors that contribute to its development, and how it serves to perpetuate their ineffective compensatory behaviors. You can use the "Doubt Conceptualization Model" from Chapter 2 (page 28) to gain a comprehensive understanding of the client's doubt formulation.

Increase Motivation and Develop Buy-In

Once you have worked to uncover how life experiences have shaped the development of a client's doubt label, operating guidelines or assumptions, and ineffective compensatory actions, the next step is to discuss motivation to change. Many clients fear change, and although they are suffering, suffering is a known commodity, whereas change is the scary unknown. Take time to appreciate the anxiety that people feel when their sense of self is called into question.

In order to increase motivation for change, one strategy is to ask clients to consider the advantages and disadvantages of modifying their doubt label versus not changing it. Completing this cost-benefit analysis helps make a case for why working toward change makes sense. Hopefully, the pros of change and the costs of not changing outweigh any reasons to keep the doubt label. As an example, consider the case of Ali, a client with avoidant personality disorder who is afraid of being hurt and rejected. Ali's belief that she doesn't matter fuels her fear and perpetuates her avoidance of social situations, where she thinks she may be judged. Although she is dysphoric as a result of her loneliness, she is unwilling to put herself out there and face rejection. Before any behavior change can happen, Ali first has to be willing to work on changing her belief that she doesn't matter, or fear will prevail and avoidance will continue. The following example illustrates Ali's cost-benefit analysis of working to modify the doubt label "I don't matter."

Advantages of Changing My Doubt Label	**Disadvantages of Changing My Doubt Label**
1. Go after the things I want	1. Might feel anxious
2. Boost my self-esteem	2. Might make someone mad
3. Get my needs met	3. Won't have an excuse to not take care of myself
4. Have the courage to say "no"	
5. Stop fearing rejection	
Advantages of Keeping My Doubt Label	**Disadvantages of Keeping My Doubt Label**
1. Don't have to face anxiety	1. Will never have the things I want
2. Avoid others being mad at me	2. Will always feel badly about myself
	3. Will never get my needs met
	4. Will never be able to say no
	5. Will live in fear of rejection and abandonment

Often, the disadvantages of change are imaginary or exaggerated, and they can be addressed through objective, guided questioning. Therefore, once clients have listed the pros and cons of change, the next step is to examine and reframe the disadvantages of change so that you can minimize clients' anxiety and solidify a commitment to change. Work with clients to develop an overall conclusion regarding the importance of change. For example, returning to Ali's example of the doubt label "I don't matter," a reframe and accompanying conclusion might look as follows:

Disadvantages of Changing My Doubt Label	Reframe
1. Might feel anxious	1. I might feel anxious, but it will be temporary.
2. Might make someone mad	2. Most likely no one will be mad, and if they are, so what?
3. Won't have an excuse to not take care of myself	3. It is time to take care of myself. I don't need any excuses not to.

Overall Conclusion: Although change might be uncomfortable, the advantages to working on modifying my doubt is worth it in the long run.

The following page contains a worksheet you can use with your clients to engage in a cost-benefit analysis regarding the advantages and disadvantages of modifying or not modifying their doubt label.

Client Worksheet

COST-BENEFIT ANALYSIS OF CHANGING MY DOUBT LABEL

• • • • • •

It can be difficult to consider making changes to your life, even when you know that such changes might be in your best interest. Use this worksheet to examine the costs and benefits of changing your doubt label versus not changing it. Once you have identified any disadvantages to modifying your doubt label, reframe these disadvantages into a more realistic statement so you can develop a more balanced conclusion regarding the importance of change.

Advantages of Changing My Doubt Label	**Disadvantages of Changing My Doubt Label**
_____	_____
_____	_____
_____	_____
_____	_____

Advantages of Keeping My Doubt Label	**Disadvantages of Keeping My Doubt Label**
_____	_____
_____	_____
_____	_____
_____	_____

Once you have identified the pros and cons of working to modify your doubt label, reframe these disadvantages into a more realistic statement.

Disadvantages of Changing My Doubt Label		Reframe
1. _____ _____	→	1. _____ _____
2. _____ _____	→	2. _____ _____
3. _____ _____	→	3. _____ _____
4. _____ _____	→	4. _____ _____
5. _____ _____	→	5. _____ _____

What's your overall conclusion about working toward change? _____
_____

Build a Confident Self-View

Examine the Data

Whether clients embrace one negative core belief or have a variety of negative beliefs, all of these beliefs are hypotheses and not facts. Try to keep in mind that these beliefs were fueled by how clients *perceived* their history, not by the history itself. Therefore, building self-confidence involves helping clients recognize that negative self-beliefs are never 100 percent true, nor are they true 100 percent of the time. Sometimes, the belief is completely false (e.g., "I am a failure") and the opposite is true (e.g., "I am a success"). More often, it is likely that a more reasonable belief is true (e.g., "I am not a complete failure" or "I'm okay"). Helping clients examine the data for and against their doubt label is the most crucial step in building a new, more accurate positive view of themselves (Sokol & Fox, 2009).

Although you can use either current or historical data as a means of testing a client's doubt hypothesis, it is easier to start with current information that supports a new, more positive belief. You also can collect data that, on the surface, *seems* to support their old belief while acknowledging that there is an alternative, and perhaps more accurate, viewpoint regarding that data. Take the case of Deja, who has obsessive-compulsive personality disorder. She sees herself as responsible for everyone and everything, and she holds herself accountable for getting everything done perfectly. She views mistakes, flaws, or shortcomings as an indicator of catastrophe and life spiraling out of control. Unable to live up to these unreasonable standards, she always falls short of her ideal, which leads her to think that she is a bad person. In therapy, Deja has been evaluating the negative belief that she is a "bad person" and has been working on developing a new belief that she is a "decent person." The following reflects the evidence that she has collected in support of the new belief, followed by a new perspective regarding the evidence that *seemed* to support the old belief.

Evidence That Supports Deja's New Belief

1. My friend asked me to watch her young son while she went to a doctor's appointment.
2. I volunteered to help my sister with her daughter's birthday party even though I was exhausted.
3. I didn't hold a grudge when my friend didn't tell me her secret.
4. I offered to help my friend with her garden.

Evidence That Seems to Support Deja's Old Belief, with a New Perspective

1. I want to go back to work instead of staying at home with my baby, but that doesn't mean I am bad. It means that I want to work outside the home, and that is a reasonable thing for a woman to do. My husband never considered not working.
2. I told my friend that I was too busy to have lunch with her, because I actually was too busy, and she understands. Besides, there will be other opportunities to see her. We have been friends for a long time and have gone out many other times.
3. I had a negative opinion of my friend's outfit, but I kept my opinion to myself, and it doesn't make me a bad person if I have a fashion opinion.
4. I made a mistake on my papers at work, but it doesn't make me a bad person. It just makes me human, as people make mistakes—and, in truth, no serious consequences resulted.

Use the following worksheet to help clients collect data for their new belief and reframe the evidence for their old belief. Always start by doing this work together in session and then asking the client to continue to collect data on their own.

Client Worksheet

BUILD A CONFIDENT BELIEF

• • • • • •

Don't let self-doubt define you. Use this worksheet to build a more confident self-view by identifying evidence in support of a more positive, accurate, and realistic view of yourself. List any characteristics, features, compliments, feedback, roles, and strengths that support this new, confident you. In addition, list any evidence that *seems* to still support the old belief, but reframe this evidence with a more accurate and objective understanding. Examples are provided below, followed by some blank spaces for you to fill in your own.

Evidence that supports the new, confident belief of "I'm likeable":

1. Sam and Zach texted me.
2. Dylan asked me to play pickle ball.
3. Liv asked me to be part of her group project.
4. Some of my friends included me in their plans for this weekend.

Evidence that seems to support the old belief of "I'm unlikable":

1. I felt uncomfortable striking up a conversation with someone I knew at the coffee shop, but that doesn't make me unlikable. It just means I'm shy.
2. I turned red when my boss asked me why I was late this morning, but that makes me human, not unlikable.
3. I sent an awkward text about plans for this weekend, but no one seemed to notice and it didn't get in the way of the plans happening.

Evidence that supports the new, confident belief of _____:

1. _____
2. _____
3. _____
4. _____

Evidence that seems to support the old belief of _____, but with a new perspective:

1. _____
2. _____
3. _____
4. _____

You also can help clients gain a more accurate perspective regarding their biased doubt beliefs by pointing out the stark differences between their extreme conclusion and the facts. For example, Jen has dependent personality disorder and believes she is incompetent. She thinks she is an especially incompetent mother. She believes she needs around-the-clock support to mother her children, as she thinks that she cannot handle it on her own. In this case, Jen's neediness comes from her failure to recognize how many things she actually does effectively handle. As the therapist, you can help her gain a new perspective by engaging in a collaborative discussion regarding the definitions of an incompetent mother (e.g., one who deprives her children of food, shelter, and clothing to feed her drug habit or allows her children to be sexually abused for drug money—or to a lesser extreme, one who is unable to shop, prepare food, or provide transit for her children). You can also have Jen compare herself against the criteria for a competent mother (e.g., one who takes care of her children, puts them first, meets all their needs) to help her recognize that she meets those same criteria.

At the same time, you can work with Jen to accept that she is not perfect, which means that she can occasionally slip and yell at her kids, or she can decide to sit on the sofa instead of playing with them sometimes, and she is still a competent mother. Most importantly, she can learn to recognize that she doesn't need help by her side all the time if she believes in her competence. Viewing behavior along a continuum allows clients to measure themselves more reasonably, which serves to increase self-confidence. The following is an example of Jen's coping card, in which she reframes her beliefs about herself along a continuum.

Jen's Coping Card

I can be lazy at times and still be a competent person.

I can lack patience sometimes and still be a competent person.

I am a competent person even if I fall short.

I have permission not to be perfect.

I can accept help when it is offered and still be competent.

These reminders keep Jen from believing that she is an incompetent person every time she is irritable with her kids, more impatient then she would like to be, or doesn't deal with stress as well as she would like. For homework, you might instruct Jen to remind herself of these new conclusions and to choose new behavioral actions in support of her gained self-confidence.

Jen's Homework

1. Tell myself: "I am a competent person, but I am not perfect."
2. Accept that I can be cranky and still be a competent person, but I can work on reducing my crankiness by better managing my stress in the following ways:
   - Accepting childcare help at times, but recognize that I don't need it around the clock
   - Reducing my hours at work
   - Coming to therapy

Brain Versus the Gut

It is not uncommon for clients to tell you that they intellectually understand this new belief but that the new view of themselves doesn't feel true. This is understandable because they have spent most of their lives filtering in data to support their negative self-view and ignoring, distorting, or minimizing data to the contrary. Accepting the positive aspects about themselves takes a lot of time and rehearsal. The key is for clients to put their rational brain in charge, rather than letting their subjective "gut" feelings take over. Therefore, once you have worked with clients to gather evidence in support of their more positive self-view, have clients practice talking back to their gut. For this exercise, it is helpful to have clients play both the brain and the gut; if they get stuck, you can make suggestions to help the brain along. The following is an example of a client talking back to their gut with their brain.

Brain: "I am not a failure."

Gut: "But I am having trouble conceiving another child."

Brain: "Getting pregnant is not the definition of success or failure. I am not a failure; I have a good job."

Gut: "But I didn't finish college."

Brain: "It's true that I didn't finish a four-year college, but I did complete a two-year program and now have a good job, earn good money, and am highly respected in my position."

Gut: "But I am not as successful as my sister."

Brain: "She might make more money than I do, but I am more successful than she is in my home life. I am a good mom, wife, and daughter. My parents are proud of me, people say nice things about me, and I get a lot more positive feedback than my high-achieving sister who is getting a divorce."

Gut: "But I have anxiety, and that makes me a failure."

Brain: "It's no wonder I have anxiety with the nightmare I had living with my ailing grandmother. Besides, I am managing my anxiety and not running away from it."

Brain Concludes: "It is my unreliable, emotional gut that is telling me I am a failure and that I am vulnerable. My brain tells me that is not true. There are piles of evidence to the contrary. I have to start acknowledging and accepting the evidence that I am not a failure and, in many ways, am truly a success!"

Historical Review of the Evidence

Sometimes, a current review of the evidence is not enough to modify a client's self-doubt, and when this occurs, an examination of historical evidence is in order. Keep in mind that many of the conclusions that clients believe about themselves are a result of personalizing and misinterpreting historical data in support of their self-doubt. Given that personality disorders are defined by their chronicity and pervasiveness, understanding the impact of early life experiences is critical in working with these clients. Imagine a mother who hits her child and tells him that he is a good-for-nothing loser, or a father who walks away from his son and wife only to start a new family in another state. When children take these situations personally, they tend to believe that it means something about them as a person. The child whose mother beat him and told him he was a loser comes to believe that he is a loser. He may also embrace aggression and disregard for others as reasonable strategies, in turn fueling the potential for an antisocial personality to develop. Similarly, the child whose father abandoned him for another family comes to believe that he is unloved and unwanted. Fearing vulnerable to rejection, he avoids getting close to others or asking for what he wants, which reinforces his belief that he is unwanted and unloved, and perpetuates the growth of the avoidant personality.

Therapy can help clients see these events through another and often more accurate lens. Perhaps the mother who hit her child had severe mental illness herself, and her paranoia made her think her child was lying, so she lashed out in fear. Maybe the father had an unhealthy codependent relationship with his wife, and the only way to protect himself was to move away even at the expense of his child. In both cases, considering this alternative view can help clients externalize the situation so they do not ascribe as much personal meaning to it. By taking a new look at historical data, clients can formulate new conclusions about the impact of their history on their self-view.

Although you can examine historical evidence at any point, it is helpful to ask clients about the earliest memories that are linked to their self-doubt and to systematically move forward in time, collecting all the historical events linked to their self-view. Taking a second look at these events means examining the evidence that seems to support clients' negative self-doubt and coming up with an alternative viewpoint that helps them draw a more realistic conclusion. It also involves pointing out any evidence that directly contradicts the negative self-doubt.

Take the example of Harlow, who held the belief that she was "bad" because her father always yelled at her, called her nasty names, and physically abused her, while never mistreating her younger sister. Her mom never protected her or took her side. Harlow also reported being bullied at school and having few, if any, real friends. On the other hand, she was a good student who took excellent care of her baby sister, seemed to be well liked by her teachers, helped around the house by doing much of the cooking and cleaning, and was an overall terrific child.

Reviewing her history helped Harlow see that her dad's behavior was not about her but a reflection of his drinking problem and the violence it unleashed. Her mother's inability to protect her came from a place of self-preservation, as she was disabled with anxiety. Her dad did not abuse her younger sister because he did not notice her and thus neglected her. While the kids at school did tend to make fun of Harlow, this was because she rejected them. Harlow feared to let anyone near her home owing to the fear of her father's wrath, so she kept others away and declined invitations. After looking over all the evidence, Harlow learned that her belief that she was a bad person made no sense, as the data indicated that she was and is an exceptionally good and responsible person. In fact, she was so excessively responsible that she developed symptoms consistent with a diagnosis of obsessive-compulsive personality disorder.

Use the following worksheet to help your clients evaluate their interpretations of their history. Direct them to list all the historical evidence they have used to confirm their negative doubt label, and then try looking at the evidence from another perspective. See what alternative conclusions they can make.

Client Worksheet

CAPTURE INTERPRETATIONS OF HISTORY

• • • • •

Our history does not necessarily define us; rather, it is our interpretation of that history that we let define us. Think back to events in your life that you retain vivid memories of, or events that you believe played a significant role in your life, and see if you can link these events to the development of your self-doubt.

1. What is your doubt label? (This label reflects the negative core belief(s) that you have about yourself as a person.)

   _____

   _____

   _____

2. What is the historical evidence that supports this belief? (This evidence might include memories of trauma, messages you received, interpersonal conflicts, housing or financial difficulties, sibling issues, stressors in the home, rejections, etc.)

   _____

   _____

   _____

3. What is the historical evidence that contradicts this belief? (Think about the many different areas of your life that reflect your aptitudes, accomplishments, interests, goals achieved, positive messages received, etc.)

   _____

   _____

   _____

4. What are alternative explanations for the evidence you found in support of the negative belief? (Think back on every piece of evidence you listed in item 2, and consider a way of looking at this historical data differently. Consider it from a more mature perspective, how someone else might look at it, what the objective facts imply, etc.)

_____

_____

_____

5. What is a new conclusion that supports a more positive self-view? (Given all the data, what is the most positive, realistic perspective?)

_____

_____

_____

Modify Doubt Beliefs Through Imagery

Once you have worked with clients to reframe evidence in support of their doubt belief into a healthier viewpoint, an advanced technique is to subsequently rescript the historical event through imagery. To do so, take clients back to a time when a memory or image evoked the doubt belief. Have them close their eyes and describe the memory in as great detail as possible so they can relive the experience. Elicit the emotions, automatic thoughts, and core beliefs that were triggered by this situation. As clients stay with the memory, facilitate cognitive restructuring by having clients engage in a dialogue with another person that enters the image. This can be an older version of themselves who comes in or an outside ally, like a therapist or a friend. The following is a sample transcript in which the therapist aids the client in gaining a new and more confident self-view by introducing the client's older self into the memory.

Therapist: "Can you remember an early memory when you felt that you were bad and worthless?"

Client: "I remember being a little girl, I was only five or six, and I was playing with my favorite doll in my room when my older brother's friend came into my room."

Therapist: "What happened?"

Client: "He pushed me into the closet and shut the door. It was so dark that I couldn't see, and he was squishing me. I couldn't breathe. He was hurting me."

Therapist: "What are you thinking?"

Client: "I'm a bad little girl. I'm bad. I'm dirty. I'm worthless."

Therapist: "Now imagine that 'big you' comes into your room. She opens the closet door and sees you. What does 'big you' do?"

Client: "'Big me' grabs him and pulls him off me. She pushes him out of the room."

Therapist: "Imagine that you are helping her push him out of the room and telling him to get out of here. Yell it: 'Get out of here!'"

Client: "Get out of here."

Therapist: "Even louder."

Client: "Get out of here!"

Therapist: "It looks like he is running away. Does 'big you' want to comfort 'little you'?"

Client: "Yes."

Therapist: "Why don't you have 'big you' hug 'little you.' What does 'big you' want to tell 'little you'?"

Client: "You are not a bad girl. You are not dirty. You are not worthless. He is the bad boy. He was bigger and stronger than you, and 'little you' was overpowered. You are a good girl; he is a bad boy."

Therapist: "Are you a good girl? Are you worthwhile?"

Client: "I am a good girl; I am worthwhile!"

If you do cognitive restructuring through imagery, make sure you have prepared clients by first examining and reframing the evidence for their doubt belief through verbal dialogue. That way, when they are facing the image, they are prepared to see the alternative, more accurate conclusion. In addition, it is important that the imagery exercise comes to a resolution. To do so, make sure to finish the memory in its entirety so that new learning can take place and clients can realize that they are no longer in harm's way. Fully processing the imagery allows clients to recognize the distortions inherent in their doubt beliefs, and it also reinforces their new, positive beliefs.

Fuel the New Belief

In order for clients to continue to grow their self-confidence and to prevent self-doubt from biasing how they process information, it is important for them to pay attention to data that supports their new, more realistic self-view (Sokol & Fox, 2009). Helping clients confirm their new, confident beliefs can happen by removing the negative filter, seeking new confirming data, and rehearsing the positive message. The following handout provides a number of ways that clients can collect data to confirm a more confident self-view regarding their competency and desirability.

Client Handout

FUEL THE NEW BELIEF DATA

• • • • •

To further grow and sustain your self-confidence, learn to pay attention to confirming information that supports your new, realistic, and positive belief. Use this handout to collect data that confirms your competency and desirability.

Confirm beliefs about competency by doing the following:

1. Objectively evaluating your school, work, or recreational performance and recording the facts (e.g., verbal or written feedback, work bonuses, responsibilities given to you, promotions, solicitation of your knowledge).

2. Recording any compliments, thank-yous, or praise you have recently received.

3. Asking yourself if any complaints, reprimands, or grievances have been filed against you, and, if so, if any of those actions are a result of outside factors.

4. Asking yourself if you have recently handled any stressors, problems, or difficult tasks.

5. Asking yourself how much you accomplished today and if you had to multitask at times.

6. Asking yourself what responsibilities, chores, or tasks you took care of today or this week.

Confirm beliefs about desirability by doing the following:

1. Noting any compliments, praise, or thank-yous you have received for being there for another person.

2. Asking yourself if you have any plans with friends or relatives, or if you have received an invite for an upcoming gathering.

3. Noting if anyone has called, texted, emailed, or snapped you.

4. Asking yourself if you have recently been a good friend by being considerate, kind, generous, thoughtful, or caring.

5. Noting whether you have reached out to a friend or relative, and observing how they responded or reacted.

6. Asking yourself what you like in other people and considering which of those qualities you possess.

Confidence Logs

The use of confidence logs is another way for clients to collect data to fuel self-confidence. Confidence logs are daily recordings of experiences and feedback that support clients' new, more realistic self-view. The logs are intended to filter in positive information and move clients away from focusing on negative data that support their old doubt label. More general logs can be used to track evidence that makes clients feel good about themselves, or more specific logs can be used to track evidence that supports a new belief (e.g., "I am strong," "I am capable," "I am desirable").

For example, consider a client with avoidant personality disorder, who is working on accepting the new belief that she is "a desirable package." First, the therapist and client could work together to come up with descriptive terms that are consistent with being a desirable package (e.g., being loyal, down to earth, funny, considerate, generous, etc.). After looking at this list, the client may conclude that she has many of these qualities and that she actually meets her definition of desirability. For homework, she might complete a log titled "I'm a desirable package," where she records data every day in support of this belief, especially evidence that supports her definition of what makes people desirable. The following is an example of what the client might record in her log.

"I'm a Desirable Package" Log

Day 1
1. I was invited to a potluck at my neighbor's house.
2. People asked me to join them at their table at back-to-school night.
3. Two people laughed at my joke.
4. I shared my lunch with a friend who forgot hers.

Day 2
1. I offered to cover a shift for someone at work so they could go to their child's game.
2. I invited a neighbor and her son over for a play date, and she said "yes."
3. A neighbor called me and asked if I wanted to join her book club.
4. A stranger smiled at me and gave me a big "hello."

The worksheet on page 205 contains a self-confidence log that you can give clients to collect data in support of their new, more positive self-view. If you are developing a diagnosis-specific log with your client, the following are some suggestions that you can consider when developing a title for the log.

Cluster A	Cluster B	Cluster C
Paranoid Personality • I am tough. • I am resilient. • I am safe. • I am okay. • I am capable. • I am strong.	**Antisocial Personality** • I am not invincible. • I can be considerate. • I can be empathetic. • I can show that I care. • I can follow the rules.	**Avoidant Personality** • I am competent. • I am desirable. • I am cool. • I am likeable. • I am lovable. • I am socially capable. • I am strong.
Schizoid Personality • I can be part of the crowd. • I am can be a team player. • I can share. • I can join in.	**Borderline Personality** • I am supported. • I have control. • I am not defective. • I am lovable. • I am not bad. • I am not powerless. • I am resilient.	**Dependent Personality** • I am strong. • I am capable. • I am competent. • I am independent. • I am not helpless. • I am powerful.
Schizotypal Personality • I am safe. • I am real. • I am strong. • I am resilient. • I am like everyone else.	**Histrionic Personality** • I am able to reign it in. • I am in control. • I am liked. • I am wanted even without my jokes or glamour. **Narcissistic Personality** • I matter. • I am cared for. • I am okay and that's okay. • I am not superior or inferior but good as I am. • I am capable of empathy.	**Obsessive-Compulsive Personality** • I am responsible. • I am powerful. • I am capable. • I don't have to be perfect. • I don't need to have complete control.

Client Worksheet

SELF-CONFIDENCE LOG

• • • • • •

In order to fuel your new self-confidence, keep a daily log of evidence that confirms your more positive and realistic self-view. First, give your log a title. It can either be a general title about growing a more positive self-view (e.g., "My Feel-Good Log"), or you can make it more specific (e.g., "I am _____ [capable/competent/strong/lovable/etc.] Log"). Then, list several things each day that build your self-confidence. Most importantly, regularly read through all the data you have collected so that your new self-view sinks in.

"_____" **Log**

Day 1

1. _____
2. _____
3. _____
4. _____

Day 2

1. _____
2. _____
3. _____
4. _____

Day 3

1. _____
2. _____
3. _____
4. _____

Confidence-Building Cards

Confidence-building cards, which contain coping statements that remind clients of the evidence in support of their new self-view, are another way to reinforce confidence. By having the coping statement written on a card or typed out on a digital screen, clients have the facts readily available in front of them, which keeps their mind from twisting information in support of a more biased viewpoint. Here are some strategies to help clients make use of their confidence-building cards, followed by some sample confidence-building statements for each personality disorder.

1. Clients can put the cards in their bathroom (e.g., posted on the mirror or sitting by the sink) and review the cards as they brush their teeth in the morning.
2. Clients can keep the cards in their wallet, purse, or back pocket and pull them out whenever they find themselves waiting around.
3. Clients can use the statements as a screen saver on their computer.
4. Clients can type the statement into the notes section of their phone.
5. Clients can text themselves the coping statement to refer to whenever they need a confidence-boosting reminder.
6. Clients can save the statements in a file on their computer.
7. Clients can write the statements on sticky notes and post them everywhere.
8. Clients can place the confidence-building cards in drawers around their home and office so they have lots of opportunities to review them.
9. Clients can leave themselves a voicemail on their phone or answering service and listen to the message whenever they check for messages.

Confidence-Building Statements

Cluster A

Paranoid Personality
- I can trust some people, especially if I have known them a long time and they have never betrayed me.
- I am safe. I can remind myself of all the things that protect me and all the people who are looking out for me.
- I am tougher than I realize. I can go out and participate in the things I want.

Schizoid Personality
- Join the crowd. It might pay off, and I might actually get more out of the experience than I predict.
- Try being a team player, as it has the potential to make things easier for me.
- I don't have to fully join in to participate. I can just go and be there with everyone.

Schizotypal Personality
- Even though it feels like I am not real, I need to remind myself that I am.
- I am safe unless there is real danger that I can identify.
- I am like everyone else even though it feels like I am totally different.
- No two people are the same, and being different is the definition of being human.

Cluster B

Antisocial Personality
- I can follow the rules and not be a sap, especially if it gets me closer to what I really want.
- I am not invincible. If I break the rules, then the consequences might be more than I can handle.
- I can try being considerate and showing some empathy. Even if I don't get any immediate results, I do get the satisfaction of knowing that I am in control of myself.

Borderline Personality
- Just because someone isn't physically there for me doesn't mean I've been abandoned.
- I am supported even if it's not 24/7. Besides, I can do it alone some of the time.
- Not all people can be trusted, but some can.
- I can mess up and still be a good person, especially if I recognize that I messed up and am willing to work on making things better.
- It is never too late to repair damage.
- I am not helpless, but if I keep avoiding, then I will never believe that.

Histrionic Personality
- I don't have to be funny or dramatic all the time for people to like me. People like me for me without all the frills.
- I can let loose some of the time but not all of the time.
- Having dignity and being in control makes me feel stronger and more powerful.
- I can count on the people who care about me even if I am not entertaining them all the time.

Narcissistic Personality
- I cannot be the most important person to everyone all the time, even though that is what I want.
- Other people have needs too, and just because I acknowledge that doesn't mean I don't matter.
- People do care about me even if they don't give me everything I want.
- I don't have to take everything so personally. Sometimes what happens has nothing to do with me, sometimes it has a little to do with me, and sometimes it has a lot to do with me. Either way, I don't need to overreact. I can think about what I want in the long run.

Cluster C

Avoidant Personality
- I am desirable even if someone doesn't want to date me, cheats on me, or isn't interested in taking the relationship as far as I would like to.
- I can tolerate distress. I am stronger than I realize. Even though it feels like I can't bear unpleasant feelings, I can.
- So what if I get rejected? I will survive, and the only way I have a chance of getting what I want is to put myself out there. Go for it.
- I am good enough exactly as I am.

Dependent Personality
- I can do things on my own.
- It feels hard, but that doesn't mean I can't do it.
- I am more capable than I give myself credit for.
- I can try and tackle it, and if I can't achieve the outcome I want, then I can always ask for help later.
- If I am counting on someone else, then I may never achieve my goals or do the things I want.

Obsessive-Compulsive Personality
- It's okay if someone doesn't do it exactly the way I want in the time I want. Don't make it a problem if it isn't.
- I don't have to take control of everything and every detail.
- Being spontaneous sometimes doesn't mean I am not responsible, or that things are going to unravel.
- I can break my routine and say yes to opportunity so I can have the social connections I seek.
- Responsible people don't have to be perfect.

Stretch the Comfort Zone

Finally, another way to fuel self-confidence is to have clients push themselves to do the things they previously feared or avoided. For example, clients with avoidant personality disorder could accept social invitations even if it makes them uncomfortable. Clients with a dependent personality disorder could eat alone in a restaurant, apply for a job with a long commute, or take public transportation on their own. Clients with obsessive-compulsive personality disorder could purposely do something less than perfect, accept a spontaneous invitation, or let someone else have control of a project or an event. Clients with paranoid personality disorder could try trusting a relative or using the health insurance provider they have been avoiding owing to confidentiality fears. Clients with narcissistic personality disorder could compromise their needs and eat dinner with someone at a time they did not prefer.

When clients stretch their comfort zone, reach for their goals, and conquer their fears, this serves to perpetuate confidence. Remind clients that goal obtainment is less important than goal direction. With no crystal balls and variables out of their control, the outcome often is compromised. However, when effort and goal-directed action are rewarded, then success is more likely.

Embrace Individuality

Although fueling new, confident beliefs is critical in helping clients move beyond their maladaptive behavioral strategies, not all labels that clients give to themselves are in need of change. Sometimes, clients have labels about themselves that they don't need to dispute, but must learn to embrace. They might call themselves weird, quirky, shy, nerdy, compulsive, unconventional, eccentric, peculiar, or odd. Instead of trying to find data to dispute these labels, we can help clients embrace themselves and not let their label get in their way. We don't want clients to judge the label or assume that it means they are undesirable or incapable in some way. Rather, we want to encourage clients to wear their uniqueness with pride. Remember that no one is average or ordinary; we are each uniquely special. The following is a coping card you can use to remind clients to embrace their individuality.

Coping Card

EMBRACE YOUR INDIVIDUALITY

I am unique. Own it! Wear my individuality with pride and never let it mean that I am less than. I can go after what I want and know that my individuality will help me get there.

Modify Ineffective Action

When treating clients with personality disorders, working to build a more confident self-view is one part of the process. Another important component of treatment involves addressing the ineffective compensatory actions that they take in response to their doubt beliefs. Their overdeveloped strategies prevent them from achieving their goals and, in many cases, actually cause them social, occupational, or personal harm. Typically, when the overdeveloped strategy doesn't work, rather than changing their approach, clients with personality disorders simply continue the ineffective behavior. They may even amplify the degree to which they engage in the ineffective behavior, believing that if they engage in the behavior more intensely or more frequently that results will follow.

Additionally, clients with personality disorders have not developed alternative behavioral strategies, so their ability to consider other choices is not always apparent. Consider the client with narcissistic personality disorder, who competes with everyone in every situation and never cheers on anyone, but then wonders why he doesn't have the support of others and why the crowd doesn't cheer him on. Or, consider an adolescent with borderline personality disorder, whose parents have told her that she is not welcome in their home if she continues to cut, break things, or berate others—and yet she continues to do all those things anyway. Helping clients realize when their behavioral strategies are self-defeating—and teaching them alternative, more effective strategies—is critical to improving functionality.

For example, consider Jansen, who is diagnosed with narcissistic personality disorder and has just returned to his country club after many months of absence. As he enters the high-stakes card room, no one stops the game to say hello or ask how he is. Jansen thinks, "I am not special; no one cares. If I were special, then they would make a fuss." In turn, he concludes, "I am not important. They don't care. I am not good enough for them. I don't need them." Although he yearns for friendship and popularity, he plans to never talk to these people again and verbally lashes out at them. In this example, Jansen's biased conclusions caused him to engage in ineffective compensatory actions by pushing everyone away. However, isolating himself results in the exact opposite of what Jansen wants and only further fuels his negative core belief that he is not important. If he continues to use these ineffective behavioral actions, then he will never have the interpersonal connections he desires.

In this case, cognitive restructuring can help Jansen realize that it is not always about him. People do not always give us what we want, but that does not mean they do not care about us. The desire to be the most important person to everyone all the time is not possible, and learning to accept that is key. Instead of lashing out and severing relationships when others don't make him the priority or do what he wants, Jansen can look at the situation through other people's perspective and consider possible reasons he could not be accommodated. Treatment can also teach him to focus on the big picture and remember past examples when his friends were there for him and included him. Instead of impulsively lashing out, he can focus on what he wants in the long run and accept that people don't always do what we want, but that doesn't mean we don't matter or that they don't care. In turn, Jansen can learn to stop overreacting with volatile anger and, instead, stay calm and accept the world as it is. These new, more effective behaviors can help Jansen sustain his friendships, which is what he really wants all along.

As another example, consider the case of Harper, who personifies the obsessive-compulsive personality. Although she excels in school, maintains impeccable grades, and has exceptional standardized test scores, she compromises extracurricular activities and her social life to make schoolwork her sole priority. As a result, she feels isolated from her friends and anxious about the future. For Harper, these ineffective behaviors are driven by the doubt beliefs that she will be "irresponsible" and "lazy" if she does not devote herself entirely to her schoolwork. Although she wants to lead a more well-rounded life, her doubt beliefs prevent her from making anything other than schoolwork a priority.

One way that treatment could help Harper overcome her rigid beliefs is to have her monitor her daily activities and accompanying mood on an activity schedule. In doing so, she can come to recognize that her mood is highest when she is socializing with her friends and that her mood is lowest when doing schoolwork. In addition, interoceptive exposure could be used to help Harper realize that her anxiety about leaving schoolwork behind is worse than actually leaving it behind. The symptoms of anxiety (e.g., sweaty, tingling, heart pounding) are nothing to fear, and even if she does nothing to address these symptoms, they will go away and not harm her.

In order for Harper to achieve a more well-rounded life, treatment would also involve the goal of reducing rigidity and increasing spontaneity. For example, Harper could devise a plan to incorporate one hour of "fun time" into her day and work on limiting unnecessary studying. As the therapist, you would also want to work with Harper on giving herself permission to take time off from schoolwork, knowing that she is exceptionally responsible, prepared, and the opposite of lazy. To do so, it would be important to teach Harper how to talk back to give-up thoughts that try to derail her from her plan (e.g., "I cannot afford to take time off" and "I'll just finish all my schoolwork first and then I can play") and to replace these with go-to thoughts (e.g., "The truth is I can take time off, as I am more than prepared" and "It's never going to happen if I don't play now"). Ultimately, the goal is not for Harper to stop being in control and thorough; rather, it is to add spontaneity, impulsivity, and flexibility to the mix.

Reduce Overdeveloped Strategies and Increase Underdeveloped Strategies

Cluster A

Paranoid Personality
Overdeveloped Strategies
- Vigilance
- Mistrust
- Suspicion
- Guardedness

Underdeveloped Strategies
- Trust
- Contentment
- Relaxing
- Believing

Schizoid Personality
Overdeveloped Strategies
- Withdrawal
- Independence
- Isolation

Underdeveloped Strategies
- Intimacy
- Reciprocity

Schizotypal Personality
Overdeveloped Strategies
- Magical thinking
- Appearing odd
- Assuming hidden motives

Underdeveloped Strategies
- Rational thinking
- Social appropriateness
- Contentment

Cluster B

Antisocial Personality
Overdeveloped Strategies
- Attacking
- Depriving others
- Exploitation

Underdeveloped Strategies
- Empathy
- Being pro-social
- Reciprocity

Borderline Personality
Overdeveloped Strategies
- Dependency
- Egocentricity
- Avoiding abandonment
- Extreme behaviors
- Rigidity
- Emotional dysregulation

Underdeveloped Strategies
- Emotional and behavioral control
- Self-sufficiency
- Social reciprocity
- Flexibility
- Concern for others

Histrionic Personality
Overdeveloped Strategies
- Being overly dramatic
- Dressing, acting, speaking seductively
- Entertaining others all the time
- Seeking adulation

Underdeveloped Strategies
- Being quiet, submissive
- Social appropriateness
- Acting less extreme
- Holding reasonable standards for others' behavior toward them

Narcissistic Personality
Overdeveloped Strategies
- Competitiveness
- Aggrandizing self-preoccupation
- Outward signs of status
- Demanding special accommodations

Underdeveloped Strategies
- Empathy
- Being supportive
- Compassion

Cluster C

Avoidant Personality
Overdeveloped Strategies
- Avoidance
- Inhibition
- Sensitivity to rejection

Underdeveloped Strategies
- Self-promotion
- Assertiveness
- Openness

Dependent Personality
Overdeveloped Strategies
- Help-seeking
- Clinging
- Over-reliance on others

Underdeveloped Strategies
- Autonomy
- Self-sufficiency
- Mobility

Obsessive-Compulsive Personality
Overdeveloped Strategies
- Control
- Responsibly
- Systematization

Underdeveloped Strategies
- Flexibility
- Spontaneity
- Impulsivity

Personality Disorders, Self-Harm, and Suicidality

When treating clients with personality disorders, remember that the ineffective behavioral actions they take may be reasonable strategies that are simply not working at a specific time (like in Harper's case), or they may be toxic actions that will never work or come with a significant cost. For example, clients with avoidant personality disorder may exhibit severe procrastination and shy away from opportunities that promote recovery, while also relying on alcohol and marijuana to self-medicate. Similarly, clients with narcissistic personality disorder may frequently threaten, attack, and cut themselves off from others in response to their inferiority beliefs.

Perhaps the most toxic and ineffective actions that clients may take involve those that involve self-harm behaviors, such as self-mutilation, substance use, and suicide attempts. This is particularly the case for clients with borderline personality disorder, who exhibit concomitant impulsivity and hopelessness, as the combination of these two traits increases the risk for self-harm and suicidality in particular. Clients with borderline personality disorder have personalized egocentric orientations (e.g., "I am entitled," "I need you"), and their impulsivity leads them to engage in extreme action-oriented behaviors (e.g., reassurance seeking, drug use, revenge, self-mutilation, suicide). Their cravings to engage in these behaviors are driven by demanding imperatives (e.g., "I have to . . . ," "I must . . . ") and permission-giving beliefs (e.g., "It's okay to act this way because I need it badly, because I am entitled, or because that person should be punished"). They also believe they have no self-control, and their "now" orientation causes them to focus on what matters in the moment, with no regard for future or past consequences. The section that follows goes into more detail on self-harm as an ineffective compensatory strategy and discusses interventions for the treatment of self-harm and suicidality.

SELF-HARM

Cognitive Model of Self-Harm

Self-harm behaviors are ineffective compensatory actions that clients use to address their distress. These ineffective coping strategies are not unique to individuals with personality disorders, as any clients who experience psychological distress or are desperate to get their needs met may be driven to self-harm or suicide. However, clients with personality disorders are more likely to regularly use these dysfunctional strategies, whereas clients with other clinical syndromes (e.g., depression, anxiety) may only resort to these extreme strategies in the acute phase of their problem. Regardless, the cognitive model behind the cycle of self-harm is the same. Typically a triggering stimulus activates an underlying doubt belief, which leads clients to misinterpret the stimulus in the form of negative automatic thoughts. These negative automatic thoughts give rise to a variety of unpleasant emotions, which trigger the urge to self-harm, and clients ultimately give in to these urges when they listen to permission-giving beliefs that rationalize the self-harm in some way.

Triggers for self-harm can come in the form of external or internal stimuli that activate the underlying doubt belief. External triggers can include breaking up with a romantic partner, losing a job, not getting a job, making a team, or getting invited to a party. Internal triggers can include strong emotions (e.g., despair, loneliness, sadness, fear, anger) or physiological sensations (e.g., sweating, racing heart, dissociation). These triggers themselves do not inherently elicit distress; rather, they provide opportunities for underlying self-doubt to surface. For example, clients who experience a breakup may interpret the rejection as proof of their unlovability or defectiveness. Alternatively, the breakup might be perceived as abandonment, which activates beliefs about helplessness and being unable to survive without the other person. Any triggering stimulus can activate self-doubt, but clients with personality disorders are most vulnerable, as their self-doubt is always present.

When clients' doubt beliefs are activated, it causes them to experience thoughts about the triggering event that are distorted, biased, or exaggerated. For example, in response to a breakup, clients who believe they are unlovable or helpless may think, "No one will ever want me. I will be alone forever," or "I cannot survive on my own. I cannot handle this." In turn, they are likely to experience associated feelings of despair, hopelessness, and fear, which increase the urge to self-harm. Clients view self-harm as a reasonable strategy in response to these unpleasant emotions when they listen to permission-giving beliefs that rationalize the dysfunctional behavior (e.g., "Cutting is the only way to deal with being upset," "Self-harming will make my partner stay with me," "Everyone cuts from time to time. It's not a big deal"). Allowing the permission-giving beliefs to rule, self-harm follows.

For example, consider the case of Kali, who is a senior in high school living at home with her father. Her mother died a few years earlier, and her older sister recently moved a significant distance away. She has been struggling with emotional issues and self-harm urges, and she has begged her father to spend more time at home with her and less time away at his new girlfriend's house, which he has agreed to do. However, the first Friday night after her father made his new promise, Kali arrived home at the agreed-upon time only to find an empty house (*triggering stimulus*), which triggered the belief, "I am unloved. I am helpless" (*doubt belief*). In turn, she thought, "My life is not in a good place. My family situation is horrible. Dad should have been here. I miss Mom. Only Mom cared about me, but she is dead. Everyone abandoned me" (*negative automatic thoughts*). She felt frustrated, angry, helpless, and distressed (*unpleasant emotions*), which triggered the urge to cut (*increase in urge to self-harm*). Believing that there was no other option ("If I feel the urge, then I have to do it") (*permission-giving belief*), she took a knife and cut herself (*self-harm behavior*). Although she experienced a momentary sense of relief, she ultimately felt worse and was admitted to a psychiatric ward.

When working with clients who have exhibited self-harm behavior, it is helpful to map their self-harm path shortly after self-harm has taken place, examine previous episodes of self-harm, and look at future triggers that might put them at risk for self-harm behaviors. Once the self-harm path is understood, the path to intervention is clear. The following section explores the cognitive model of self-harm in greater detail and discusses points of intervention along the way.

Intervention

Whether self-harm is driven by personality pathology or other clinical issues, the interventions to address this dysfunctional strategy are the same. The first step in addressing self-harm and specifically self-mutilation involves helping clients embrace the goal of extinguishing these behaviors. However, clients who engage in self-harm often do not view the behavior as problematic and, in turn, may not be invested in changing it. For example, individuals who engage in cutting frequently view this behavior as the only way to alleviate emotional pain, control pain, refocus pain, or demonstrate to others that they are in pain. Therefore, it is not uncommon for clients who engage in self-mutilation to minimize or discount its associated risks, believing that it is "no big deal." Help clients see how problematic self-harm is in order to increase their desire to extinguish the behavior.

To aid clients in more accurately assessing the risk of self-harm, you can use cognitive restructuring to help them develop more accurate conclusions about the consequences of self-harm. For example, guided questioning can help them appreciate that cutting is destroying their skin by scarring it for life, and it could also accidentally result in serious harm or death. Cutting also may bring them unwanted attention or put them in an uncomfortable position of responding to other people who are curious about their scars. Similarly, cognitive restructuring can make clients see that self-mutilation gets in the way of healthier coping strategies and only reinforces the bad habit. It also blocks them from opportunities (e.g., jobs, school, relationships) and could land them in a situation they are trying to avoid (e.g., hospitalization, different living situation). Returning to the example of Kali, cognitive restructuring helped her recognize that self-harm was a negative choice that resulted in the opposite of what she wanted. Rather than feeling better and having more time with her dad, she felt worse, and her actions put even greater distance between her and her father. In turn, she was able to realize, "I was in a lot of distress and had no answers at that moment, so I impulsively had to do something about it. I know it was a bad choice, and I want to work on it."

Once clients acknowledge the problems associated with self-harm, then they will be more receptive to working on reducing and eliminating the behavior. To do so, you can use your client's path to self-harm as a guide, as each point of understanding on the path is a point of intervention. Although the triggering stimulus does represent the first step in the path, it is not reasonable to predict all of the external and internal triggers that might activate self-doubt. Instead, the key is to help clients develop an awareness of what is likely to activate their doubt beliefs and, more important, to use cognitive restructuring to directly evaluate and modify these beliefs and accompanying automatic thoughts. Aid clients in building self-confidence by asking them to collect evidence that contradicts their underlying doubt beliefs, as well as evidence that supports a more positive self-view.

Returning to the example of Kali, coming home to an empty house was not a trigger that she could have predicted, as her father said he would be there. However, had she been aware that someone not being there for her would activate her self-doubts, she could have intervened instead of reacting. For example, she could have gone to a nearby diner where she wouldn't feel alone or called a friend to come over. In time, therapy can help Kali address the underlying doubt belief that she is unloved and evaluate the validity of her automatic thoughts (e.g., "Only Mom cared about me," "Everyone abandoned me") by collecting data to the contrary. For example, therapy can help her see that her dad does care, but he is so caught up in his own grief that he is unable to be there for Kali. Additionally, she can recognize that her friends also care and want to be there for her, as they were upset when she didn't reach out to them for help. Using this data, Kali can accept that it is not 100 percent possible for her to be unlovable and that she may even be loved.

In addition to addressing underlying doubt beliefs and automatic thoughts, treatment for self-harm involves helping clients find behavioral alternatives when the urge to self-harm erupts. Some examples of behavioral alternatives are relaxation (e.g., deep breathing, mindfulness, progressive muscle relaxation) or distraction techniques (e.g., exercising, cooking, reading, knitting, going on the internet, watching television). You can also implement social alternatives, such as asking clients to connect to others, listen to a recording of a therapy session, or hold reminders of love or competence (e.g., a gift from a loved one, a trophy they won, a diploma). In the process of eliminating self-harm behaviors, you can also temporarily have clients use alternative strategies that simulate what they gain from self-harm but are not physically harmful. For example, instead of cutting, clients can crack raw eggs on their body or write with a fat red marker on their skin. Over time, work with clients on reducing their reactivity by teaching them emotion regulation skills to bring down their emotional temperature so they can effectively use problem-solving strategies.

Helping clients identify their permission-giving beliefs (and replace these with more valid and rational beliefs) is also a critical point of intervention, as these beliefs rationalize the urge to engage in self-harm. Work with clients to develop rebuttals to their permission-giving beliefs and have them read these rebuttals on a daily basis. For example, Kali believed that if she had any self-harming thoughts then she had to act on them. Like many others who self-harm, she also believed it was the only way to make her distress go away. Treatment can help her understand that these beliefs are all hypotheses to be tested, not facts. For example, Kali can see that it is possible to have an urge and not act on it, such as when she is in school and is able to resist the urge by painting her nails, drawing pictures, or lacing her shoes together. Kali learned that there were other ways to reduce her distress, refuting her harm hypothesis.

Ultimately, the goal is to replace self-harm with adaptive coping. To do so, you can ask clients to make a list of all the alternative behavior options to self-harm you have discussed throughout treatment (e.g., relaxation, distraction, self-soothing). Then, ask clients to practice using these alternative strategies and keep track of when they were able to successfully resist (or delay giving into) the urge, as well as times in which they encountered obstacles. For example, Kali replaced cutting with connecting with friends and reading her therapy coping cards.

Identifying the consequences of the self-harm behavior can solidify clients' investment in reducing future self-harm. Hospitalization, incarceration, eviction, or losing custody of a child punctuate the danger and dysfunction of self-harm. Additionally, the consequences not only pull clients away from their goals, they compromise the person they want to be for themselves and others. Kali's cutting behavior resulted in an unpleasant hospital stay and friends upset with her. Kali's motivation to never return to a psychiatric unit in a hospital and her investment in her friendships are strong deterrents to her self-harm prevention. Kali's deterrents were recorded and regularly reviewed.

In order to identify your client's path to self-harm, as well as the specific cognitive and behavioral interventions you can use at each point along the path, use the worksheet on the following page.

Clinician Worksheet

PATH OF SELF-HARM

● ● ● ● ● ●

Work with your client to map their specific path for self-harm. Then, at each point on the path, record any interventions that could help put your client along an alternate path.

1. Triggering Stimulus: _____

_____

> **Intervention:** _____
>
> _____
>
> _____

2. Doubt Belief: _____

_____

> **Intervention:** _____
>
> _____
>
> _____

3. Negative Automatic Thoughts: _____

_____

> **Intervention:** _____
>
> _____
>
> _____

4. Unpleasant Emotions: _____

_____

> **Intervention:** _____
>
> _____
>
> _____

5. Increase in Urge to Self-Harm: _____

_____

> **Intervention:** _____
>
> _____
>
> _____

6. Permission-Giving Beliefs: _____

_____

> **Intervention:** _____
>
> _____
>
> _____

7. Self-Harm Behavior: _____

_____

> **Intervention:** _____
>
> _____
>
> _____

8. Consequence: _____

_____

> **Intervention:** _____
>
> _____
>
> _____

SUICIDALITY

Hopelessness, which is defined as a general set of negative expectancies about oneself and the future, is one of the strongest predictors of suicidality (Beck, 1986; Weishaar & Beck, 1992). When clients perceive that they are in unending psychological pain and feel hopeless that there is no solution, suicide becomes the answer in their mind. Suicide risk is particularly pronounced among clients with personality disorders—especially borderline personality—as the chronic and pervasive problems that these individuals experience put them at particular risk for depression and hopelessness. This risk is further exacerbated by the impulsivity and present-orientation that characterizes many of the personality disorders, as it renders them unable to consider past and potential future consequences (Beck, Davis, & Freeman, 2015).

The primary goal when working with clients who are suicidal is ensuring the client's survival, and a variety of possible interventions can achieve this goal, including intensive outpatient therapy, medication, or inpatient hospitalization. The following section focuses on interventions as they pertain to outpatient treatment, though this is not always the preferred path of treatment. Rather, this determination should always be made by the treating clinician on a case-by-case basis and in accordance with what is in the best interest of the client.

Intervention

Conduct a Suicide Risk Assessment

The first level of intervention when working with clients who exhibit suicidality is to conduct a thorough suicide risk assessment (Weishaar & Beck, 1992). In addition to hopelessness, some risk factors for suicide include a family history of mental illness or suicide, drug and alcohol abuse, availability of firearms, physical illness, and loss of a parent or significant figure during childhood. Clients are also at increased risk for completing suicide if they are male; over the age of 45; living alone; separated, divorced, or widowed; unemployed or retired; or have previously attempted suicide (Wenzel, Brown, & Beck, 2009). You can use a variety of tools to conduct a suicide risk assessment, such as the Scale for Suicide Ideation (Beck, Kovacs, & Weissman, 1979), the Columbia Suicide Severity Rating Scale (Posner, Brown, & Stanley, 2011), or the Suicide Assessment Five-Step Evaluation and Triage (SAFE-T) plan (Fochtmann & Jacobs, 2015).

In addition, given the link between suicide and hopelessness, you can specifically assess the severity of clients' perceived hopelessness using the Beck Hopelessness Scale, which is a psychometrically valid measure of hopelessness (Beck et al., 1974). The scale assesses feelings about the future, loss of motivation, and expectations. The Beck Hopelessness Scale has been reported as a sensitive indicator of suicide potential, as it was able to identify 16 of 17 patients who eventually committed suicide (94.2 percent) in a study of 1,958 outpatients using a cutoff score of nine or above (Beck, Brown, Berchick, Stewart, & Steer, 1990).

Develop a Suicide Safety Plan

In the early phases of treatment, develop a safety plan in collaboration with clients, which contains a series of escalating steps that clients should follow if they begin to experience the urge to harm themselves or experience an acute suicide crisis (Wenzel, Brown, & Beck, 2009). The Safety Planning Intervention (SPI; Stanley & Brown, 2012) is one such tool that can help stop the suicide crisis, keep it from escalating, or get clients through the moment. The SPI is considered to be a best practice by the Suicide Prevention Resource Center (www.sprc.org) and the American Foundation for Suicide Prevention (https://afsp.org).

The **first step** in the SPI plan involves identifying the thoughts, images, mood, behaviors that represent warning signs for suicide. Helping clients identify their early warning signs provides them with an opportunity to intervene when they begin to experience suicidal ideation. In particular, these warning signs present opportunities to intercede by reducing hopelessness and ongoing risk. Once the crisis remits, it is also an opportunity to collect warning signs that you were previously unaware of that triggered suicidality. Some of these warning signs include the following:

1. Making vague comments about not being around
2. Giving away possessions
3. Talking about feelings of hopelessness or feeling trapped
4. Increased substance use
5. Withdrawing from friends and social activities
6. Writing farewell notes
7. Putting finances and business affairs in order
8. Canceling sessions
9. Calling themselves negative labels of self-doubt

For example, consider a client who recognizes that he is at risk for suicide when he feels exhausted, calls himself his doubt labels (e.g., failure, wimp, defect), stays in bed, ignores his phone, and declines all invitations. By implementing the first step in his safety plan, he can use the principles of behavioral activation to mobilize himself toward action whenever these warning signs arise. He can put action before motivation, get up and dressed, and tackle the goal of having lunch with his sister and meeting a friend at the movies. He might also tell himself that his negative label is the voice of depression and that these labels are not 100 percent true (and probably not true at all).

The **second step** in a thorough suicide safety plan includes a list of internal coping strategies that clients can use on their own when they start to experience these warning signs. The intent is to distract themselves until the urge to act subsides. Distraction makes it more difficult for clients to think about suicide and is the most effective way to circumvent a crisis (G. Brown, personal communication, May 9, 2019). Therefore, work collaboratively with clients to develop a list of internal coping strategies that they can use in the event of a suicide crisis (e.g., taking a hot shower, exercising, going for a walk, playing video games, listening to music, watching a movie or TV show, playing with a pet, doing a crossword puzzle, reading, yoga, preparing a meal). In addition, work with clients to forecast, address, and remove any obstacles that prevent implementing these coping strategies. Although the goal of these activities is to distract clients from their suicidal ideation, they also serve to give clients a sense of accomplishment and pleasure. When clients cope on their own, they increase their self-efficacy and empower themselves to gain control over their suicidality (Stanley & Brown, 2012).

It is possible that these internal strategies can prevent suicidal ideation from escalating. Indeed, we want to encourage clients to be their own therapist by first trying to address suicidality on their own. However, if internal action is not sufficient, then clients would move on to the **third and fourth step** in their plan by seeking out the assistance of external resources (Stanley & Brown, 2012). In step 3, clients can create a list of family members, friends, or acquaintances who can provide them with distraction from the crisis, or social settings where they can put themselves amongst other people (e.g., AA meeting, gym, place of worship, supermarket, mall). In step 4, they can specifically seek out support or ask for help. Make sure that clients include phone numbers and other contact information on the safety plan so that it is easily accessible to them in a time of crisis.

If outside assistance is not helpful or accessible, the **fifth step** in the safety plan is developing a list of professional resources that clients can contact if they are suicidal. This list should include the names of mental health professionals (including you as their therapist), as well as local emergency departments or national suicide prevention hotlines. Ensure that relevant addresses and phone numbers are listed on the safety plan for these resources as well.

The **sixth step** in a thorough suicide safety plan is ensuring that the environment is safe. In order to reduce the potential that clients will have access to lethal means, you can ask them what method they would consider using during a suicide crisis, making sure to specifically ask if they have access to a firearm. You may want to tell clients to remove or restrict their access to these methods, or to collaboratively identify ways for a responsible person to limit access or secure them. You can also ask clients to get help from family members or roommates to make sure that items with the potential for injury are taken out of the home or locked up in a way that is inaccessible to the client. Ask clients to write this arrangement on their safety plan.

A sample template you can use with clients to develop a suicide safety plan is provided on the following page.

Client Worksheet

SAFETY PLAN

· · · · · ·

Step 1: Warning signs:

1. _____

2. _____

3. _____

Step 2: Internal coping strategies – Things I can do to take my mind off my problems without contacting another person:

1. _____

2. _____

3. _____

Step 3: People and social settings that provide distraction:

1. Name_____ Phone_____

2. Name_____ Phone_____

3. Place_____

4. Place_____

Step 4: People whom I can ask for help:

1. Name_____ Phone_____

2. Name_____ Phone_____

3. Name_____ Phone_____

Step 5: Professionals or agencies I can contact during a crisis
1. Clinician/Agency Name_____Phone_____
Clinician Pager or Emergency Contact #_____
2. Clinician/Agency Name_____Phone_____
Clinician Pager or Emergency Contact #_____
3. Local Emergency Service _____
Emergency Services Address_____
Emergency Services Phone _____
4. Suicide Prevention Lifeline: **1-800-273-TALK (8255)**
5. Other: _____

Step 6: Making the environment safe
1. _____
2. _____

Step 7: (optional): Reasons for living - The things that are most important to me and worth living for are:
1. _____ 2. _____ 3. _____
4. _____ 5. _____ 6. _____

Reproduced with permission (@ 2008, 2012, 2016 Barbara Stanley, Ph.D. & Gregory K. Brown, PhD.).
To register to use this form and for additional training resources go to www.suicidesafetyplan.com

Identify Reasons for Living

Following completion of the safety plan in the acute phase of treating suicidality, you can move on to directly addressing the hopelessness associated with suicide risk. One treatment strategy that has been used to increase hope is to have clients list all of their reasons for living. This can be a difficult task for clients who have already attempted suicide, as these clients often enter treatment not wanting to live. Give credence to their inner experience while also developing their willingness to work on being alive. Clients may not have wanted to live in the past and may not want to live in the present moment, but most will acknowledge that they may want to want to live in general, and that is a solid starting point.

The goal of living is enhanced when you can help clients see the rationale for doing so. Work with the client to create a list of reasons to live, as those reasons may not be readily apparent to them in their time of distress. Help clients examine all the spheres of their life (e.g., social, occupational, personal, academic, romantic, etc.) that provide them with reasons to live. Seek data from their life that remind them about the people, places, and things that matter. For example, you can remind clients that it makes sense to live by helping them recognize that they care about (and are cared about by) their family, friends, and pets; there are things they want to do now and in the future; and there are things they enjoy and bring them a sense of accomplishment. Use the worksheet on the following page to help clients identify some of these reasons.

Client Worksheet

REASONS TO LIVE

• • • • • •

List all the reasons it makes sense to fight to live. The following are some reasons that might make sense for you, followed by some space for you to write your own specific reasons.

1. No one will love and care for my pets as well as I do. They need me.

2. If I kill myself, then I will never have a chance to actually have the things I want like a partner, home, or job.

3. People do care about me, and I care about them. I want to be there for them.

4. My therapist believes I can overcome this, and if I quit now, I will never know if he or she is right.

What are some of your reasons for living?

1. _____

2. _____

3. _____

4. _____

5. _____

The use of coping cards is another helpful strategy to enhance the desire to live and negate suicidal intent. Coping cards contain statements that acknowledge and encourage acceptance of the distress, point out its temporary state, remind clients of resources within and outside of themselves, specify constructive action, and state what they might say to someone else they care about in their shoes. The following are some sample coping cards that clients can use to get through a distressing moment.

Coping Card

LIVING GOAL

I proclaim my goal is to want to live. I want to have purpose in my life, have a social life, feel joy, and look forward to activities. I have felt better in the past, and there is no reason I won't feel better again. Thinking of these things makes me want to be around.

Coping Card

NO JUDGMENT

When despair knocks me over, I can acknowledge it without letting it get the best of me. I can accept it by not making it more than it is. It's temporary; it will pass. I can do something to distract myself or talk to someone to move beyond the despair. I can remind myself that my hopelessness is coming from my depressive biased thinking, so it is probably irrational and untrue. If my friend were thinking of killing herself, I would tell her not to because she is too important to too many people and the truth is, I know that is true for me too.

Coping Card

CHOOSE TO LIVE

When a suicidal thought shows up—regardless of whether I am flirting with it, embracing it, or it is just a fleeting thought—I can acknowledge it. I will tell it "no." It may always be there at some level, but that doesn't mean it has to be. I can remember all the reasons I have to be around. Maybe there is some hope for a decent future. People care, and I am going to choose to live.

Reframe Suicidogenic Beliefs

We cannot ignore that clients also have reasons to die, but often these reasons are flawed distortions of reality, as their thinking is often negatively biased by depression. Therefore, addressing suicidality also involves working with clients to modify their reasons for dying and helping them see the thinking errors behind their suicidogenic beliefs (Wenzel et al., 2009). Clients who are suicidal have a variety of reasons for which they think dying makes sense, and our job as clinicians is to help them see that these suicidogenic beliefs may be flawed.

Often, the hopelessness behind these beliefs may be associated with more specific automatic thoughts (e.g., "I will never pass this exam"), or it may stem from broader underlying beliefs (e.g., "Life won't get any better," "I have nothing to look forward to").

Validate the distress clients are experiencing without validating these distorted beliefs. For example, let clients know that you understand how hard it has been for them or how much pain they seem to be in. At the same time, resist validating the hopelessness. For example, you might say, "What a horrific situation you have had to face. I can only imagine how awful it was. It's no wonder you want to give up, but you're here because you don't want to give up, and we can find ways to make your life what you want it to be."

Then, instead of accepting these beliefs as true, work with clients to reframe the errors in their thinking and consider an alternative view. Death is not a solution but an escape, and working on viable solutions is the better alternative. The following are some sample reframes for some common suicidogenic beliefs:

1. "No one cares about me, so I'd be better off dead."

   Reframe: "Although it feels like no one cares about me, the truth is lots of people do care about me. My parents tell me they care and want me to be with them. My friends and relatives would be emotionally scarred by my death, especially my sister, because they all care about me."

2. "I have nothing to look forward to. I will never have what I want, so what is the point of living?"

   Reframe: "It feels like I will never have what I want, but that doesn't make it a fact. I am working on ways to manage my emotions and have the courage to try new things, so if I hang in there, it's possible that one day I may have what I want."

3. "I am a burden to others and would be better off dead."

   Reframe: "Just because I cannot contribute in the ways I have in the past doesn't mean I can't provide for others. I have time to listen to others, and I can provide the people I care about with a voice of encouragement."

4. "Things will never get better. Death is the only solution to my problems."

   Reframe: "Death is not a solution. It is an escape. If I want a solution, then I need to be here to experience it."

5. "I deserve to die."

   Reframe: "No one deserves to die because they are struggling and in pain. I deserve compassion and help."

6. "If I kill myself, other people will finally understand all the pain they have caused me. I have to teach them a lesson."

   Reframe: "It's likely they will never understand no matter what I say or do, and I can work on accepting this."

Use the worksheet on the following page with your clients to modify their suicidogenic beliefs and provide more accurate reframes regarding their reasons for dying.

Client Worksheet

REFRAME YOUR REASONS FOR DYING

• • • • • •

It is possible that your reasons for dying are negatively biased by feelings of hopelessness or depression. Use this worksheet to list your reasons for dying, and then work with your therapist to develop an alternative and more reasonable perspective. Let your objectivity replace your emotional view. For example:

Belief: "The world would be better without me."

Reframe: "Even the small things I do make a difference. The woman I held the door for, the help I gave my friend, and the tech support I gave my mom mattered to them. The world is a better place anytime anyone, including me, does something positive."

Now it's your turn:

Belief: _____

Reframe: _____
_____

Belief: _____

Reframe: _____
_____

Belief: _____

Reframe: _____
_____

Copyright © 2019 Leslie Sokol & Marci G. Fox, *The Comprehensive Clinician's Guide to Cognitive Behavioral Therapy*. All Rights Reserved

SUMMARY

Working with personality disorders and intervening in the face of life-threatening behaviors is challenging. However, developing a clear conceptualization of your clients and their problems makes it easier to connect with them, feel compassion for them, and find a clearer path for their recovery. When a suicide crisis occurs, be prepared to review all of the factors that contributed to their feelings of hopelessness and prompted their suicidal action. Although it is important to discuss what specific cognitive and behavioral tools they can use to reduce future crises, be careful not to lose sight of more life-enhancing goals. Work to increase clients' social connections and push them to reach out and accept invitations. Help them find pleasure in life by trying new things, seeking out meaningful and productive activities, and keeping an open mind.

PSYCHOSIS

With contribution from Aaron P. Brinen

For some clinicians, a chapter on the application of CBT to psychotic disorders sounds impossible. In many areas of the mental health field, psychotic experiences are considered purely biological, and psychosocial treatments are at best palliative. However, over 20 years of research exists in the application of CBT to psychosis and schizophrenia spectrum diagnoses, which is commonly referred to as CBT for psychosis (CBTp). Although the primary goal of CBTp is to reduce the distress associated with the positive symptoms of psychosis (e.g., hallucinations and delusions), Aaron T. Beck has recently led his team to extend CBTp to individuals who experience prominent negative symptoms as well (Brinen & Beck, 2018). This extension of CBTp is known as Recovery-Oriented Cognitive Therapy (CT-R), and it focuses on helping individuals who are struggling to regain their desired life. This chapter highlights the utility of both these interventions for the treatment of schizophrenia spectrum and psychotic disorders, and also discusses the application of the cognitive model as it pertains to psychosis.

PSYCHOTIC DISORDERS

Schizophrenia spectrum and psychotic disorders are characterized by the presence of at least one of the following abnormalities: hallucinations (e.g., auditory and visual perceptual disturbances), delusions (e.g., fixed beliefs that are bizarre in nature), thought disorder (e.g., disorganization of speech, including tangentiality and incoherence), disorganized motor behavior (e.g., catatonia), and negative symptoms (e.g., flat affect, avolition, asociality) (APA, 2013). Although psychosis is the defining feature of schizophrenia, psychotic symptoms also can occur in the context of the manic state of bipolar disorder, ethanol withdrawal, psychedelic intoxication, cocaine/methamphetamine abuse, PTSD, and traumatic brain injury. It is important to note that psychotic symptoms that result from substance use or an underlying medical condition differ from primary psychotic disorders in terms of etiology, course, and onset. When the offending substance is removed, or the underlying medical condition is resolved, then the symptoms typically subside (APA, 2013). However, the individual might maintain worries or compensatory strategies established during the psychotic episode, as described in the following cognitive model of psychosis.

THE COGNITIVE MODEL OF PSYCHOSIS

At the core of the cognitive model is the notion that thinking influences emotion and behavior, and this concept can be applied to psychotic symptoms as well. In particular, schizophrenia spectrum diagnoses are associated with a core set of beliefs that influence how individuals experience and respond to the world. Broadly speaking, these beliefs involve the assumption that the world is threatening (e.g., that others are rejecting, threatening, or dominating), that the self is defeated (e.g., defective, helpless, vulnerable), and that the future contains more of the same (Beck, Stolar, Rector, & Grant, 2009). Although anxiety disorders are also maintained by beliefs that the world is dangerous and that the individual is incompetent, the beliefs associated with psychosis and schizophrenia spectrum diagnoses are at an additional degree of intensity.

Individuals with psychosis experience others as rejecting and, in response, they take in data from the environment that causes them to see the world as threatening and dominating (e.g., they search out rejection and overinterpret others' behavior). In addition, unlike anxiety beliefs (which are satiated through avoidance), clients with psychosis believe that danger is always lurking, which causes them to be in a state of constant hypervigilance. When the threat system is constantly activated in this manner, it taxes clients' cognitive resources (e.g., attention, memory, planning) and leads them to misinterpret small stressors as large problems. In turn, clients engage in a variety of compensatory strategies in response to these stressors that generally follow a theme of self-protection.

For example, clients avoid feared situations and employ behaviors to neutralize the danger associated with the feared situation (e.g., rituals, safety behaviors). Additionally, clients over-incorporate information in an attempt to respond to danger more quickly, which leads to many false positives of danger. Consider a client who believes that the FBI is monitoring all of his movements and who stays inside to avoid being killed or abducted. As a result, he becomes hypervigilant to sounds and has anxious images of the FBI abducting him, which confirms his fear that the FBI is conspiring against him and that he is unsafe.

In conjunction with seeing the world as rejecting and dangerous, clients with psychosis also view themselves as defeated. For these clients, life experiences have conferred that little benefit is held in attempting tasks due to the likelihood of failure. This belief is associated with under-engagement in tasks, which leads to actual failure and reinforces the belief that the client is defeated. Over time, clients view themselves as defective, helpless, or vulnerable, leading to a reduction in pursuit of purposeful activity or social connection. This decrease in activity reduces opportunities for clients to gather new data and increases the time they have available to focus on aberrant experiences. Given time, stress, and focus, these odd experiences develop into what is thought of as psychosis. According to the cognitive model, the symptoms associated with schizophrenia spectrum diagnoses arise from this basic formulation, and the cognitive model may better account for psychotic symptoms than genetics and biology (Bentall, 2009).

INTERVENTIONS FOR PSYCHOSIS

Although antipsychotic medication is considered the first line treatment for individuals with schizophrenia, medication does not appear to be able to improve social or vocational functioning on its own. Rather, evidence suggests that the use of medication in conjunction with cognitive interventions is necessary in producing enduring changes in positive symptoms and targeting negative symptoms more directly (Grant, Huh, Perivoliotis, Stolar, & Beck, 2012; van der Gaag, Valmaggia, & Smit, 2014; Wykes, Everitt, Steel, & Tarrier, 2008). Some research even suggests that CBT for psychosis can be effective in the absence of medication (Morrison et al., 2014). Cognitive-based interventions are specifically useful because they help clients learn more accurate thought patterns by correcting the false assumptions associated with their symptoms, and they help clients plan behavioral routines incompatible with symptom maintenance.

When treating psychosis within a CBT framework, the goal is not to eliminate the hallucinations or the delusions but to reduce the distress and impediment to life associated with them. Individuals are taught to evaluate the cognitive, affective, and behavioral reactions they have in response to their hallucinations and delusions—and to correct these response patterns—which reduces their impact and salience. Teaching individuals to contextualize the experience of these symptoms, rather than seeking a cure, is at the core of CBT. In psychosis, it is not the symptom that is the problem, it is the emotional and behavioral consequences (Beck et al., 2009).

The key in treating psychotic symptoms is active and experiential learning. Treatment must involve actively testing out the client's core beliefs in the context of a desired life. In a treatment that is focused on achieving a desired life, clients increase the amount of time they spend in productive activity during the day, which limits the time they have to attend to hallucinations or ruminate on delusional content (Grant et al., 2012). Additionally, engaging in masterful, pleasurable, and social activity provides evidence that contradicts their underlying core beliefs that are maladaptively met through delusions or other compensatory strategies.

As clients work to live a desired life, hallucinations and delusions become dwarfed by clients' aspirations, and the salience and intensity of these symptoms reduce. At this point, treatment can focus on developing routines and skills that make the hallucinations and delusions less threatening by altering the meaning behind them. For delusions, a gentle, collaborative, and Socratic style is used to weaken the beliefs and behaviors empowering the delusion. For hallucinations, the goal is for clients to correct any unhelpful beliefs they have about the voices or visions, as well as to modify any behaviors that strengthen or maintain the experience of the hallucination itself. This basic treatment protocol inherently addresses the underlying negative symptoms that also accompany the schizophrenia spectrum disorders. However, for clients whose negative symptoms persist, therapists can use a functional analysis to determine the beliefs or assumptions maintaining the symptoms and develop a series of behavioral experiments to correct them and promote a new, more active pattern of behavior.

The following section discusses some of the basic principles of CT-R for the treatment of negative symptoms, as well as those underlying CBTp for the treatment of hallucinations and delusions, in greater detail.

Negative Symptoms

The core beliefs associated with negative symptoms (e.g., "Time with others is not worthwhile," "Others are not interested in what I have to say," "Others will reject me") and their associated behaviors (e.g., lack of connection, avoidance, poverty of speech) create a fundamental block to starting treatment. Further, they create a fertile environment for a range of other psychotic symptoms to develop, as clients who self-select out of engaging with others and spend most of their time inert have ample opportunity to hear voices. Therefore, forming a therapeutic relationship is critical for the treatment of negative symptoms, as simply connecting with you as the therapist demonstrates the benefits of social connection and pushes back against some of these core beliefs (e.g., "Others are not interested in what I have to say").

Cognitive work for negative symptoms should initially begin with experiments around energy, connection, enjoyment, and success through human experiences that prime the client to consider alternate possibilities. Simply taking a walk with a client can provide data against an inertia hypothesis (e.g., "I must reserve my energy") or an anhedonia hypothesis (e.g., "Nothing is enjoyable") if you use collaborative empiricism in guiding the client to new conclusions. For example, you could help the client come to a new conclusion by stating, "After that big walk, you have more energy and are okay. Does that seem weird? Shouldn't you have less energy? We should check that out."

These initial experiments create the foundation for an activity schedule, which can then be used to help clients become more active and reclaim their life. As clients reframe their beliefs about motivation and social connection, you can work with them to generate aspirations for the future and collaboratively explore how negative symptoms block action toward these goals. You can then continue to add activities to their daily schedule that increase their chances of attaining their goals. Keep in mind that the overall goal is to increase functioning in life and, by extension, reduce distress.

Hallucinations

When clients experience hallucinations, they develop beliefs related to these hallucinations and engage in a variety of dysfunctional compensatory strategies that reinforce those beliefs. More than the hallucinations themselves, it is the beliefs that clients have about these hallucinations that are associated with dysfunction. Therefore, the goal of treatment is to make the hallucinations less threatening by altering the meaning associated with the voices or the visions. The following are the three broad categories of beliefs that clients ascribe to their hallucinations, as well as the compensatory behaviors associated with these beliefs:

1. **Control:** Clients believe that the hallucinations are in control of when they come and go. In turn, clients isolate out of the fear that they will experience auditory or visual hallucinations while out in pubic (making them look "weird" or causing them to get hospitalized). However, isolation actually makes it more likely that clients will hallucinate because it heightens anxiety and increases their perceptions of threat. When clients subsequently hear voices or see visions, this reinforces the belief that the hallucinations are in control ("If I had gone out, the voices would have come, and it would have been terrible"). In response, clients isolate more. Beliefs surrounding control are most associated with dysfunction.

2. **Credibility:** Clients believe that the hallucinations are telling the truth, so they constantly monitor for voices so as not to miss them. This monitoring behavior, in turn, makes it more likely that they will experience auditory hallucinations. Typically, people do not listen for something they do not expect to hear. When clients finally do hear a voice, they conclude, "If I had missed the message, it would have been terrible, so I need to listen." Clients with credibility beliefs have no reason to doubt the veracity of the message, so they do not check its truthfulness.

3. **Power:** The content of auditory hallucinations can be scary, threatening, or commanding. These voices are only a concern when clients believe that the voices have the power to follow through on the threat. When this occurs, clients either comply with the demand or engage in a ritual to neutralize the threat and prevent its outcome. For example, clients who hear a voice saying, "If you leave the house, then I'll kill your friends" may take one of two options. They may either stay home and, when their friends are safe, conclude, "Had I left the house, my friends would have been killed by the powerful voice." Alternatively, they may try to neutralize the threat by performing a ritual, like praying. When clients pray repeatedly, they are less likely to hear voices, which leads them to mistakenly conclude that praying stopped the danger.

The belief that the voices are external has not been found to relate to dysfunction, yet clinicians often target that belief first. Targeting the belief that the voices are external yields the least benefit and will most likely alienate clients. Rather, it is most effective to address beliefs surrounding control, power, or credibility—and running behavioral experiments is the key to testing these beliefs. Because these beliefs are deeply engrained, they require a slow accumulation of concrete evidence to shift the client's perspective. One way to accumulate this evidence is to have clients engage in activities regardless of the voices, as this pushes back on beliefs about control, power, or credibility. For example, simply talking with you in session will likely reduce the volume of the auditory hallucination, and this experience serves as an initial test of whether the client has control of the voices. As you talk together in session, you can point out to clients that simply talking made the voices quieter. Ask them what would have happened if the two of you hadn't talked and what it means about who controls the voice's loudness. Clients may conclude that they have some control over the voice's loudness, allowing you to set up more experiments to test this hypothesis.

Over time, work with clients to start evaluating the credibility or power of the voices as well. For example, consider a client who hears a voice saying, "Don't leave the house or I will hurt you." In turn, this client feels fear and does not leave the house, thereby confirming his belief. When he does leave the house, he feels pain in his leg, which confirms the belief that the voice is powerful. In this case, the voice itself is not the problem; rather, the client's interpretation of the voice is. By helping the client realize all of the reasons why leaving his home makes sense (e.g., it is consistent with his goal of leading a desired life), he may be willing to leave despite the warnings. Although the leg pain may or may not disappear, the client can learn that he does not have to let the voice stop him from doing what he wants. Eventually, he may conclude that the leg pain was just stiffness from lack of exercise—and even if the pain does persist, he can learn to not let it get in the way because it was worthwhile to go out in spite of the pain. As a result, the power of the voice becomes limited.

After clients have conducted some experiments that push back against their maladaptive beliefs, you can further fortify clients by having them schedule activities that are incompatible with hearing voices or seeing visions. In particular, ask them to intentionally schedule one full day of structured activities and one day without any structured activities. The structured day should include a diverse list of activities, including those associated with mastery, pleasure, and social connection. The underlying key is to have clients make a note of when the hallucinations decrease in frequency and intensity across both days, and to record what that means about their ability to control the hallucinations. You want clients to conclude that increasing their level of activity decreases hallucinations and, in turn, decreases their distress. Once clients come to this realization, they can begin to regularly plan a scheduled routine that helps inoculate them against symptoms. The following pages contain activity schedules you can use with clients to complete this exercise.

Client Worksheet

COLLECT THE DATA

• • • • • •

Use this worksheet to collect data in two steps:

1. First, record two days of activity from the previous week: one day that included lots of structured activities, and one day that was largely unstructured and open.
2. Then, intentionally plan one day of scheduled activities and one day of unstructured activities.

At the end of each day, rate how you felt, and also make a note of the intensity and frequency of any auditory or visual experiences you had.

	Structured Day	**Unstructured Day**
6–7 a.m.		
7–8 a.m.		
8–9 a.m.		
9–10 a.m.		
10–11 a.m.		
11–12 p.m.		
12–1 p.m.		
1–2 p.m.		

2–3 p.m.		
3–4 p.m.		
4–5 p.m.		
5–6 p.m.		
6–7 p.m.		
7–8 p.m.		
8–9 p.m.		
9–10 p.m.		
10–11 p.m.		
11–12 a.m.		
12–6 a.m.		
How did you feel? How worthwhile was your day? (0 = *not at all worthwhile*, 10 = *very worthwhile*)		

On which day were the auditory or visual experiences stronger? _____

On which day were the auditory or visual experiences more frequent? _____

Client Worksheet

CREATE A BETTER WEEK

• • • • • • •

Based on the data you collected in the previous worksheet, plan some activities you can do on a routine basis that improve your mood and reduce the auditory or visual experiences.

	Monday	Tuesday	Wednesday	Thursday	Friday	Saturday	Sunday
Morning							
Afternoon							
Evening							
Night							

Copyright © 2019 Leslie Sokol & Marci G. Fox, *The Comprehensive Clinician's Guide to Cognitive Behavioral Therapy*. All Rights Reserved

Refocusing Hallucinations

As discussed, it is not the hallucinations themselves that lead to distress, vigilance, safety behaviors, and avoidance. Rather, it is the appraisals that clients make about these hallucinations in terms of control, power, and credibility. One way to test these beliefs is to ask clients to conduct a functional chain analysis, which identifies the factors that increase or decrease their hallucinations. For example, consider a young man who was taking a walk with his father when he saw a pack of demons ready to attack him. He became frightened, and they returned home. When discussing the situation with his therapist, the young man described "seeing" the demons at the edge of the woods. When the therapist had the man revisit the specific memory in great detail, he described the following chain of events:

- He was walking with his father.
- His father was talking about people at work.
- He struggled to understand what his father was saying, and his heart started racing.
- He started to hear muttering.
- He connected the distress with the muttering and concluded it must be demons.
- He saw the edge of the woods and the darkness. He became more anxious.
- He looked down at the ground to avoid the "demons."
- He had an image in his mind of demons at the edge of the woods.
- He retreated home.

By going through this functional chain, this client was able to realize that regardless of demons or not, he does not get a lot of time with his father and this was time lost. In addition, he recognized that looking down prevented him from evaluating the situation and left him with his internal fears surrounding demons. In turn, the client agrees to take another walk near the woods with his father, where he teaches his father some mindfulness skills he has learned in session. Teaching and practicing mindfulness are incompatible with the father talking too quickly and the client becoming overwhelmed. Teaching his father this new skill also helps prime the underlying belief that the client is capable and of value, which opposes his beliefs of incompetence and insignificance that were activated during the initial walk. Activation of these beliefs increases the tendency for rumination and withdrawal from the interaction. As the two of them practice mindfulness and walk together, the client takes in more data from the environment, which reduces his stress and allows him to remain interactive with his father.

Following this behavioral experiment, cognitive restructuring work in session helped the client realize that he could withstand the anxiety of the situation and that he was actually quite helpful to his father and others. He also realized that his stress often came from false perceptions of threat and that emotional reasoning further exacerbated this distress. In time, he took in more experiences with his father, and the woods began to seem quite irrelevant. Fortified with the idea that he was not in danger and was in fact safe, the client began to do hallucination exposures in session to demonstrate his ability to manipulate the hallucinations (e.g., imagining the last time he saw the demons vividly and then being quiet for 30 seconds). This exposure allowed the client to realize that he could make the hallucinations louder and quieter at his initiation, which reduce their perceived control. Eventually, he was able to conclude that the hallucinations were not worth fearing because they were in his control.

As the therapist, you can also help clients develop more accurate and helpful appraisals through the use of Socratic dialogue. Through this process, clients can recognize that their hallucinations are untrustworthy, even though they may seem familiar and helpful. For example, consider a college student who often heard voices that told him scary things (e.g., that the police were on their way and that everyone hated him). Distracted by the voices, he was unable to focus in class and often spent time listening for the voices and preparing for the warnings. Sitting in the therapy office, the clinician asked this client about the people who purportedly hated him. As the man struggled to come up with examples, the clinician pushed the client to come up with the name of at least one person. The man kept struggling. At this point, the clinician asked the man how he felt (and what he did) whenever "these people" (aka the voices) told him that everyone *hated* him. The man reported that it caused him to feel sad and paranoid, and that he responded by isolating. The clinician adopted a strong Socratic approach by observing that "these people" ran their mouths saying that everyone hated him, which made him feel terrible and led him to isolate. But worst of all, between the clinician and the man, they couldn't find one hater! The clinician then asked, "What does that mean about these people?" In response, the man said, "They must be stupid," and the clinician added, "Or liars?" The two concluded that regardless of the reality of these voices, they were not worth the man's time, and they started developing a plan to stop attending to the voices.

Doubt Beliefs and Hallucinations

In addition to beliefs surrounding control, power, and credibility, auditory hallucinations may also reflect a client's own doubt beliefs or automatic thoughts. For example, consider the example of a college student, who lacks self-confidence and doubts his social desirability. The voices tell him that other people are calling him nasty names and insulting his sexuality, which makes him angry and anxious, as he fears it will make him a social pariah. He responds by avoiding students, standing close to the walls, and sitting in the back row of class. However, this behavior makes the voices more intense, as sitting at the back row provides him with ambiguous information about social cues (e.g., he can only see the back of students' heads) and increases his anxiety. He tries to get the voices to stop by begging them inside his head, but after this effort fails, he yells at the students to stop. He is removed from class by campus security, which reinforces his social ostracism.

Therapy can work to increase this student's self-confidence by helping him understand that social insecurities are a normative experience that can be exacerbated by the stress of college. In addition, treatment can evaluate the utility of his safety behaviors and demonstrate how they are unhelpful in perpetuating the voices. By conducting behavioral experiments, he can realize that when he is in a small class and encouraged to engage, that he feels better. In turn, he develops a plan to drop his safety behaviors and engage with people in and outside of class. He also develops a more accurate reframe regarding his social anxiety: "Regardless of what other people think, worrying about it isn't going to make the situation better, so I need to focus on the people I am connected to." With this reframe, he can identify potential social connections or existing acquaintances whom he is discounting. Not only does building his self-confidence reduce the volume of the voices and shift its contents, but it also fortifies him against the voices so that he does not have to fear anyone else's judgment.

Delusions

Delusions are the result of information-processing biases brought on in response to threatening beliefs about the world (Beck et al., 2009). Specifically, when clients are faced with irrelevant information (e.g., people laughing, hearing whispers, heart racing), they ascribe personal meaning to the event (*self-referential bias*) and construct an explanation surrounding the event in which the actions of others are viewed as intentional and malevolent (*intentionalizing bias*). Finally, the individual takes the event and attributes it to an external cause (*externalizing bias*).

In combination, this trio of biases bends information and distorts reality, which leads to the development of the delusion. Once the delusion is established, the belief is sustained the same way other symptoms are sustained: through a confirmatory bias. In particular, clients accrue evidence in support of the delusion and overlook or minimize disconfirming evidence as flukes. For example, a student is sitting in class and hears whispering among other students (*self-referential bias*), which leads him to believe that everyone in the class is judging him (*intentionalizing bias*) because he has a history of demons possessing him (*externalizing bias*). In turn, he keeps to himself and looks at the class handouts instead of interacting with his classmates (*safety behavior*). He becomes anxious when people do not talk to him and concludes that everyone in the class hates him, exacerbating his thoughts about rejection and the demons possessing him (*confirmatory bias*).

However, delusional beliefs may be amenable to reason and can be explored using a gentle and non-interrogative Socratic style. There might be some truth in the delusional beliefs, so be careful not to jump to your own conclusions. As with all disorders, beliefs feel true to the client, and even if they are not factually true, aggressive confrontation of the belief can compromise treatment and cause clients to become defensive. Rather, identify the specific times when the delusion is interfering with taking action toward a desired life, as this can uncover the thoughts, feelings, and behaviors maintaining the larger belief system. By gaining a good understanding of the function behind the delusion, you can develop a strategy that targets its smaller, maintaining factors and increases functioning.

For example, returning to the student who believes that others know about his history of demon possession, you could use Socratic questioning to help the student consider the helpfulness of his delusion (e.g., it makes him feels worse, socially embarrassed, and prevents him from interacting with people to test their acceptance). Upon deciding that it is unhelpful, he can develop a plan to engage at parties regardless of others' judgment. In time, he finds that most people like him. In this example, the clinician does not challenge the delusion but, rather, attacks one part of the delusion that increases the isolation. With more social interaction, the student has less time to ruminate on the delusional beliefs, which causes them to become less salient.

For other clients, delusions serve to compensate for low self-esteem. In these situations, you need to identify the client's core beliefs, find out what need the delusion is meeting, and develop a different routine to meet the need in the long run. For example, consider a client who maintains the delusion that he owns the hospital where he resides. You can start by asking, "What is good about owning the hospital?" By posing this question, you are not endorsing the delusional belief that he owns the hospital, as any person can answer this question. The client answers, "You have a role and get respect." This answer provides you with two pieces of information: (1) the need to be met, and (2) an idea of the core belief. In particular, this client has a need to have a role and experience respect, which indicates that he likely has underlying core beliefs about being irrelevant and helpless. The delusion meets that need and compensates for his core beliefs, even with the amount of ridicule that he experiences from others by maintaining this delusion.

In this situation, the therapeutic approach follows a series of steps. To start, the clinician engages the client with the therapeutic relationship to prime new beliefs regarding capability and respect (through activities together and the interchange of ideas). This priming meets the need served by the delusion, and the client's focus on the delusion is reduced. In time, these interactions serve as examples to create routines that meet the need of the delusion. These routines are placed into an activity schedule to systematize the routines, and the client can ultimately restructure beliefs about capability and respect based on the experiences in the routines.

CBT AND MEDICINE

In addition to helping to address psychotic symptomology, CBT also can play a significant role in medication adherence, as it helps clients take a constructive approach to dealing with medication, consider the pros and cons of various medications, and make informed decisions about medication usage. CBT assists clients in recognizing that regardless of whether they believe they need medication, inconsistent medication usage is not going to be to their benefit. Initially, clients might adopt a plan to stay on medicine while "getting CBT up to the full dosage," and then work with their psychiatrist to titrate down. Others may choose to remain on medicine indefinitely, though the evidence on the long-term usage of antipsychotics implies a limited benefit (Harrow, Jobe, & Faull, 2012).

Regardless of whether individuals choose to take medication on a short-term or long-term basis, the goal of treatment for psychosis to help clients reclaim their lives. Often, it is necessary to assist them with reentry into the social world by helping them repair damaged relationships, reconnect to people from their past, and make new connections. Gradual reentry into the occupational world, even if only voluntary, is important for clients to develop self-efficacy and gain a sense of accomplishment. When living with the ebb and flow of distress that is inevitable in life, it is critical for them to find joy in life, reestablish past pleasures, and explore new opportunities.

REFERENCES

> For your convenience, purchasers can download and print worksheets and handouts from www.pesi.com/SokolFox

American Psychiatric Association. (2013). *Diagnostic and statistical manual of mental disorders* (5th ed.). Arlington, VA: American Psychiatric Publishing.

Beck, A. T. (1964). Thinking and depression II: Theory and therapy. *Archives of General Psychiatry, 10*(6), 561–571.

Beck, A. T. (1983). Cognitive therapy of depression: New perspectives. In P. J. Clayton & J. E. Barrett (Eds.), *Treatment of depression: Old controversies and new approaches* (pp. 265–289). New York, NY: Raven Press.

Beck, A. T. (1986). Hopelessness as a predictor of eventual suicide. *Annals of the New York Academy of Science, 487*(1), 90–96.

Beck, A. T. (1999). *Prisoners of hate: The cognitive basis of anger, hostility, and violence.* New York, NY: HarperCollins.

Beck, A. T., Brown, G., Berchick, R., Stewart, B., & Steer, R. (1990). Relationship between hopelessness and ultimate suicide: A replication with psychiatric outpatients. *American Journal of Psychiatry, 147*(2), 190–195.

Beck, A. T., Butler, A., Brown, G., Dahlsgaard, K., Newman, C., & Beck, J. (2001). Dysfunctional beliefs discriminate personality disorders. *Behavior Research and Therapy, 39*(10), 1213–1225.

Beck, A. T., Davis, D. D., & Freeman, A. (Eds.). (2015). *Cognitive therapy of personality disorders* (3rd ed.). New York, NY: Guilford.

Beck, A. T., & Emery, G. (2005). *Anxiety disorders and phobias: A cognitive perspective* (Rev. ed.). New York, NY: Basic Books.

Beck, A. T., Kovacs, M., & Weissman, A. (1979). Assessment of suicidal intention: The scale for suicide ideation. *Journal of Consulting and Clinical Psychology, 47*(2), 343–352.

Beck, A. T., Rector, N. A., Stolar, N., & Grant, P. (2009). *Schizophrenia: Cognitive theory, research, and therapy.* New York, NY: Guilford.

Beck, A. T., Rush, A., Shaw, B., & Emery, G. (1987). *Cognitive therapy of depression.* New York, NY: Guilford.

Beck, A. T., & Steer, R. A. (1993a). *Manual for the Beck Anxiety Inventory.* San Antonio, TX: Psychological Corporation.

Beck, A. T., & Steer, R. A. (1993b). *Manual for the Beck Hopeless Scale.* San Antonio, TX: Psychological Corporation.

Beck, A. T., Steer, R. A., & Brown, G. K. (1996). *Manual for the Beck Depression Inventory-II.* San Antonio, TX: Psychological Corporation.

Beck, A. T., Weissman, A., Lester, D., & Trexler, L. (1974). The measurement of pessimism: The Hopelessness Scale. *Journal of Consulting and Clinical Psychology, 42*(6), 861–865.

Beck, A. T., Wright, F. D., Newman, C. F., & Liese, B. S. (1993). *Cognitive therapy of substance abuse.* New York, NY: Guilford.

Beck, J. S. (2011). *Cognitive behavior therapy: Basics and beyond* (2nd ed.). New York, NY: Guilford Press.

Bentall, R. P. (2009). *Doctoring the mind.* New York, NY: New York University Press.

Brinen, A. P., & Beck, A. T. (2016). Cognitive Behavior Therapy for Psychosis (CBTp) and Recovery-Oriented Cognitive Therapy (CT-R): What is the difference? *Beck Institute for Cognitive Therapy.* Retrieved from https://beckinstitute.org/cbtp-ct-r-whats-difference/

Burns, D. D. (1995). *Therapist's toolkit: Comprehensive treatment and assessment tools for the mental health professional.* Philadelphia, PA: Author.

Clark, D. M. (1986). A cognitive approach to panic. *Behavior Research and Therapy, 24*(4), 461–470.

Clark, D. A., & Beck A. T. (2010). *Cognitive therapy of anxiety disorders.* New York, NY: Guilford.

Clark, D. M., & Ehlers, A. (2004). Posttraumatic stress disorder: From theory to therapy. In R. L. Leahy (Ed.), *Contemporary cognitive therapy: Theory, research, and practice* (pp. 141–160). New York, NY: Guilford Press.

Daley, D. C., & Marlatt, G. A. (1992). Relapse prevention: Cognitive and behavioral interventions. In J. Lowinson, R. Ruiz, R. Millman, & J. Langrod (Eds.), *Substance abuse: A comprehensive textbook* (2nd ed., pp. 533–542). Baltimore, MD: Williams & Wilkins.

Dobson, K. S. (2012). *Cognitive therapy.* Washington, DC: APA Books.

Ellis, A. (1962). *Reason and emotion in psychotherapy.* New York, NY: Lyle Stuart.

Foa, E. B., Hembree, E. A., & Rothbaum, B. O. (2007). *Prolonged exposure therapy for PTSD: Emotional processing of traumatic experiences.* New York, NY: Oxford University Press.

Fochtmann, L. J., & Jacobs, D. G. (2015). Suicide risk assessment and management in practice: The quintessential clinical activity. *Academic Psychiatry, 39*(4) 490–491.

Grant, P. M., Huh, G. A., Perivoliotis, D., Stolar, N. M., & Beck, A. T. (2012). Randomized trial to evaluate the efficacy of cognitive therapy for low-functioning clients with schizophrenia. *Archives of General Psychiatry, 69*(2), 121–127.

Harrow, M., Jobe, T. H., & Faull, R. N. (2012). Do all schizophrenia clients need antipsychotic treatment continuously throughout their lifetime? A 20-year longitudinal study. *Psychological Medicine, 42*(10), 2145–2155.

Kagan, J. (1989). Temperamental contributions to social behavior. *American Psychologist, 44*(4), 668–674.

Kingdon, D. G., & Turkington, D. (1994). *Cognitive-behavioral therapy of schizophrenia.* New York, NY: Guilford.

Liese, B.S., & Franz, R.A. (1996). Treating substance use disorders with cognitive therapy: Lessons learned and implications for the future. In P. M. Salkovskis (Ed.), *Frontiers of cognitive therapy* (pp. 470–508). New York, NY: Guilford.

McLellan, A. T., Lewis, D. C., O'Brien, C. P., & Kleber, H. D. (2000). Drug dependence, a chronic medical illness: Implications for treatment, insurance, and outcomes evaluation. *JAMA, 284*(13), 1689–1695.

Morrison, A. P., Turkington, D., Pyle, M., Spencer, H., Brabban, A., Dunn, G., . . . Hutton, P. (2014). Cognitive therapy for people with schizophrenia spectrum disorders not taking antipsychotic drugs: A single-blind randomized controlled trial. *The Lancet, 383*(9926), 1395–1403.

Newman, C. F., Leahy, R. L., Beck, A. T., Reilly-Harrington, N., & Gyulai, L. (2001). *Bipolar disorder: A cognitive therapy approach.* Washington, DC: American Psychological Association.

Posner, K., Brown, G. K., & Stanley, B. (2011). The Columbia-Suicide Severity Rating Scale: Initial validity and internal consistency findings from three multisite studies with adolescents and adults. *American Journal Psychiatry, 168,* 1266–1277.

Rector, N., & Beck, A. T. (2001). Cognitive behavior therapy for schizophrenia: An empirical review. *Journal of Nervous and Mental Disease, 189*(5), 278–287.

Rector, N., Seeman, M. V., & Segal, Z. V. (2003). Cognitive therapy for schizophrenia: A preliminary randomized controlled trial. *Schizophrenia Research, 63,* 1–11.

Salkovskis, P. M. (1996). Avoidance behavior is motivated by threat beliefs: A possible resolution of the cognitive-behavior debate. In P. M. Salkovskis (Ed.), *Trends in cognitive and behavioral therapies* (pp. 25–41). Chichester, UK: Wiley.

Segal, Z., Kennedy, S., Gemar, M., Hood, K., Pedersen, R., & Buis, T. (2006). Cognitive reactivity to sad mood provocation and the prediction of depressive relapse. *Archives of General Psychiatry, 63,* 749–755.

Sokol, L., & Fox, M. G. (2009). *Think confident, be confident: A four-step program to eliminate doubt and achieve lifelong self-esteem.* New York, NY: Perigee.

Stanley, B., & Brown, G. K. (2012). Safety planning intervention: A brief intervention to mitigate suicide risk. *Cognitive and Behavioral Practice, 19,* 256–264.

van der Gaag, M., Valmaggia, L. R., & Smit, F. (2014). The effects of individually tailored formulation-based cognitive behavioural therapy in auditory hallucinations and delusions: A meta-analysis. *Schizophrenia Research, 156*(1), 30–37.

Weishaar, M., & Beck, A. T. (1992). Hopelessness and suicide. *International Review of Psychiatry, 4,* 185–192.

Wenzel, A., Brown, G. K., & Beck, A. T. (2009). *Cognitive therapy for suicidal clients: Scientific and clinical applications.* Washington, DC: APA Books.

Wykes, T., Steel, C., Everitt, B., & Tarrier, N. (2008). Cognitive behavior therapy for schizophrenia: Effect sizes, clinical models, and methodological rigor. *Schizophrenia Bulletin, 34,* 523–537.

Young, J., & Beck, A. T. (1980). *Cognitive Therapy Scale: Rating manual.* Unpublished manuscript, University of Pennsylvania, Philadelphia.

Young, J., & Beck, A. T. (1988). *Revision of Cognitive Therapy Scale.* Unpublished manuscript, University of Pennsylvania, Philadelphia.

Zubin, J., & Spring, B. (1977). Vulnerability: A new view on schizophrenia. *Journal of Abnormal Psychology, 86*(2), 103–126.

www.ingramcontent.com/pod-product-compliance
Ingram Content Group UK Ltd.
Pitfield, Milton Keynes, MK11 3LW, UK
UKHW050414240426
12048UKWH00020B/1499

9 781683 733201